411895

THE TRIAL
OF PATROLMAN
THOMAS SHEA

THE
TRIAL
OF
PATROLMAN
THOMAS SHEA

THOMAS HAUSER

THE VIKING PRESS   NEW YORK

Library of Congress Cataloging in Publication Data
Hauser, Thomas
The trial of Patrolman Thomas Shea.
1. Shea, Thomas Joseph, 1937-   2. Glover, Clifford, 1963-1973.
3. Trials (Murder)--New York (City)
I. Title.
KF224.S46H38   345'.73'02523   79-22612
ISBN 0-670-73013-0

Printed in the United States of America
Set in Computer Times Roman

Elise and Harry Nordlinger,

Their Book

CONTENTS

PART ONE

1

ADD ARMSTEAD

Add Armstead is the product of an America that should have died a century ago. The elderly midwife present at his birth in Fredericksburg, Virginia, on June 14, 1922, had been raised in slavery. The eighth of nineteen children, he dropped out of school in second grade and can neither read nor write.

Armstead grew up in the American South before the Montgomery bus boycott, sit-ins, and freedom riders. It was an era when most blacks were forbidden to vote and it was a crime punishable by ten years in prison for a black and white to intermarry. His formative years were spent under the heels of political and economic barons who had a vested interest in keeping his people ignorant, uneducated, and superstitious. At age twenty-one, he moved north to New York, where he has worked as a laborer for more than thirty years.

Armstead is five feet six inches tall, of wiry build, with skin the color of bitter chocolate. His face is thin with high cheekbones and a pencil mustache. The majority of his teeth are missing, leaving gaping holes on each side of his mouth. His eyes are dull, and his hair is cropped close where it has not receded. A gold crucifix dangles from a chain around Armstead's neck just to the left of an ugly three-inch scar. His hands are the hands of a laborer—extremely large for someone his size, scarred from an endless series of metal slices, dirt perpetually under the nails. He is an unremarkable man who, as the result of a single horrifying moment in the dreary predawn hours of April 28, 1973, was ripped from obscurity and brutally exhibited before the American public until the same public wearied of him.

His voice is deep. He speaks in rushes.

"Shea! Yeah, I know that name. He made a pact with the devil. You see, God and Satan be sittin' in heaven with suitcases full of souls, and they trade them back and forth. And the devil, he's got another suitcase with every kind of temptation you can imagine. Shea made a pact with the devil. The devil took his soul, and now Shea does his bidding. I know because I was there the morning Shea shot my boy. If I'd been drunk or causing trouble, it might have been different, but there weren't none of that. Me and Clifford was just walking along when Shea killed him dead. Some nights I still wake up and hear the bullets whistling over me.

"After Shea killed my boy, there was a time when any man with a uniform and badge was my enemy. Every cop, I hated. Then God called me. I was sitting in church, cursing God for everything that had gone wrong, when I felt my breath growing short. My throat closed up and I couldn't breathe. Right then I heard the voice of God. He said, 'Add, the devil could have killed you that Saturday morning, but I saved you to preach the Gospel.' I heard God's voice, and I begged for forgiveness. I said, 'Lord, I surrender everything. Lord, I'll give you everything. Lord, I'm in your hands.'

"That's the way it's been now for five years. All the trouble I went through was for God. Without God, you don't got

4

nothing. You can give me a Rolls-Royce and I'll say that's mine but it ain't. That's God's car because, if God takes the breath out of me, if God takes my life right then, that car ain't worth nothing. I'd rather do what God tells me than live in a palace because what I got now, money can't buy. God came in and put peace and love in my heart.

"Peace and love—that's the message of the Lord. If all of us were united, not just here in America but in the whole world, if we could sit down and talk out our problems, then we'd have peace. But we can't get the world united. We got countries fighting with countries. We got rich fighting with poor, black fighting with white. It don't make sense. Everybody should get on the train and ride together with Christ. He's the conductor and, when you got Christ, you have everything.

"Hate tears up a man's insides. When Jesus was on the cross, He said, 'Father, forgive them, for they know not what they do!' That's why I forgive Shea. God says that Shea's my brother. If Shea walked in this door right now and said, 'I'm hungry,' I'd give him something to eat. There's no way a man can love God if he hates his own brother. That's what matters to me now—loving God. But there's more you came to ask me, so I'll tell you more.

"I was born in nineteen hundred and twenty-two on a farm in Fredericksburg, Virginia. There were nineteen children in the family. I got five brothers and four sisters still living. Nine of them are dead. I'm the oldest living son.

"My mother's name was Sarah. She was a big woman, weighed a little more than two hundred pounds. At hog-killing time she worked in the yard, but the rest of the time she stayed at home. I guess raising nineteen of us was work enough. She was born a Baptist, lived like a Baptist, and died a Baptist—always told us to go to church, and I never gave her no trouble except once. One Sunday, instead of praying like I was supposed to, I went fishing with George Young.

The canoe turned over and I couldn't swim, nearly drowned before George saved me. Right then I figured the Lord was trying to tell me something. That's the last time I ever went fishing on Sunday.

"My father hauled wood for a living. His name was Add, and I look a lot like he used to. He and my mother ran out of names by the time they got to me so they named me Add, Junior. My father was a hard man, but he taught us the best he knew how. He gave us what he could and we didn't have no palace, but what we had was all right. I was never ashamed.

"My father worked us hard when we was children. I didn't get much book learning because he made me quit school in second grade so I could help him out at work. Every day except Sunday him and me would chop down a load of trees. Then we'd saw them into eight-foot sections and bring them back by horse and wagon to the yard, where my brothers cut them down some more. Finally, we'd load the wood back on the cart and take it to people's houses for their stoves. It was hard work but honest money. We got five dollars a load, three or four loads a day.

"Plenty of times I got tired of working, but my father made me keep going. If he told me to do something, I did it. That's how it was with all of his children. Once he came home at midnight and I hadn't chopped up some logs, so he woke me up and made me to go outside in the snow to do it. Another time we was repairing a piece of machinery and he told me to lift something heavy. I just looked like I wasn't going to do it and he hit me on the head with a hammer. I still got the scar to prove it. My mother told him, 'You're going to kill that boy,' but it was for my own good. My father said, 'You have it hard now and it will be easier later on.' He was right. Sixteen years I've been able to hold onto the same job because of what he taught me. Children today don't have that. Everything comes too easy to them. That's why there's so much juvenilism. There are more young junkies in jail today than ever before because they don't have good fathers that keep on them. I laugh at some of those kids, the way they misbehave, but deep down inside it breaks my heart. All I had to do was just look like I wasn't going to do what I was told and I got the belt. But I'll say this about my daddy and mama—none of their children ever went wrong. Nineteen of us, and none of us ever went bad.

"There was some hard times back when I was young. We never had money for nineteen pairs of shoes, and once I got frostbite walking through the snow. Sometimes we only had cornpone and boiled potatoes for dinner, but I usually made out okay. If I was hungry, I walked along the road and looked for empty soda bottles to turn in at the store for bread and cheese.

"Most folks was good to us. Most folks left us alone. There wasn't much problem with color. Up here in New York, people throw rocks and hide their hand. They talk like they're your friend, but they treat you like a nigger. Down south, if a man don't like you because of your color, he says so. Down south, if a colored man is working for a white and lands in jail, his boss calls the sheriff and says, 'Let my nigger go.' I got nothing against the civil rights movement. Things are better now because of it but, at the time it was going on, it never crossed my mind.

"About the time I was seventeen, I left home and went to work for a man named Mr. Cupid. He put a cot and stove in his hen house, and I got along there just fine. Then, maybe three years later, my brother Joe moved up north. After a while he come home to visit and told us how good things were, so I decided to see for myself. It was cold when I got to New York, and I almost went back home, but after a while I decided to stay. The first job I had in the city was driving a cab. Then I cleaned cesspools for a couple of years and carted coal. After that I worked as a longshoreman. Partway through World War II, I went to work for a man named Jack Reynolds at a wrecking yard on Springfield Boulevard in Queens. I worked with Mr. Reynolds for fourteen years. About the time we got started, I met Lola. Her father owned a grocery store near where I lived, and sometimes I'd go over and give a big red apple to her mother. Christmas Eve of 1945 I went by to give Lola her present. We stayed up late talking and fell in love; got married the first Tuesday in 1946.

"We had a lot of nice years together, me and Lola. We had, I'm not sure but I think it was eight children—three boys and five girls. The first boy died from asthma when he was two months old. My daughter Margie was shot to death by her husband. The other children are still alive. I loved Lola, but I did some running around that maybe I shouldn't have. She told me once, 'I'll forgive you but I won't forget.' Then, in 1959, I had a bad accident on the New Jersey Turnpike. I was in the hospital for almost a year and, when I got out, Lola was gone. She'd fallen in love with someone else and lived with him until Easter Sunday 1971, when she died. Heart trouble, it was. I was the one they called to the morgue to identify her body. I loved that woman.

"After Lola left me, I went near crazy from being alone. I lived with my brother for a while, but that didn't work out, so I lived alone again. Then my mother died, and after that my father passed away. I went home for his funeral and gave the undertaker the only suit I had so my daddy could be buried proper. Right after that I met Mrs. Glover.

"Mrs. Glover was a nice woman, very good with children. We met in a little restaurant on South Road and New York Boulevard in Queens. One day she came in when I was having lunch, and I bought her something to eat. Then a friend of mine told me, 'Don't mess with her because she's married.' After that I was perfectly proper. I didn't do anything, but we stayed friends. I bought her lunch almost every day, and once someone broke into her home, so I helped fix

8

the lock on the door. Another time something in the bathroom broke, so I fixed it. Then her husband ran out and left her with two children—Clifford and Henry—both of them babies. I started seeing her more, and she had two more children—Patricia and Darlene. Both of them are mine. Finally, about 1971, she asked me to move in.

"I liked all of Mrs. Glover's children, but me and Clifford got along the best. He was eight years old when I moved in, and he took to me real good. Mr. Reynolds had died by then, and I'd gotten another job at a junkyard right by our home. Most of the time I cut up old cars with a torch. It was the best job I ever had. The boss sold all the radiators, batteries, and motors, but I could keep anything else I wanted. One day I made sixty-seven dollars selling copper wire and a heater I found in a car.

"Working in a junkyard gets in your blood. I figured that Clifford could learn it real good, so when he turned ten I started bringing him along. Every day after school he'd come down to the yard and stay until I got off. Then, if I went for a beer, he'd come keep me company. He was a nice boy, very intelligent. He'd have been a good mechanic someday. Saturdays he'd come to work the whole day. That's where we was going when Shea killed him.

"I suppose I'm lucky. If I'd died that morning, hell would have been my home. I was a sinner, but Clifford had no sin on him. He was pure. Right now he's by the side of the Lord. That's all I want. That's all any man needs. To die and be by the side of the Lord. You see, someday you and me gonna pass away. The houses we live in and this city gonna pass away. But the Word of God will live forever. Remember that, my friend. The Word of God will live forever. There might not be no justice in this world, but don't you worry none. They got plenty of it in the next. I'm getting on in years, and someday me and Clifford gonna meet up again. Lord, that'll be the day."

9

2

THE MAKING OF A COP

No two cops come out of the same mold. Like everyone else, they are the product of family and friends, schooling and the neighborhoods they live in. They are as varied and complex as other men, and each one must be seen in light of his own peculiar origins.

Thomas Joseph Shea was born in New York City on March 28, 1937. His father rewound commercial generators for I. W. Bliss, Inc., but lost his job when the company moved to Ohio. After a brief period of unemployment, Joseph Shea found work as a security guard and messenger for the First National City Bank in Brooklyn. At age sixty-one he died of cancer.

Shea's mother was a supervisor in the billing department of the Eclipse Mattress Company. "My mother was a great person," Shea remembers. "Her name was Charlotte. She never got past eighth grade, but she had beautiful handwriting. She did the income tax for our family; she worked; she was one of the greatest people I've ever known."

Charlotte Shea suffered from tuberculosis during her early and mid-forties. After the condition was arrested, she contracted cancer and died at age forty-nine. "Back then," Shea continues, "doctors believed in keeping their patients alive for as long as possible. We lived with death for almost a year, my mother lying in bed, her stomach all bloated up like she was eight months pregnant. Then, one morning, my father called and told me we were about to lose her. By the time I got there she'd stopped breathing. I started pounding on her chest, giving her mouth-to-mouth resuscitation the way I'd learned at the Police Academy, but it was too late. I don't know why I did it. I knew she was gone, but I didn't want to let her go. Maybe I just wanted to hold her."

Shea grew up in a low-income polyglot section of Brooklyn which reflected his family origins. Of his own grandparents, one was Irish, one French, one English, and one German. His father was Catholic; his mother, Protestant. Shea was brought up as a Methodist.

For most of his childhood, Shea's family lived in a small flat adjacent to an elevated train station in Brooklyn. He attended elementary school P.S. 65, Junior High School 171, and East New York Vocational High. He was a less-than-average student, totally uninterested in his studies. His playground was the street and, like his contemporaries, he skipped classes and got into street fights with random frequency. Generally, he tried to be part of the crowd but was self-conscious with girls because of a severe case of acne. Later in life, he would stand five feet nine inches tall, 190 pounds, with a ruddy face and fighter's nose. He had no brothers and one sister, three years his junior.

"The thing I remember most about my childhood," Shea says, "is that I always wanted to be a policeman. My parents taught me respect for law and order. I never stole or destroyed anything. I did what cops told me. If I was playing stickball in the street, which was against the law, and a cop drove by, the bat and ball disappeared. When a cop walked by, I said, 'Hello, Officer.' If I had ever come home with a

11

policeman chasing after me—and I never did—my father would have given me a shellacking. Just the sight of a cop in uniform would have done it."

At age seventeen, Shea dropped out of high school and enlisted in the United States Air Force. He wanted to be an air policeman, but an aptitude test revealed him to be "overqualified" and, at the urging of his commanding officer, he began training to be an aircraft technician. Stationed in Japan, he worked mostly with ground instruments while studying for a high school equivalency diploma. In April 1958, after being honorably discharged, he returned to New York and took the next qualifying examination given for admission to the New York City Police Department. Then, while waiting for the results, he worked for Northwest Airlines, loading luggage and servicing planes. In April 1959, during services at St. Andrew's Church in Brooklyn, an attractive green-eyed blonde sitting in a pew nearby captured his attention. Later that day the minister approached him and said, "Tom, you're a nice young man, but it's disconcerting to preach while you sit there staring at a young lady. If it's all right with her parents, I'll introduce the two of you to each other. If I'm not mistaken, she also had her eye on you."

On their first date, Shea brought Bonnie Stevenson to the annual Blue and Gold Cub Scout Dinner, where he was serving as a volunteer scoutmaster. They were married on December 23, 1959.

Shea's credentials as a police applicant were average at best, but the numbers were on his side. The New York City Police Department in 1959 was midway through a hiring campaign that would raise its ranks from 18,800 to 31,000 men. Of the applicants who took the test with Shea, 60 percent passed, compared with 45 percent over the following three years. After the written examination, Shea underwent a series of personal interviews, and his wife was required by police investigators to sign a statement saying that she and Tom had not engaged in sexual intercourse prior to their marriage. Several years earlier Shea had received a traffic ticket for an illegal turn on Mott Street in Chinatown. The Department required him to provide written proof of payment. It wasn't until eighteen months after his job application had been filed that Shea was called for a physical examination. On May 4, 1961, he was appointed to the Department, assigned Shield Number 22737, and instructed to report to the Police Academy in Brooklyn for recruit training.

By and large, Shea's fellow recruits had backgrounds similar to his own. They were from lower-middle-class New York City families striving to move up a rung on the economic and social ladder. Virtually none had attended college. Twenty percent had received their high school diploma, which was mandatory for appointment, in an equivalency program. In general, their motivation in joining the force was twofold—they wanted the salary, job security, and pension offered by the Department, and they sought the respect, prestige, and authority that they associated with being a cop.

The Police Academy training program lasted eighteen weeks. Fifty-six classroom hours were devoted to firearms training; 192 to physical conditioning and defense techniques; 312 to general academic instruction. "The first thing we learned," Shea recalls, "is that in order to remain viable, society needs police. Our job was to preserve the fabric of society and, toward that end, we were to be given the power, where warranted, to use force. Then we learned about the risks that go along with being a cop. It's the only profession in the world, except for the military in time of war, where a person faces unknown violence every day. When a fireman responds to an alarm, he knows how big the fire is and what has to be done to put it out. If a fireman dies, it's a tragedy but it's an accident. When a cop answers a call, he doesn't know what lies ahead. It could be a shotgun blast in the stomach or a knife in the gut, a two-foot machete or a can of lye in his face. They taught us self-protection early, and it was a lesson they made stick. We all knew that once we were cops, any minute someone could be shooting at us."

Self-protection was thus an integral part of Thomas Shea's police training. A cop, he learned, should not run up a flight of stairs when responding to an emergency call. If he does, he will be too winded to defend himself properly in the event of an attack. If a policeman uses his flashlight while pursuing a suspect, it should be held at arm's length away from the body—a suspect is more likely to shoot at a light than at its holder. A siren, Shea learned, is not a license to speed or drive recklessly. Its purpose is to bring a cop to the scene of a crime as quickly as possible without endangering his own life. A cop should never keep papers or other material above the sun visor of his patrol car. In a high-speed chase they might shake loose and fall in his face.

Police brutality and the use of unnecessary force, the recruits were told, were to be avoided at virtually any price. But if a fight did arise and a cop's life was in danger, rules of fair play were to be ignored. In a life-and-death struggle, a cop is expected to use any weapon at his command, including thumbing an adversary in the eye, kneeing him in the groin, and butting an opponent's nose, preferably splattering it all over the attacker's face.

However, the most important lesson in self-defense was the "Eleventh Commandment"—cops protect each other. "You men," the recruits were told, "will develop a warmth and camaraderie among yourselves simply by virtue of the fact that you are cops. You'll eat together, work together, frequent the same after-hours bars together and, in a few

14

terrifying instances, die together. You'll be praised and looked up to by some, hated and feared by others. But in the end, when the chips are down, you'll be alone. Whenever one of your brothers is in trouble, move as though your own life depended on it. Someday it will."

Shea graduated from the Police Academy on September 17, 1961. "It was a very proud moment," he recalls. "I felt good. Being a policeman was an honored profession and an opportunity to serve the public. It was something I had always wanted, and finally I had attained my goal. It was the first time in my life I had done something that my family and I could be proud of."

Shea's first police assignment was with the newly created Tactical Patrol Force. In the eyes of the media, the TPF was a select group of six-foot-tall karate-trained experts who were New York City's "roughest," if not finest. Shea was five feet nine inches tall with unprepossessing physical skills and minimal knowledge of martial arts. In truth, 40 of the unit's 125 men were rookies straight out of the Academy. Unlike most cops, they were not permanently assigned to a particular precinct. Instead, they were on city-wide alert, assigned to precincts on a day-to-day basis, according to need. Whenever a major crowd-control problem threatened to escalate into a riot, the TPF was called to maintain order. If the city was calm, TPF patrolmen were pressed into decoy duty.

It was as a police decoy that Shea made his first arrests. His uniform consisted of a red wig that had belonged to his mother, a scarf, raincoat, black skirt, blouse, women's shoes, and falsies. His badge was pinned to a pair of Bermuda shorts beneath the skirt. Once, as Shea was sitting with his pocketbook on a bench near Central Park West and 108th Street in Manhattan, a man, taken in by the disguise, tried to seduce him. Several days later, at the same location, another suspect sat down next to him and began rummaging through Shea's pocketbook.

"We couldn't arrest someone until they actually took something and ran," Shea recalls, "so I just sat there and pretended not to notice. The first thing this guy found was my police memo book, and I said to myself, 'Shit, I blew it. Now he knows I'm a cop.' But it didn't seem to matter. He kept working his way through my things until he found my wallet and took off. My backup partner arrested him on the spot. It turned out the guy didn't speak English so, when he saw the memo book, he didn't know what it was."

After two and a half years with the TPF, Shea was reassigned to the 90th Precinct in the Williamsburg section of Brooklyn. Then, in April 1965, he was transferred to Brooklyn's 79th Precinct. As with most cops, the vast majority of his hours were spent on "preventive assignment"—supervising an area in the hope that his mere presence would deter crime. When he was called to act, his performance was largely "service-oriented," entailing situations which did not involve the commission of a crime—controlling traffic, administering first aid, giving directions, escorting parades, caring for lost children, delivering babies, and resolving disputes between cabdrivers and fares. Blaring radios had to be silenced late at night. If a fire broke out, Shea or a fellow cop called in the alarm, held back the crowds, sealed off the street from traffic, and guarded the building afterward to protect against looting. The average street fight was broken up without an arrest. Family quarrels were generally disposed of in similar fashion.

Still, if police work was frequently service-oriented and dull, on occasion it could also be extremely dangerous. "I had a friend in the Ninetieth Precinct," Shea recalls, "a cop named Jerry Shrimpf. He had the bad habit of reaching into other people's cars to shut the motor off when he stopped them for questioning. One day Jerry stopped someone for speeding and reached in like he always did. The motorist rolled his window up and took off at seventy miles an hour with Jerry's arm caught between the window and the frame of the door. After two blocks Jerry fell off and slid under the car. The back wheel took his head off. Then the driver hit another person straight on and killed him. Two people dead —the driver pled guilty to manslaughter and got seven and a half years.

"I was afraid after that," Shea remembers, "but I guess that's a healthy reaction. Any cop out on the street who doesn't have a certain amount of fear is crazy. It's not like I was trembling every minute, but the fear was always there —like riding a motorcycle. Anybody who rides a motorcycle and isn't afraid will get hurt. It's the same thing with being a cop. If you think you're above getting hurt, that's when it happens."

"It" almost happened twice in 1967. On July 11, 1967, while on radio-car patrol, Shea responded to a routine call regarding a "disorderly person" and was attacked by a former mental-hospital patient armed with a meat cleaver. For the first time in six years on the force, Shea fired his revolver, striking his assailant once in the abdomen.

Four months later, on November 25, 1967, Shea was on motor patrol in the same area when a pedestrian flagged him down to report that an addict was shooting heroin in a nearby building. After following the informant inside, Shea climbed the stairs to the apartment in question and looked through a crack in the door. The room was small and dimly lit. Narcotics and narcotics paraphernalia littered the floor. Shouting, "Don't move. Police," Shea kicked open the door and trained his gun on the lone suspect inside. The man froze, and Shea shoved him against a wall, then "tossed" him for weapons. Finding none, he ordered the suspect outside. As they reached the top of the stairs, the man whirled

17

around, pulled a linoleum cutter from his sleeve, and ran a six-inch gash across Shea's uniform just above the heart. At the end of its arc, the knife sliced through the skin between Shea's thumb and second finger.

As Shea reeled back, the addict turned and ran for the fire escape. Chasing after him, Shea fired three shots, hitting him once in the leg. The perpetrator was convicted of assault and sentenced to two to five years in prison. The drug charge against him was dismissed because during the fight and shooting Shea had lost sight of the narcotics. Thus, there was no "chain of custody," and the heroin was not admissible into evidence. At trial, the judge told Shea that, when he left the room, he should have carried the narcotics with him.

Shea's work in the 79th Precinct won him recognition as a tough, "street-smart" cop, and in December 1967 he was promoted to the Brooklyn North Task Force Narcotics Unit. Thirty-one months later he was transferred again—this time to the Department's Taxi-Truck Surveillance Unit. Taxi-Truck operated out of Flushing Meadow Park in Queens. It was responsible for the prevention and investigation of motor-vehicle-related thefts on a city-wide basis, and Shea considered it his best assignment ever because of the flexibility it involved. For twenty months he performed in exemplary fashion. Then near disaster struck.

Shortly after midnight, on March 19, 1972, two off-duty policemen allegedly assaulted and shot at neighborhood youths outside a bar and grill in Woodside, Queens. Shea was not involved in the initial assault. However, in arresting one of the youths (a fourteen-year-old Hispanic) for criminal mischief, he reportedly struck the boy twice on the head with the butt of his revolver. Shortly thereafter departmental charges were filed against him.

Then, fifteen days later, Shea was involved in a far more

serious incident. While on patrol-car duty on the West Side of Manhattan, he and his partner (a cop named John Fitzgerald) were confronted by a man who shouted that he had been robbed and pointed toward another pedestrian. When the suspect (a twenty-three-year-old named Felix Tarrats) fled, Shea chased after him. The pursuit covered several blocks and, as Tarrats crossed the intersection of Broadway and 84th Street, Shea fired twice, hitting Tarrats once in the neck. On the basis of Shea's testimony that he had shot in self-defense and only after the suspect had fired at him, Tarrats was indicted for attempted murder. The fly in the ointment was that no gun belonging to the suspect was ever found. Then Shea's own partner, John Fitzgerald, conceded in court that he had not seen the alleged gun. The attempted-murder charge against Tarrats was soon dismissed. The question of Shea's future was unresolved.

In a police department where most cops never fire a gun at a suspect in their entire career, Shea had shot and wounded three men and allegedly pistol-whipped a fourth within fifty-seven months. In the course of fifteen days he had been involved in two incidents which were questionable at best. Still, in the eyes of those who held his fate in their hands, Shea had much to recommend him. A lot of cops come to hate their job after five or ten years on the force. Indeed, for many, the only thing that keeps them going is a pension plan which allows retirement at half pay after twenty years. The bosses felt that if a cop liked his work it was a plus factor, and no one liked it more than Shea. He loved it. He was a tough cop, who had made more than 200 arrests in eleven years—twice the city-wide average. He wasn't polished, but he gave the Department eight hours of work each day, and then some. "If told to go out and capture six lions running wild in the streets," one colleague said, "Shea will try. He might bring back only five, but he'll go after all six."

Shea was the type of cop the police brass wanted on the

force. The bosses felt that there was a place for him. The only question was where. After caucusing to decide his fate, they decided that Thomas Shea should be transferred to the predominantly black 103rd Precinct in South Jamaica, Queens.

3

IN THE GHETTO

To many, the city of New York is synonymous with Manhattan. But beyond the skyscrapers and Wall Street, away from the theater district and deluxe Fifth Avenue stores, lies a different reality.

New York City is comprised of five boroughs, the largest of which is Queens. Manhattan covers 22 square miles; Queens, 119. Manhattan has a population of one million five hundred thousand; Queens more than two million. Manhattan is known for its diversity but, in many respects, the variations within Queens are greater.

Queens embraces forty-four distinct geographic entities, each a community within itself. It is a mid-station between Manhattan and the affluent suburban communities of Long Island—an amalgamation of one- and two-family houses, apartment buildings, industrial plants, and stores. Its "good" areas are home to almost two million white middle-class residents who seek the amenities of semisuburban life on a limited budget without leaving New York. In the midst of this middle-class milieu, however, lies a socioeconomic blight of monstrous proportions.

South Jamaica is the ghetto area of Queens. A disproportionate number of its 100,000 residents are on welfare. Several thousand are known to be addicts on the basis of public records alone. Its population, which is more than 90 percent black and Hispanic, suffers from an infant mortality rate twice that of other Queens residents. Their life expectancy is six years shorter. Three times as many of their households are headed by women. Unemployment among them is twice the national average. They are, a 1978 *New York Times* study found, "a permanent underclass, people who are wards of the government, living out unproductive lives under conditions that most Americans, if they think about them at all, consider unacceptable."

New York City's 103rd Precinct lies in the heart of South Jamaica. In 1973, the year Thomas Shea was to shoot and kill Clifford Glover, the precinct's 5.47 square miles were the site of 11,919 reported felonies. Of eighty-two police precincts in the city of New York, only two were more lawless. That year the 103rd Precinct had 45 percent more murders than the city-wide precinct average, 167 percent more rapes, twice as many felonious assaults, three times as many robberies and motor-vehicle thefts. To combat this wave of crime, the New York City Police Department amassed a formidable force. The 103rd Precinct boasted more police manpower than any other in the city—356 patrolmen, 57 superior officers, and 50 civilian employees—all to little avail. Only 22.6 percent of the reported felonies committed in the 103rd Precinct in 1973 were solved. For grand larcenies and burglaries, the total was one in fifty. Meanwhile, relations between the predominantly white police and black community were a source of increasing tension. One focal point for antipolice sentiment was the cops' apparent inability to protect the citizenry and enforce the law. Even more compelling though, was black concern about alleged police brutality.

Most South Jamaicans believe that cops view black lives

more cheaply than white. Capital punishment in New York State was abolished by the legislature in 1965. That same year, in New York City alone, cops shot and killed twenty-seven people. A subsequent study by the New York City Police Department revealed that a grossly disproportionate number of white patrolmen and black victims were involved in these shootings—a trend that has continued unabated.

In the early 1970s four plainclothes New York City policemen were mistaken for criminals, shot, and killed by other policemen in the line of duty. In each instance, the victim was black and his attacker white. On April 3, 1972, at 4:00 P.M. in the South Jamaica section of Queens, a black detective named William Capers, who was on duty in civilian clothes, ordered a just-apprehended felon to lie flat on the ground during a frisk for weapons. Moments later a white cop assigned to the 103rd Precinct arrived on the scene, approached Capers from behind and, without identifying himself, ordered Capers to "drop it." When Capers turned to learn the identity of his challenger, the cop fired once, killing him instantly.

Many of the area's residents fear the police as they would soldiers in an occupying army. On the streets, it is firmly believed that cops enjoy pushing people around, and one often hears the refrain "Cops are *bad* people." Legends abound of police who carry toy guns so that, in the event they shoot an unarmed suspect, a "weapon" can be dropped by the body to justify a claim of "self-defense." Other reports tell of cops who, after shooting an armed suspect, fire the victim's weapon in the air to establish that they were fired upon.

One black attorney who resides in South Jamaica tells of being stopped by a white policeman for a minor traffic violation: "I reached into an inside jacket pocket for my driver's license and, as I did, the cop tensed and moved his hand toward his gun. Right then I remembered what color we both were. I told him very slowly and clearly, 'I am reaching into my pocket for my wallet. I do not have a gun.' "

Within South Jamaica the tendency of police to cover up the use of unnecessary force in making an arrest is taken for granted. The victim, it is felt, is invariably arrested and the charges against him tailored to justify whatever police action transpired. Thus, a citizen injured by a cop in a minor scuffle will be charged with resisting arrest, and additional charges added on to increase the chances of a guilty plea through the plea-bargaining process. Another often-alleged police practice is pushing a suspect down a flight of stairs. Handcuffed, the victim cannot break his fall, yet the arresting officer can claim that the suspect slipped, tripped, or twisted free and stumbled, all of which may account for his injuries.

All the aforementioned acts constitute crimes but, as a practical matter, prosecution rarely results. Even when a case of police brutality is well documented, the matter is usually left for internal discipline by the Department rather than criminal action by the district attorney's office. Strong predictable sanctions in cases of police wrongdoing are seldom imposed.

"When all is said and done," notes one black clergyman in South Jamaica, "only a small percentage of New York City cops are prone to violence. But it's a big department, and one percent of thirty thousand cops is three hundred men. That's three hundred screwballs scattered around New York with guns and the authority to use them. They can hurt a lot of people.

"Something happens to most men who put on a uniform and join a paramilitary system," the clergyman continues. "They change. A cop should undergo psychological testing every few years, but the Department's medical resources are totally inadequate. You know who a cop is sent to if he has a drinking problem? A police chaplain. That's where the force is at. And the problems are getting worse, not better.

Ten years ago being a cop was an honored profession. Now, after Vietnam, Watergate, and the urban riots, idealistic young whites don't want to be cops anymore. Nowadays the New York City Police Department gets the butchers."

"Butchers," one patrolman from the 103rd Precinct remarks bitterly. "That same preacher would have a fit if you called someone from his congregation an animal, but he's pretty free with labels, isn't he? I know the people who live in South Jamaica are human. But I'm human too, and they seem to forget that. I walk down the street, and all I hear is 'Hey-y-y, motherfucker.' I walk it at night, and I'm lucky if I don't get hit with a bottle coming off a roof. I bleed too you know. I got a wife and kids to feed too.

"Civic cooperation in the 103rd Precinct is virtually nonexistent," the same cop continues. "Community members should be a cop's allies in fighting crime but in South Jamaica, nothing could be further from the truth. Stop a guy in a white neighborhood to make an arrest, and there's no problem. Stop him in South Jamaica, and there's a big racial altercation. The first thing you know, you've got a crowd on your hands and you're lucky to get out alive. Then witnesses to the crime say they saw nothing and are unwilling to testify. Victims refuse to press charges. I hate to say this, but let's face it. We're in an adversary relationship with the people we're supposed to protect. And don't give me that crap about social grievances. Even if they hate cops, that doesn't explain why they throw bricks at firemen."

Since the urban riots of the 1960s, course work at the Police Academy has been altered to include heavy emphasis on police-community relations. A continuing theme, which has become a standard part of police indoctrination, is the one sounded by former Police Commissioner Vincent Broderick at a promotion ceremony in 1965:

If you believe that a police officer is somehow superior to a citizen because the citizen is a Negro or speaks Spanish, get out right now. You don't belong in the Police Department.

If you will tolerate in your men one attitude toward a white citizen who speaks English, and a different attitude toward another citizen who is a Negro or who speaks Spanish, get out right now.

If you will tolerate physical abuse by your men of any citizen, get out right now.

If you do not realize the incendiary potential in the racial slur, if you will tolerate from your men the racial slur, get out right now. You don't belong in the Police Department.

Yet no amount of indoctrination can shake the belief among many cops that, once in the ghetto, they are dealing with people who are lawless, uneducated, and irrational—people who regard arrest as a mere inconvenience. "There are people in South Jamaica," one cop contends, "who don't see any stigma at all to a conviction for mugging. And that's how they're bringing up their children. There are twelve-year-old kids who are in jail for four or five days before their parents even know they're missing."

Disrespect, hostility, mutual antagonism. With elements like these, a small spark can precipitate a crisis. The cops in New York City's 103rd Precinct are aware of this. They know that it is "just plain stupid" to engage in acts of brutality and, by and large, they avoid them. But there is an additional, extremely unpredictable element at work—fear.

Most white cops on duty in South Jamaica are afraid. They have ridden the side streets off New York Boulevard to the accompaniment of rocks thudding against patrol-car windows, and they remember the case of a young cop paralyzed from the neck down by a brick that crushed his skull. They know that routine fistfights have ended in death when one of

26

the participants grabbed a knife and plunged it deep into the chest of an intervening officer. They have learned to open police patrol boxes with their faces turned away, just in case some kid has placed a firecracker inside or a bomb has been planted by someone even more dangerous and deranged.

During the past fifteen years, seventy-one New York City policemen have been killed in the line of duty. In response, less than one percent of all police fire their guns in combat each year. But despite their restraint, most cops live in fear of an attack, and many of them have been conditioned to believe that, when it comes, the attacker will be black.

On May 19, 1971, Patrolmen Thomas Curry and Nicholas Binetti were standing guard in a police car outside the Manhattan home of New York County District Attorney Frank Hogan when a passing motor vehicle sprayed their car with machine-gun bullets. Both men survived, although Curry's face was permanently disfigured and portions of his brain destroyed. Within hours the *New York Times* and radio station WBLI-FM received identical notes which read: "The domestic armed forces of racism and oppression will be confronted by the guns of the Black Liberation Army."

Two days later, on May 21, 1971, Patrolmen Waverly Jones and Joseph Piagentini were patrolling a Harlem street when a pair of black men walked up behind them and fired two bullets into Jones (who was black) and twelve into Piagentini. That night WBLI-FM received a second note stating, "Revolutionary justice has been meted out again by the righteous brothers of the Black Liberation Army with the death of two gestapo pigs."

On January 28, 1972, Patrolmen Gregory Foster (a black) and Rocco Laurie were gunned down by three black men on a Lower Manhattan street in much the same fashion as Piagentini and Jones. Laurie was shot six times; Foster, eight. After Foster fell, his assailants turned him over and shot out both his eyes. The following day United Press International

27

received a note which read: "This is from the George Jackson Squad of the Black Liberation Army about the pigs wiped out in Lower Manhattan last night. No longer will black people tolerate oppression and exploitation. This is the start of our offensive. *There is more to come.*"

The effect of the Black Liberation Army executions on police morale in the 103rd Precinct was galvanic. Cops are viewed by many as pillars of strength, but the reality is considerably less imposing. Many are in their early and mid-twenties and inexperienced. None are bulletproof. Functioning in a precinct where a large percentage of residents carry guns and knives and virtually all are black, most cops in South Jamaica feared for their lives. Yet, just when they had the greatest need for reassurance, a new irritant was thrown into their midst. On April 2, 1973, a black police captain named Glanvin Alveranga was appointed Commanding Officer of the 103rd Precinct.

Born in Harlem, the son of immigrants who had moved to New York from the Caribbean island of Jamaica, Alveranga represented a "new breed" of police brass. His father had been a cabdriver; his mother, a member of the International Ladies Garment Workers Union. After graduating from high school, Alveranga spent two years in the United States Army and two more with the Port Authority of New York Police. On November 1, 1955, he joined the New York City Police Department and was assigned to a precinct in East Harlem. Thereafter, while moving up the ranks, he served as a Police Academy instructor, consultant to the New York State Crime Control Commission, and Commanding Officer of the 88th Detective Squad in Bedford-Stuyvesant and Fort Greene in Brooklyn. By 1972 he was one of the city's few black police captains. In April 1973, at age forty-five, he became the first black precinct commander in the history of Queens. At the time of his appointment, in a city that was more than twenty percent black, black cops made up less than eight percent of the Department's manpower. In the 103rd Precinct, which was the greatest minority bastion in Queens, only thirteen out of 413 cops were black.

Alveranga's appointment brought a generally negative response from cops in the 103rd Precinct. Stocky, five feet ten inches tall, with a deep voice and heavy jowls, he had a tendency to make cops summoned to his office wait while he leafed through papers on his desk. He had a thick black mustache that hung heavy on his upper lip and a full head of hair which one white cop described as being "combed back with some sort of pomade." Some of Alveranga's men defended him as being studious and reserved; others saw the same qualities as arrogance and "false pride."

Alveranga knew that his appointment was unpopular among the precinct's white cops. "The Police Department," he later said, "is a reflection of the rest of our society. Black-white friction on the force is the same as anywhere else. All I wanted from my men was professionalism and respect. I had a wife and two teenage children I could go to for love."

But the respect Alveranga sought was not forthcoming. Many white cops viewed his appointment as "political" and a "sellout" to appease the black community. Others complained that their new Captain was more concerned with protecting "his people" than doing a proper job. Some cops openly declared that Alveranga himself was a racist.

The fact of the matter is that many cops in the 103rd Precinct simply weren't ready to accept a black commander. The mistrust which existed between them and the black community had reached feverish proportions, and they felt that only a white commanding officer could be fully on their side. Thus, with Alveranga's appointment, the siege mentality which existed in the decrepit red-brick station house which housed "South Jamaica's finest" accelerated still further. With hostility and antagonism on all sides, the 103rd Precinct had become a festering sore waiting to burst.

4

BEFORE DAWN — APRIL 28, 1973

The appointment of Glanvin Alveranga, while engendering deep division within the Department, went largely unnoticed by the black community. South Jamaicans had jobs to perform and families to rear. To area residents, who had always regarded the police with deep suspicion, the addition to the force of one man made little difference. As the new Precinct Commander's first month in office neared an end, few citizens were aware of his existence, let alone encouraged by it. "I didn't know Alveranga from no one," Add Armstead later said. "I was concerned with making out a living, not running the police."

Armstead's concern was well founded. Two years earlier he had moved into a small two-story wood frame house at 109-50 New York Boulevard in South Jamaica with Eloise Glover and her four children. He was the sole means of support for Clifford (age ten), Henry (eight), Darlene (six), Patricia (two), Mrs. Glover, and himself.

The Armstead-Glover union filled needs in both parties. Born in Mobile, Alabama, in 1937, Eloise Glover had been unable to achieve stability or security on her own. Her father had been a seaman; her mother, a household domestic. For reasons she does not recall, she was brought up by an aunt on a farm outside Mobile. Marrying in her mid-teens, Eloise Glover bore four children, after which she was divorced. She then worked as a domestic for three dollars a day. In 1960 she moved to New York, leaving her four children with a relative in Alabama.

A large, gap-toothed woman weighing close to 200 pounds, Mrs. Glover was unable to cope with the pressures of big-city life. Soft-spoken and shy, extremely vulnerable to the world around her, she found temporary work in New York as a domestic but was forced to resign after contracting diabetes. Moving to Queens in 1963, she joined the ranks of South Jamaica residents receiving public assistance. Then she met Henry Blackman, who fathered two of her children —Clifford (born November 16, 1962) and his younger brother, Henry. She married Blackman in 1963, but he left several months later.

For the next few years, Eloise Glover survived largely on welfare and private handouts. Every Christmas the St. Albans Congregational Church gave her a generous supply of canned food and clothing. As "church mother" for the Temple Gates of Prayer Community Church (the job entailed opening the church on Sundays and keeping it clean), she came to rely on "care packages" from that church's congregation. In 1965 she met Add Armstead and subsequently bore two of his children—Darlene in 1967 and Patricia in 1970. In 1971 Armstead moved into her home.

"I know some people make a fuss about the way I've lived my life," Eloise Glover says softly, "but a good man is hard to find. Add helped us with money, he was good with the children, and he didn't beat me none. The two boys needed a man they could look up to, and he was the only one."

Armstead and Glover lived the subsistence life that characterizes much of South Jamaica. Their house was rotting and run-down. Gaping holes pockmarked the living-room walls. Monday through Friday, Armstead worked at the Pilot Automotive Wrecking Company from 7:00 A.M. to 5:00 P.M. Saturdays he worked from 7:00 A.M. till noon. Armstead was one of three steady employees. By 1973 he had worked there for eleven years—four years longer than his employer, Tony Minutello, who had bought the business in 1966 and kept Armstead on as a "burner," whose job it was to extricate car parts with an acetylene torch.

On Friday, April 27, 1973, Armstead left the junkyard at his customary hour of 5:00 P.M. His mood was buoyant. Friday was payday, and in his pocket he had almost one hundred fifty dollars in cash. Stopping at a bar, he had several beers, then made his way home for dinner. After the meal he gave Mrs. Glover thirty dollars for groceries and turned on the television. The show bored him. The plot line was confusing, and he had already begun to think about the morning ahead. His boss had told him to get in early so they could load a shipment of motors onto a truck before noon, and it was Armstead's responsibility to make sure the crane was in working order. He even had his own key to open the yard.

At 9:00 P.M. Armstead turned off the television, removed his shoes, and went to sleep on the living-room sofa. Two hours later he awoke and put the set back on to watch *Perry Mason.* Then, at midnight, he fell asleep again, unaware that within hours his life would be irrevocably altered.

As Add Armstead slept, Thomas Shea's workday had just begun. It was almost 11:00 P.M. on Friday when Shea arrived at the squat four-story concrete and red-brick building which housed the 103rd Precinct police. His mood was not good. On Thursday night he and his partner, Walter Scott, had made an arrest which necessitated his spending the better part of Friday in court. It wasn't until late afternoon that Shea had gotten home, and now, after only two hours' sleep, he was on the job again.

In many respects, the station-house layout underscored police-community tensions. Located catercorner from a large municipal parking lot, it seemed designed to shield what went on inside from probing eyes. Visitors entered the station house through a single door which opened onto a small reception area dominated by a long chest-high wood counter. Behind the counter, a raised platform six inches off the floor gave the desk officer an appearance of height to any civilian who entered. A heavy iron bar in front of the counter kept visitors a minimum of two feet away. Only one chair was available for civilians—a clear indication that they were not expected to linger. If a visitor had legitimate business at the station house, it was transacted in the labyrinth of corridors and rooms which radiated from the reception area. Several lights dangled from the ceiling with yellowed globes muting their glow. The walls, once ivory cinder block, were now gray. A huge American flag hung behind the counter. Otherwise, the reception area was bare save for two plaques opposite the door. One read:

Police Department, City of New York
58th Precinct Station House*
Borough of Queens

Erected 1927
James J. Walker, Mayor

The other plaque was more sobering:

*New York City's police precincts were renumbered after the station house was built.

34

103rd Precinct Honor Roll
In Memory of Those Killed in Line of Duty

William Long
Shield No. 15186
Appointed December 1, 1954
Called to Rest September 2, 1956

Kenneth Nugent
Shield No. 16022
Appointed November 11, 1958
Called to Rest August 21, 1971

William Capers
Shield No. 945
Appointed January 1, 1953
Called to Rest April 3, 1972

Passing through the reception area, Shea waved to the officer on duty, then went directly to the roll-call room in back on the first floor. Most cops dressed for duty in the second-floor locker room, but one month earlier Shea and Scott had drawn a permanent plainclothes assignment. Tonight, as always, they would wear civilian clothes—Shea, dungarees and a brown CPO jacket buttoned down the front with a gray sweat shirt underneath; Scott, jeans and a navy blue windbreaker.

The roll-call room was large and well lit. Two dozen metal frame chairs dominated the center with several vending machines off to the side. Shea checked the bulletin board for descriptions of wanted and missing persons, then thumbed through his memo book to make certain he had enough blank pages to cover a busy night. Joseph Kossmann, the night Operations Lieutenant, walked by and nodded hello. A rotund man of medium height with bright red hair, he had a bulging stomach of monstrous proportion and a rear end described by one cop as "the biggest butt in history." From

35

11:30 P.M. until 7:30 the following morning, Kossmann would be the commanding officer of the 103rd Precinct, responsible for supervising the station house and all cops on patrol.

One by one, the cops filed into the roll-call room, their heavy New York accents filling the air. Despite having been assigned to the precinct ten months earlier, Shea did not know many of their names. Nonetheless, he felt a strong sense of camaraderie with each of them. As always, there was a high visibility of guns. Police regulations mandate that a loaded service revolver be carried at all times. For a cop to leave home without it would be akin to a Wall Street lawyer appearing in court without a tie. As a practical matter, most cops, Shea included, carried two guns.

At 11:15 P.M. Sergeant Joseph Kennedy called roll. Shea knew him by name and sight, nothing more. Still, Kennedy had a reputation as someone who looked after his men, and Shea liked him. For the coming night, Kennedy would be one of three sergeants responsible for supervising patrol-car duty. Thomas Donohue and Robert Bennett were the others.

As Kennedy called roll, the cops strained to hear him. He had a deep, gravelly voice extremely low in volume, and no one wanted to miss an assignment. Most of the men would spend the next eight hours in uniform patrolling an assigned section of South Jamaica by car. However, Shea and his partner, Walter Scott, had a different task.

Eighteen months earlier the Department had implemented an "Anticrime Program" which placed hundreds of cops on duty disguised as drunks, blind men, Hasidic rabbis, taxi drivers, telephone linemen, and the like. The theory underlying Anticrime was that, without their giveaway blue uniforms, these cops would be better able to gather information and enforce the law. However, in South Jamaica after midnight, any white man was suspect as a cop, and thus in the

103rd Precinct late-night anticrime details were conducted by motor patrol.

Shea and Scott had been partners on the late-night anticrime shift since March 1, 1973. Their initial assignment had been general in nature, but in late March they were instructed to concentrate on stolen cars. An automobile-theft ring was operating virtually unchecked in the 103rd Precinct. Rather than steal cars in their entirety, the thieves stripped them. Every day four or five residents would come out to the street and find their automobiles without doors, hoods, or fenders. These parts, the police presumed, were sold to neighborhood body shops which had "requisitioned" them, but a check of shops in the area had proved futile. And one additional item was particularly galling. The thieves always escaped police detection. Not once had they been caught in the act by a passing patrol car. Thus, the precinct command had come to conclude that the "other side" had access to a police radio, enabling it to know exactly when and where the cops were on duty.

Careful monitoring by the opposition required a resourceful response. For the upcoming night, Shea and Scott had been instructed to radio the station house at 4:00 A.M. and announce that they were going off duty for a meal break. However, rather than leave the streets, they would then cruise anonymously in the hope that the car thieves would strike. Their real meal break would come an hour later at five.

As Shea and Scott left the station house at 11:30 P.M., they walked by prearrangement to Scott's car. Every evening they drove separately to work, Shea in an ivory-colored Volkswagen, Scott in a white Buick Skylark. Then, after roll call, they would ride the streets together until 7:30 A.M., when they separated and drove home. The previous night they had used Shea's car, and he was glad tonight was Walter's turn.

"You tired?" Scott asked as they pulled away from the curb.

"Yeah."

"It shows . . . cheer up. We've got the next two nights off."

As the car moved slowly through the streets, Shea stared out the window . . . burned-out shops . . . abandoned buildings . . . cracked sidewalks with whole chunks of concrete torn away. Idle men holding bottles in brown paper bags stood huddled together, all of them black, each a potential adversary. During their first shift together, Shea had told Scott, "If I ever get shot, I want you to take me to Queens General Hospital. The emergency room there is better than the one at Mary Immaculate."

Almost without thinking, Shea checked the position of his guns. One, a six-shot service revolver, was strapped over his left shoulder. The other, a snub-nosed revolver holding five bullets, was in a pants holster on the right side of his back. Both were .38-caliber models.

"Thank God the next two days are off," Shea told himself. Maybe then he could catch up on his sleep and spend some time with his children. Tuesday had been his younger daughter's birthday. Lynn was eleven now, one year younger than Cindy. The balloons from the party he had missed were still up in the garage. Being a cop was detrimental to family life. He knew that, and it bothered him. Generally, when he got home from work, he ate breakfast, slept for four hours, then got up to socialize or run errands. After that he'd take a three-hour nap, eat supper, watch television with Bonnie and the kids, and go off to work again. At one point, when Bonnie was finding it particularly hard to cope with the demands of semi-single parenthood, their family doctor had suggested he switch to daytime hours. But, somehow, the suggestion had never been implemented, largely, Shea knew, because he had wanted to keep working nights.

For a dozen years Shea had always sought out late-night hours. Most cops derided the midnight to 8:00 A.M. shift, calling it the "witches' watch," "late show," or "graveyard hours." The fact that it was a direct descendant of the famous Dutch Night Watch, which had guarded New Amsterdam from dusk till dawn 300 years earlier, did nothing to spur their civic fervor. But Shea was happy with it. "That might sound strange," he says, "but I joined the force because I wanted to do police work. Nighttime is when crime is at its peak. That's when I wanted to be on the job. Besides, the time always seemed to go faster when I was busy." His tour began as evening workers—cleaning women, printers, waiters—were going home. Bars were letting out, their patrons easy prey. Generally, the first two hours were the busiest. Then, as the night wore on, the numbers thinned. By four the last bars had closed, and there was time for reflection before the pace picked up again. Leaving work each morning at eight, Shea and his partner saw most of the world moving in an opposite direction.

They were an odd couple, Shea and Scott. Both were physically unprepossessing. Scott, in particular, was a graceless man—five feet nine inches tall, 200 pounds, with short, stubby fingers and heavy thighs. Like Shea, he had always wanted to be a cop. Born in Queens, the son of a film technician, Scott had joined the force at age twenty-two in January 1969 and served in Manhattan's 9th Precinct until February 1972, when he was reassigned to South Jamaica. In two evaluation reports, superior officers had graded Scott among the "bottom quarter" of their men. On one occasion his hand had been broken by a pimp who struck him with a metal pipe. Rather than arrest the assailant, Scott had thrown him through a plate-glass window. Several years later the Civilian

Complaint Review Board had cautioned him about a report that, while issuing a traffic summons to a sixteen-year-old black, he had held a cocked gun to the youth's head.

Within any given precinct, certain men get reputations as the kind of cops others don't want to ride with. Some are unnecessarily aggressive and abrasive. Others fail to back up a partner in trouble. Generally, word gets around, and a cop whose own partner is on vacation will tell the roll-call officer, "I don't want to work with so-and-so. Give me someone else until my partner gets back, or I'll call in sick." Eventually one of three things happens to these unwanted men: They mend their ways, get station-house desk jobs, or pair up with each other. Shea and Scott were partners. Neither had enjoyed a steady companion in the 103rd Precinct until they found each other. By late April 1973 they had ridden fifty tours together.

As the night wore on, conversation between Shea and Scott began to wane. Both men were tired and, by 3:00 A.M., what little dialogue there was came from the police walkie-talkie nestled on the seat between them. It was a compact one-pound model and, through it, they were able to monitor communications between precinct headquarters and the other radio-patrol cars on duty in South Jamaica. Walkie-talkies were treated with great respect. In addition to their communications value, they each cost the Department $750. Any cop who lost one was docked five days' vacation.

At 4:00 A.M. Shea flipped on the transmitter of his machine and, as prearranged, radioed headquarters that he and Scott were breaking for a meal. Then Scott turned the car down a narrow side street and continued cruising. Moments later the walkie-talkie sounded.

"I got a signal twenty-one on an auto," the dispatcher intoned. "Two black males stole a cab. The location is Van

Wyck Expressway and Liberty Avenue. Can someone meet the complainant in the Exxon station nearby?"

As Shea and Scott listened, one of the other cars on patrol responded in the affirmative. Several minutes later a preliminary report of the incident was on the air:

RADIO CAR: Have units in the 103rd and surrounding precincts on the lookout for a yellow and red 1970 Chevrolet four-door Buzz-a-Ride Cab. It was stolen approximately fifteen minutes ago from Liberty Avenue and Van Wyck Expressway.

DISPATCHER: Any description on the perpetrator?

RADIO CAR: It was stolen by two male Negroes about twenty-three, twenty-four years of age.

DISPATCHER: Any weapon?

RADIO CAR: Possibly a gun.

At 4:22 A.M., more information came over the walkie-talkie: *"One perpetrator was wearing a white hat and black overcoat; the other a brown leather jacket.* The cab has been recovered. The alarm is still active on the two male Negroes."

There is nothing unusual about a taxicab robbery in the 103rd Precinct, and the one which occurred in the predawn hours of April 28, 1973, was no exception. Shortly before 4:00 A.M. a twenty-one-year-old cabdriver named Frank Damiani had picked up two black men outside a bar on the corner of South Road and Waltham Avenue. When they arrived at their destination, one of the men pulled a gun, pushed it against Damiani's ribs, and announced, "This is a rip-off." Evincing more concern for his money than his life, Damiani leaped with his cashbox from the car and ran. Instead of firing or chasing after him, the two men simply drove off with the cab.

Damiani ran to the nearest telephone and dialed 911 to report the theft. The abandoned car was found shortly thereafter. No sooner had it been recovered than the walkie-talkie sounded again, this time with a report of shots at the Step Inn Bar on Hillside Avenue. Almost concurrently, Shea turned to Scott and banged his fist on the dashboard in frustration. Directly in front of them, by the curb at 115-20 142nd Street, stood a blue 1970 Chevrolet stripped of its doors, hood, and fenders.

Gritting his teeth, Shea noted the license plate number on the car, flipped a switch on his walkie-talkie to "transmit," and radioed headquarters: "Anticrime to Central. Can we have a ten-fifteen on New York registration two-four-five QFT?"

"Ten-fifteen" was a request that the dispatcher check his computer to learn whether or not the car in question had been reported stolen. A ten-sixteen reply would mean "yes." Ten-seventeen would mean "no."

"Are you holding?" the dispatcher asked.

"Yes."

"Stand by."

Seconds later the first police unit to arrive at the Step Inn Bar radioed for an ambulance to be rushed to the scene. At 4:46 A.M. the dispatcher came back on again. "Anticrime, ten-seventeen on that New York plate [not reported stolen]."

"Can we have a name on that?" Shea asked.

"Stand by."

The unit at the Step Inn Bar interrupted again to report that two persons had been critically wounded.

"Anticrime," the dispatcher intoned, recapturing the air-waves. "The registered owner on that auto is Harry Heyman, 87-40 Francis Lewis Boulevard."

42

The unit covering the shooting at the bar asked for a supervisor to be sent to the scene.

"Can you tell us what precinct 87-40 Francis Lewis Boulevard is in?" Shea asked.

"One-oh-seven," the dispatcher answered.

Sergeant Joseph Kennedy interrupted to broadcast over the patrol-car radio that he would respond to the Step Inn Bar, where one man lay dead and another dying.

Shea climbed from Scott's car to inspect the stripped vehicle. The owner didn't even know it had happened. Leaning through what had once been the right front door, he reached into the glove compartment and pulled out the insurance card. "Let's go back to the station house and call the owner," he told Scott. "Then we can break for meal."

"Come on, boy. Get up! Time to go."

The alarm had rung five minutes earlier, ripping Add Armstead from a heavy sleep. Now at 4:45 A.M., he was trying to awaken his son Clifford.

For almost a year Armstead had taken the boy to work on Saturday mornings. Initially Clifford had been reluctant to go. An awkward bashful child deeply affected by the loss of his natural father, he had been suspicious of this man who lived with his mother. But in time his mistrust had faded. Armstead was the only father he had known, and before long the boy was going to the junkyard not only on Saturdays but after school as well. It gave him a sense of accomplishment, and occasionally the boss even paid him a dollar for running errands.

"Wake up, boy. No time for dreams. We gotta be movin'. Gotta get up and go to work if you want to learn to be a mechanic."

Shaking the cobwebs from his head, Clifford climbed from

43

bed. In anticipation of the moment, he had slept fully clothed except for his shoes. Reaching down, he picked a deck of playing cards, a miniature wrench, and a plastic ornament bearing the words "Aloha Hawaii" off the floor. Then, after stuffing his bounty in a pants pocket, he pulled his boots on.

"Go quiet so you don't wake your mother," Armstead cautioned. The boy was dressed in brown trousers, green nylon socks, and a long-sleeved brown shirt with a purple collar. The boots were black suede with two-and-one-quarter-inch heels. He was ten years old, five feet tall, and weighed ninety-eight pounds.

At the hall closet, Armstead stopped and pulled out a brown leather coat for himself, a mustard-colored jacket for Clifford. "Put this on," he said. "It's cold out."

The boy obeyed.

"Better wear something on your noggin too, so you don't catch cold."

Clifford reached for a white cotton fatigue hat and pulled it over his head.

It was 4:50 A.M.

Outside, Armstead buttoned his coat to guard against the chill early-morning air. The temperature was fifty-three degrees, but dampness and dew made it seem colder. The junkyard was slightly more than a quarter mile away. Sometimes on Saturdays they took the bus. Sometimes they walked.

"I got it in my mind we should take the bus today," Armstead said as they reached the street, "but I don't see none coming. It ain't but six or seven blocks. We can walk."

New York Boulevard fronted an incongruous combination of industrial buildings and battered wood frame houses. It was an ill-paved, rutted road with two lanes running in each direction. The man and boy walked along the sidewalk with Armstead near the curb. Past the corner of New York Boulevard and Mathias Avenue, the sidewalk gave way to a trail of cracked slate. To the right, a large vacant lot stood littered with paper, tin cans, and broken glass. Five trees fifty to sixty feet tall rose out of the trash. Around the trees, rough underbrush one to two feet high extended to a burned-out garage in back. A narrow dirt path that had been worn into the underbrush by people crossing the lot extended from the street past the garage and through a break in a waist-high chain-link fence which divided the lot. All totaled, the area was fifty by seventy yards in size.

Walter Scott turned the white Buick Skylark north on New York Boulevard and cast his eyes aimlessly across the dreary landscape: dilapidated stores . . . crumbling houses . . . a run-down service station. As the car crossed 112th Road approaching Mathias Avenue, two figures walking in the opposite direction caught his eye. Both were black. One was dressed in a brown leather jacket. The other was wearing brown pants, a mustard-colored jacket, and white hat.

Turning his head to the side, Scott nudged his partner. "Hey, Tom. Over there on the far side of the road, those are the two guys from the taxi stickup."

The destinies of Clifford Glover and Thomas Shea were about to collide.

5

DAYBREAK— APRIL 28, 1973

After calling roll, Sergeant Joseph Kennedy smoked a Chesterfield to the butt, then left the station house at 11:30 P.M. to go on patrol. The night was unusually quiet and, breaking for a meal just before 4:00 A.M., Kennedy and his partner (a six-year patrolman named Richard Gray) commented on how calm it had been. Then the Step Inn Bar erupted in gunfire. Kennedy and Gray were en route to the scene, their radio at full volume, when the voice of Walter Scott punctured the night air.

"Anticrime, ten-thirteen, 112th and New York Boulevard."

Immediately the Step Inn Bar was forgotten. "Ten-thirteen" takes precedence over any signal a cop might hear. It means that a fellow officer is in trouble.

Almost instantaneously the radio dispatcher repeated the call: "Ten-thirteen, 112th and New York Boulevard. 112th and New York Boulevard, ten-thirteen, plainclothes."

Before Kennedy could flip his transmitter on, another unit answered, "Three Charlie on the way."* Two near-identical

---

*The 103rd Precinct was divided into several sectors for purposes of patrol. "Three Charlie" meant unit number three, assigned to Section C.

responses followed. Gray gunned the car north along New York Boulevard toward 112th Road, seven blocks away. In less than a minute they were there. The streets were empty, no one in sight.

"Keep going," Kennedy instructed. "Maybe they're further on."

As they drove north, another patrol car passed in the opposite direction, its siren wailing.

"Hey, central," a voice called over the radio, "where's the unit for the ten-thirteen?"

"Anticrime," the dispatcher asked, "what's your location on that ten-thirteen?"

Inside the lot, Thomas Shea and Walter Scott stood hidden from view, huddled by the body of a ten-year-old boy.

"The backyard," Scott answered into the walkie-talkie by his side.

Kennedy turned toward Gray. "Turn the car around, and go back down New York Boulevard."

"Location? What address?" another cop radioed.

"We're on Dillon Street [on the far side of the lot]," Scott answered.

"We just passed there. We don't see nothing."

"Come over to Dillon Street," Scott shouted. "You'll see a green Javelin or something out front of a house."

Shea stood up from a kneeling position and looked at his partner. "I'll go out and flag someone down."

Kennedy and Gray were passing the lot for the second time when Shea emerged with a floppy white hat clutched in his left hand. "There he is," Kennedy said. "Hold it here." Gray jammed on the brakes, and the Sergeant exited from the car, meeting Shea at the curb. "What happened?" he asked.

"I had to shoot someone back in the lot."

"Are you okay?"

"Yes."

Kennedy turned toward Gray. "Call the ten-thirteen off. Otherwise, every cop in South Jamaica will be here." Then he turned back to Shea. "Where's the victim?"

Shea pointed toward the center of the lot.

"Is he alive?"

"I think so."

"Let's go," Kennedy ordered.

The two men began walking toward the trees.

"What happened?" the Sergeant asked a second time.

"My partner and I were driving down New York Boulevard when we saw two men who fit the description of the guys who pulled the taxi job. Walter made a U-turn. I got out and, when I identified myself as a cop, they ran. I chased after them, and one of them pulled a gun. I fired in self-defense."

"Did you recover the gun?"

"No. As he was falling, he tossed it to the other perpetrator. The second guy got away."

One hundred fifty feet into the lot, they reached Clifford Glover, who lay moaning on the ground. Walter Scott stood over him, gun in hand. Kennedy knelt down and examined the blood that poured from wounds in the boy's back and right shoulder.

"Where are you hurt?"

There was no answer.

"Can you walk?"

Clifford squirmed but said nothing. Two more cops, Sergeant Thomas Donohue and Patrolman John McCabe, approached. Spotting Scott with his gun still out, Donohue walked over and put a hand on his shoulder. "Take it easy, Walter. It's all over. Put your gun away."

Scott opened the cylinder of his revolver and ejected a spent shell. For the first time, Kennedy realized that Scott too had fired. Two more cops, Frank Alvy and Ralph

Panico, walked into the lot. While circling on Dillon Street, they had passed a black man standing in the center of the road waving his arms and pointing toward the lot. Panico, who was driving, slowed down enough to hear the word "shooting," then sped toward the lot, believing that a fellow officer was in trouble. The old man had been left standing in the road.

"What happened?" Panico asked.

"He pulled a gun," Shea answered. "We stopped to question him about the taxi robbery, and he pulled a gun."

Donohue bent over to examine the boy's wound. Just then Richard Gray, who could no longer stand the suspense of waiting in Kennedy's car, joined the group. "What happened?" he queried.

Before anyone could answer, Donohue stood up. "Come on," he said to Shea. "Let's take a walk."

"Okay."

"You too," Donohue said, pointing to Scott.

The three men walked toward New York Boulevard, Scott in the middle, Shea and Donohue on either side.

"What happened?" Donohue asked.

"We found a stripped car and were on our way to the station house when we saw two guys," Shea began. "They fit the description of the guys who pulled the taxi holdup, so we stopped them. I got out of the car, identified myself as a cop, and flashed my shield. Then the one who got shot said, 'Fuck you, you're not taking me,' and both of them ran. I chased after them and the guy who said, 'Fuck you,' pulled a gun from inside his jacket and started to turn. I fired in self-defense."

"Did you recover the gun?"

"No. As he was falling, he passed it to the other man. I stayed with the one who was shot. Walter chased after the second guy, but he got away."

Donohue turned toward Scott. "Is that right?"

"Yes, sir. I chased after him but, when we reached the burned-out garage in back of the lot, he fired a shot at me. I put my arm across my face and, when I took it down, he was gone."

On Dillon Avenue, behind the lot, a fourth patrol car arrived, its siren and domed red light flashing. The driver, Al Farrell, was a large, red-faced Irishman who had been on the force for twenty years. Friendly and outgoing, he had worked in South Jamaica for more than a decade. At his side sat Thomas Scott, a sixteen-year veteran who had transferred to the 103rd Precinct one month earlier.

Looking up Dillon Street, Farrell saw a black man frantically waving his arms. With no one else in sight, he stepped on the gas and pulled alongside. The man was nearly incoherent. "Help! Help! Shooting! My son! My son!"

Both Farrell and Tom Scott got out of the car, guns drawn, and frisked him. Scott found a nine-inch white metal wrench and removed it from the man's pocket.

"Help! My son! My son! Shooting!"

Neither cop could fully understand him. "Did your son shoot at you?" Scott finally asked.

"No, no, no, no! Backyard! My son! Help!"

Like a frightened dog, the man grabbed hold of Farrell's arm and began tugging at his sleeve, trying to lead him toward the lot. Farrell pulled free and pointed toward the car. "Get in," he ordered.

After flinging the door open, the man half flew into the back seat. Tom Scott slid in alongside him, and Farrell got behind the wheel. Quickly he put the car in reverse and backed up 200 feet along Dillon Street until he reached an entrance to the lot.

"What's your name?" Scott asked.

"Armstead."

On 112th Road a fifth police car pulled to a halt by the southern edge of the lot. Its driver, Eddie Anderson, was a five-year veteran of the force. He was the first black man to respond to the scene. With him was John Higgins, twenty-five years old, three years as a cop. Higgins had ridden with Shea on three previous occasions.

After parking their car, Anderson and Higgins walked toward the center of the lot. Just as they arrived at the chain-link fence where Clifford Glover lay, Donohue returned with Shea and Walter Scott, and Armstead rushed into the lot with Tom Scott and Al Farrell.

"That's my son," Armstead cried, pointing to Clifford.

Shea looked up startled. "That's the other guy. Where's the gun?"

"He didn't have one," Farrell said.

"Did you toss him?"

"Yes."

"Toss him again," Shea demanded.

Farrell did as told. "There's no gun," he said.

Anderson stared down at the crumpled form of the boy lying on the opposite side of the fence. "Has anyone called an ambulance?"

"Yes," someone told him.

"How long ago?"

"A couple of minutes."

"Why don't you take him to the hospital?" Kennedy interrupted.

The black cop nodded.

Kennedy bent over and scooped the boy up, holding one forearm under Clifford's back and the other beneath his thighs. As he did, Walter Scott reached down and picked the floppy white hat off the ground where Shea had dropped it and placed it on the boy's chest. Clifford groaned, and Anderson turned away. Kennedy handed the boy across the fence to Higgins, who carried him to the car. With Tom Scott helping, Higgins slid him across the back seat, and Eddie Anderson slipped in alongside. Higgins then climbed behind the wheel and began to drive toward Mary Immaculate Hospital. The boy moaned.

"Hush," Anderson told him, stroking his forehead. "You'll be all right."

Higgins radioed the hospital to have a doctor waiting. Clifford squirmed and tried to sit up.

"Lie still," Anderson ordered. "You'll be all right." He ran his hand down the boy's cheek till it came to rest just above Clifford's chest. Then, noticing which way the boy's shirt was tearing, he turned toward Higgins. "He's been shot in the back. He was shot in the back, and the bullet exited in front."

The ride to the hospital took ten minutes. Clifford was bleeding badly. At the in-patient entrance he was placed on a portable stretcher and wheeled to the emergency room with Higgins and Anderson by his side. Two nurses checked his pulse and blood pressure. Both were unrecordable. An attending physician made an incision in the right side of his chest and inserted an endotracheal tube to drain 2,500 cc of blood. At the same time a transfusion was given, and attempts at cardiac recuscitation were begun. "It's critical," the doctor announced. "The chances for survival are not good."

Back in the lot, a dozen cops had gathered. Taking six of them aside, Sergeant Kennedy ordered a search for the gun. Fifteen minutes later, when no weapon had been found, he told his driver to radio the Department's Emergency Services Squad for help. Then, after instructing that the area be secured, he ordered Farrell and Tom Scott to bring Armstead back to the station house and the remaining cops to resume patrol. "All except you two," he said, pointing to Shea and Walter Scott. "You'd better go back to the station house and wait."

Both men nodded, retreated to Walter Scott's car (which was parked on Dillon Street), and drove off alone. As he watched them disappear, Kennedy wondered for the first time why the car had been parked on Dillon if Armstead and Glover were apprehended on New York Boulevard.

Farrell and Tom Scott ushered Armstead into the back seat of their car and began driving toward the station house. Farrell was behind the wheel. Tom Scott was at Armstead's side.

"Do you want to tell us what happened?" Farrell asked.

Armstead nodded. "I was going to work. My boss told me to be in early to open up the shop, and I brought the boy. He always comes with me on Saturdays."

"Where do you work?"

Armstead reached into his pocket and pulled out a card bearing the name Pilot Automotive Wrecking Company. "I don't remember the name so good, but this is the place."

Farrell nodded.

"We was walking to work," Armstead continued, "when a car pulled up and a man got out. He hollered, 'You black son of a bitch,' and I run. I had my pay from yesterday, and I thought he be going to rob me. Then he started shooting, and I fell by the fence with my boy. My pliers fell out of my pocket."

"Forget about the pliers," Farrell told him. "What happened next?"

"I run to Dillon Street and a police car come by but it didn't stop. Then you two come by and helped me."

In the station house, Joseph Kossmann was breaking for a meal in the first-floor lieutenant's office. Sitting at a desk wedged between four lockers and the wall, he was about to devour his sandwich when someone banged on the door. Kossmann looked up and Sergeant Robert Bennett rushed into the room. "We have a shooting."

"What kind?"

"A bad one. Tom Shea shot a suspect who's been taken to Mary Immaculate Hospital."

Leaving his sandwich behind, Kossmann hurried to the front desk in the reception area, where Shea and Walter Scott had just arrived. The time was 5:45 A.M.

"What happened?" Kossmann asked.

Shea repeated his story for the third time.

"Okay," the Lieutenant told him. "You'd better fill out some forms." Then Kossmann retreated to his office, where, as a matter of course, he called Leonard Flanagan, the on-duty Captain for Queens, and advised him of the shooting. As he hung up, Farrell and Tom Scott arrived with Armstead.

"Take him into the roll-call room in back," Kossmann ordered, "and stay with him."

The two men did as told, instructing Armstead to sit in a metal frame chair by the vending machines. Moments later Walter Scott stuck his head into the room. "Keep an eye on him," he warned. "That man's my prisoner."

"Yeah, right," Farrell said.

In the reception area up front, Thomas Shea was completing a Firearm Discharge Report. After filling in his name, shield number, and the date, he came to the words "Describe the incident in detail": "Officer observed two m/n [male Negroes] who fit description of past armed robbery," he wrote. "After officer IDed self, one m/n stated, 'Fuck you, you're not taking me,' and started to flee into vacant lot. Officer pursued. At this point, same m/n took revolver from his pocket and attempted to turn in officer's direction. I fired."

Completing the form, Shea realized that there was blood on his hands and went to the lavatory to wash them. Simultaneously, Sergeant Donald Bromberg entered the station house and walked to the roll-call room, where Walter Scott had joined Farrell, Tom Scott, and Armstead. A seven-year veteran of the force, Bromberg had been called to the lot shortly before 6:00 A.M. His half-hour search had revealed nothing but a pair of pliers embedded in the earth five feet from the chain-link fence. After surveying the scene, Bromberg decided to visit the station house and talk with the participants. Approaching Walter Scott, he asked the now-familiar question: "What happened?"

"Who the hell are you?" Scott demanded.

"I'm Detective Sergeant Donald Bromberg assigned to the Fifteenth Burglary and Larceny Squad."

"Good for you," Scott told him. "I'm not answering any more questions until I see a lawyer."

Bromberg began a slow boil. "Look, stupid! I don't know what went on out there, but your partner might be in a little trouble. Tell me what happened, and let's get it over with."

"I'm not saying anything," Scott answered. Walking from the room, he rejoined Shea, who had begun filling out arrest forms on Armstead and Glover. Sergeant Kennedy walked by.

"What are the charges?" Kennedy asked.

"Attempted murder, possession of a dangerous weapon, and reckless endangerment," Shea told him.

Kossmann appeared in the doorway. "Captain Flanagan is here. He'd like some details and wants to see you in Alveranga's office."

Wearily, Shea stood up, preparing to tell his story for the fourth time.

"You too," Kossmann told Scott.

"Okay, okay."

Inside Alveranga's office, Leonard Flanagan sat waiting. Normally assigned to the 108th Precinct, on the morning of April 28, 1973, he was the on-duty Captain for the Borough of Queens. He had been a cop for twenty-eight years. As Shea and Scott entered the room, he stood to greet them, then asked, "What happened?"

Shea began. "My partner and I were on a late-night tour assigned to Anticrime. We had just found a stripped car and were on our way to the station house to report it when we saw two people who fit the description of the men who stole a cab earlier in the evening. Their clothes were the same. We made a U-turn and, when I got out to identify myself, one of them said, 'Fuck you, you're not taking me.' Then they ran."

Flanagan interrupted. "Where did you stop your car?"

"On New York Boulevard north of 112th Road."

"Go on."

"Anyway, the men ran into the lot. Walter and I followed for a few steps, and then Walter ran back to the car and drove it around the corner to head them off. He stopped on 112th Road and came back into the lot."

As Shea talked, Flanagan began to diagram the lot on a piece of paper. "Could you show me where you ran?"

Leaning forward, Shea took the pencil from the Captain's hand and drew a straight line from New York Boulevard to the center of the lot.

"Go on," Flanagan said.

"Just then one of the suspects reached into his pocket and pulled out a gun. I fired three times. He passed the gun to the other suspect and fell. Then the second man fired a shot at Walter and got away."

Flanagan turned toward Scott. "Did you see the suspect pull a gun and pass it to the other man after he was shot?"

"Yes, sir."

The Captain stared down at the makeshift map in front of him, then looked directly at Shea. "I don't see how Patrolman Scott could have driven his car around to 112th Road, gotten out, and run back into the lot in time to see the shooting."

There was a long silence.

"Well," Shea said at last, "I didn't draw the line exactly

56

right. The two of them didn't run straight. It was a zigzag chase, sort of a curve."

"How did your car get to Dillon Street?"

Another long pause.

"I drove it," Scott volunteered. "After the second man took the gun, he fired a shot. I pegged one back, then ran back to the car and drove over to Dillon to head him off, but he got away."

Flanagan looked down at his hands. "Do you know how old that boy was?"

Neither man answered.

"He was ten years old. Couldn't you see he was a kid?"

"It was dark," Shea mumbled. "He was wearing a white hat that shaded his face."

"Let me see your gun."

Just then Kossmann entered the room. "Patrolman Anderson called from the hospital, sir. The boy is dead."

6

MIDDAY—
APRIL 28, 1973

Shortly before 8:00 A.M., Harold Cannon arrived at the 16th
Homicide Division wearing the rumpled fifty-dollar suit that
was all but mandatory for New York City detectives. He
would be responsible for investigating any homicide which
occurred in the 103rd, 105th, 107th, or 113th precinct during
the next eight hours.

Cannon was black. Five feet eight inches tall, round-faced
with receding gray hair, he was slightly overweight and decidedly non-physical in appearance. He had been born in
Delaware and raised in New Jersey. After graduating from
high school, he apprenticed as a tool and dye maker and
served four years in the United States Navy, then returned
to work as a machinist. In 1953 he joined the New York City
Police Department because, in his words, "it was the only
decent job I could get."

As Cannon entered the Detectives' Room, Morty Edelson,
who worked the midnight to 8:00 A.M. shift, was pecking
away at the keys of a typewriter. "Good morning," Cannon
said cheerfully.

"Ugh!"

"Boy, you must have had a bad night."

"It was rough," Edelson answered. "First there was a homicide in the 107th. Then two guys got shot at the Step Inn Bar. After that there was another call from the 103rd Precinct. I haven't even had time to answer that one."

The telephone rang, and Edelson picked up the receiver. "I'll be there, I'll be there. I'm typing up reports on two other homicides. If I don't get them in by nine, the press will scream and the public relations people will have my ass."

Cannon's face wrinkled up in a smile. He was a genuinely nice man who, more often than not, was willing to share the burdens that had been placed on a fellow officer. "What's that all about?" he asked when the conversation ended.

"The 103rd again. Some father-and-son stickup team robbed a cab. The cops shot one of them, and it turned out to be a kid."

"Tell you what," Cannon offered. "You've had a long night. I'll take the last homicide."

"Sold."

Cannon noted the time on his memo pad, then walked toward the door. "Hey, Harold," Edelson said, looking up from his typewriter. "Thanks."

"Don't worry about it. You owe me one."

As Cannon left the 16th Division detectives' room, the 103rd Precinct station house had begun to stir. After notifying Leonard Flanagan of Clifford Glover's death, Joseph Kossmann had telephoned Glanvin Alveranga, who arrived at the station house within the hour. Next, Kossmann telephoned Inspector Robert Johnson (the Commanding Officer of the 16th Division), who arrived ninety minutes later. Johnson's appearance meant that Alveranga had been superseded as top cop on the case. Like Alveranga, Johnson was black.

Meanwhile, after leaving Edelson, Cannon drove directly

to the lot and found fourteen men from the Emergency Services Squad combing the area for a gun. Taking charge, the detective radioed the station house and asked that Shea be sent to help. Shea, who had just finished an interview with Sergeant Donald Bromberg, arrived with a second cop minutes later and reenacted the shooting for Cannon. As he finished, Inspector Johnson arrived, and Shea repeated his story again, after which Johnson ordered that ground and aerial photographs of the area be taken. Shea was pleased that Alveranga had been superseded by Johnson. The inspector (although black) was popular among white cops and had a reputation as "a pretty decent guy." Johnson, for his part, thought Shea seemed "a lot less shook up than most cops would be after killing a ten-year-old boy."

As the search progressed, more and more cops filtered into the area. Shortly after 10:30 A.M., a large balding man with burly forearms and heavy jowls approached Shea and extended his right hand.

"Hi, I'm Charlie Peterson, the PBA Trustee for Queens County."

The name was familiar. Each precinct had several cops who served as delegates to the Patrolmen's Benevolent Association and reported to a borough trustee. Notified of the shooting by a PBA delegate, Peterson had driven from his home to the station house, then to the lot.

"What happened?" the trustee asked.

Shea repeated his story.

"Have you made any statements?"

"Yes."

"Who did you talk with?"

Shea told him.

"I wish you hadn't done that," Peterson said. "Even if there's nothing to hide, it's hard to think straight right after a shooting. You've been through a traumatic experience, and you should have waited a few hours to calm down. Now, if you change your story, it will be held against you."

"But I told them everything that happened."

"You told them everything you remember," Peterson corrected. "You might think of something else later."

Shea shrugged his shoulders. "Okay! I'm sorry."

The trustee looked around the lot at the dozen or so cops searching through broken glass, cardboard, and tin cans. The sky was gray overhead. "Don't worry about it," he said. "Let's go back to the station house. I've arranged for a PBA lawyer to meet us there."

Minutes after Peterson and Shea left the lot, Harold Cannon did likewise. The boy's death was a tragedy, but Cannon didn't see what more could be done about it. Even if the search for a gun came up empty, it wouldn't be the first time in his experience that a weapon had disappeared. Any one of the neighbors could have taken it. All that remained was a *pro forma* questioning of the father. Then Armstead would be booked for robbery, possession of a deadly weapon, or some other offense, and the investigation could be closed.

Driving along New York Boulevard toward the station house, Cannon was planning his schedule for the day ahead when he passed the Glover-Armstead home. Suddenly he wondered whether anyone had notified Eloise Glover of her son's death. If not, as the detective who had "caught" the case, it was his responsibility. Slowing to a halt at 109-50 New York Boulevard, he took several deep breaths and approached the front door. Moments after he rang the bell, Mrs. Glover answered. Cannon introduced himself and asked if she knew about her son.

"I heard," she told him. "Someone from a newspaper called maybe an hour ago."

A sorrowful misunderstanding was in the making. The reporter who called had told Mrs. Glover that Clifford was shot in a robbery but that his injuries were minor.

"I'd like to go to the hospital to see him," she told Cannon.

The request did not strike the detective as unusual. On numerous other occasions a parent had asked to see the body of a deceased child.

"I'll call the hospital to see if it's all right," he said. "Could I use your telephone?"

She nodded and led him to the kitchen, then went to the living room to wait. Several minutes later Cannon reappeared. "It's too late," he said. "Your son's body has already been taken to the morgue."

As Cannon and Mrs. Glover talked, Thomas Shea sat with Charlie Peterson in a diner across from the 103rd Precinct station house. Peterson was eating scrambled eggs. Shea picked at a hamburger and french fries. Despite not having eaten since the previous evening, he wasn't hungry. He'd slept two hours in the past two days and wanted to go home.

"What do you think will happen next?" Shea asked.

"They'll investigate for a couple of hours," Peterson told him. "Then they'll let you go. Maybe you'll get a reprimand."

"A reprimand wouldn't be fair," Shea said. "I was only doing my job. Walter and I didn't have to stop. We could have driven right by those two guys, but we were doing our job. They robbed a cab, and then one of them pulled a gun on me."

"We think they robbed a cab," Peterson said. "Let's face it. You've got two problems. One, the kid was ten years old; and two, he was black."

"A reprimand wouldn't be fair," Shea said again.

"Don't worry about it. Finish your hamburger and let's go see the lawyer."

The lawyer was James Cahill. Heavyset, of medium height with thick sideburns and gray hair, Cahill looked very much like a retired cop. Born in Brooklyn, he had attended St. John's College, served in the United States Army, and worked as an insurance-claims adjuster before returning to St. John's to study law. After that he had engaged in private practice, served as an assistant district attorney in Brooklyn for seven years, and finally joined the legal staff of the Patrolmen's Benevolent Association. The only visible trace of his years in the District Attorney's office was a .38-caliber Smith & Wesson revolver worn in a holster looped over his belt. Cahill had started carrying it when forced to travel into rough neighborhoods alone on investigations. Once he owned it, he felt that it was safer with him than in a closet or desk drawer, where his two children might stumble upon it.

Informed at home of the shooting, Cahill promised his wife he would be back for lunch, then drove to the station house in South Jamaica. Like PBA trustees, PBA attorneys were always summoned in the event of a police shooting, and Cahill anticipated nothing out of the ordinary. When Shea arrived, Cahill handed him a mimeographed form headed "PBA Legal Program" and waited while Shea filled in the blanks:

NAME: Thomas J. Shea
RANK: Patrolman
SHIELD #: 22737
COMMAND: 103

Then, for what seemed like the hundredth time, Shea repeated his story, closing with the words "I didn't know he was young until I leaned over the body. I didn't learn he was ten until I got back to the station house and they told me he had died. I have two kids just about the same age. I didn't know. Honest!"

"Are you sure you identified yourself as a cop?"

"Of course, I'm sure. An undercover cop was killed in this

precinct last year because he didn't identify himself. I always say I'm a cop when I stop someone. The person I'm stopping might be a cop too."

Cahill started to ask another question, but Shea interrupted. "Before we go any further, I'd like to call my wife. I should have been home hours ago, and she'll start to worry. I don't want her to think I've been shot."

"Okay," Cahill said. "Tell her not to be concerned. This kind of investigation is normal. You'll be home by the end of the day."

As Shea and Cahill talked confidently on the first floor, a different scene was unfolding upstairs. Several weeks earlier New York City Police Commissioner Patrick Murphy had resigned to become President of the National Police Foundation in Washington, D.C. His successor, Donald Cawley, was anxious to avoid any charge that he had mishandled the first "incident" of his tenure.

Upon being notified in midmorning of Clifford Glover's death, Cawley telephoned Chief of Detectives Louis Cottell and instructed him to look into the shooting. Cottell then telephoned Chief of Operations Hugo Masini and asked for his assistance. Masini and Cottell arrived at the 103rd Precinct shortly before noon. With their appearance, it was apparent that this was no longer a "normal" case. As Chief of Operations, Masini was the highest-ranking uniformed cop in the Department, responsible only to the Commissioner himself. Cottell, as Chief of Detectives, was one level below Masini in the police hierarchy and was charged with the administration and control of New York City's entire 3,000-man Detective Division.

Wasting no time, Cottell took control of the investigation. Tall, with graying hair and heavy dark-rimmed bifocals, he looked like a noncombatant, but his voice and manner were unmistakably tough. Upon his arrival in South Jamaica, he spoke first with Robert Johnson and Glanvin Alveranga, then with Al Farrell and Tom Scott. "No one here has any balls," Cottell complained to Masini when the questioning concluded. "Everyone is acting as though no police procedure or law was broken."

"Was it?" Masini asked.

"I don't know, but we'd better find out. Too many people in this city believe that the police always provide the elements necessary to justify a killing of this sort. I don't want any allegations of a cover-up on this one."

"What do we do?"

"We talk with the participants," Cottell answered.

At 12:30 P.M. Add Armstead was ushered into a conference room on the second floor of the 103rd Precinct station house. Seven cops sat at the table in front of him. One by one, Inspector Robert Johnson introduced them: Glanvin Alveranga, Commanding Officer of the 103rd Precinct; Leonard Flanagan, the on-duty Captain for Queens; Louis Cottell, Chief of Detectives; Hugo Masini, Chief of Operations; William Braunstein, Deputy Commissioner for Queens; John Wilson, Detective Inspector for Queens; Harold Tyson, Deputy Inspector for Queens. An eighth man, police stenographer Vincent Tummarello, sat off to the side with a Stenorette tape recorder.

Three of the men present outranked Johnson, but they had agreed to defer to him for the purpose of interrogating the suspect. In twenty-seven years on the force, the Inspector had acquired a reputation for professionalism and calm which merited respect. Born and raised in Manhattan, the son of a valet to Broadway actor Robert Hilliard, Johnson had fought in wartime Europe under General George S. Patton. Of the experience he later said, "Patton was a good commander. When he said, 'Move,' you moved." More than incidentally, Cottell, Masini, and Braunstein also felt that Armstead might be more open if questioned by a black.

"Mr. Armstead," Johnson began, "we are here to get the facts of what happened this morning. How old are you?"

"I be fifty-one on June fourteenth."

"What is your full name?"

"Add Armstead."

"Where do you live?"

"109–50 New York Boulevard."

Wasting no time, Johnson turned to the hour before dawn. "What time did you leave your home this morning, Mr. Armstead?"

"Ten minutes to five."

"Where were you going?"

"115–05 New York Boulevard. I work there."

"Was your son with you?"

"Yes."

"How big is your son?"

"He stands about like this," Armstead answered, holding his hand four and a half feet off the floor.

"What does he weigh?"

"About a hundred."

As the attending officers scribbled notes, Johnson went on. "Did someone approach you on New York Boulevard?"

"When I got to this lot, a car pulled up in back of me. A man jumped out and said, 'You black son of a bitch.' Then he fired a gun. Me and my son started running."

"Along New York Boulevard?"

"Through the lot. I ran through the lot. My son ran behind me."

"Did you know they were police officers?"

"I didn't know who they was. It was just a car. When he said, 'Black son of a bitch,' and fired the gun, I started

66

running. If they had told me they was police officers, I would
have never run."

Wilson and Braunstein exchanged glances. Alveranga was
looking down at the table.

"What else happened?" Johnson asked.

"I ran over to Dillon. I seen an officers' car."

"Where were you?"

"I was on Dillon. They came up, and I told them my son
is shot. They said, 'All right, get in the car.' "

"You got in the car there?"

"I got in the car, and we came around."

"Your son was lying on the ground?"

"That's right."

Johnson shifted his line of questioning. "Are you married,
Mr. Armstead?"

"My wife has been dead three years last Easter. I live
common law."

"How long have you been common law?"

"Been living common law from seventy-one."

"Does your son live with you?"

"Yes."

"Has your son ever been in trouble?"

"No, he's a smart boy."

Oh, sweet Jesus, Alveranga thought suddenly. *He still
doesn't know the boy is dead.*

"Have you ever been in trouble?" Johnson asked.

"In sixty-four, I bought a car along 116th Avenue and I
found a plate. I put it on the car, and an officer stopped me.
I got busted for that, so I put in twenty-three days on Rikers
Island. Then I got framed with a girl, so I got four months."

"What for?"

"Statutory rape. I put in four months on Rikers Island."

"Those were the only times you were ever arrested?"

"Those were the only times I was ever arrested."

Deputy Commissioner William Braunstein interrupted.

"Mr. Armstead, when you were stopped this morning, did you start running immediately?"

"No."

"When did you start running?"

"When he said, 'You black son of a bitch,' and shot."

"Did they say anything to you when they got out of the car?"

"All he said was 'You black son of a bitch,' and he fired the gun."

"Did he show you anything?"

"He didn't show me nothing. If he would have showed me a badge or told me, 'I am a police officer,' I wouldn't have run. All he said was 'You black son of a bitch,' and he fired the gun."

Johnson picked up the questioning. "Then what happened?"

"I started running."

"Did you hear any other shots?"

"I heard shots fired."

"How many?"

"I don't know, about five. All I know is I was running."

"Where was your son?"

"Right in back of me." Armstead's voice trembled slightly. "In back of me, right in back of me."

"When did you discover that he wasn't there?"

"When I got on Dillon. I didn't see my son, and I saw the officers' car. I flagged for them. They carried me over to where the other officers were, and I saw my son."

"In other words," Braunstein interrupted, "once you started to run, you didn't stop until you saw the radio car?"

"No sir. I didn't stop. I was scared. I was scared when I didn't see my son."

It was 1:05 P.M. The interrogation had lasted thirty-five minutes. Johnson sent Armstead back to the roll-call room, then turned to Alveranga. "Get me Shea."

At 1:07 P.M. Thomas Shea entered the second-floor conference room with James Cahill and Charlie Peterson on either
side. Unshaven, dressed in anticrime clothes, having had two
hours' sleep in the past two days, he looked awful. As he was
seated, Johnson addressed him.

"Officer, state your full name, shield number, and command."

"Patrolman Thomas J. Shea, Shield Number 22737, 103rd
Precinct."

"What was your assignment last night?"

"Neighborhood anticrime."

"Officer Shea," Johnson began, "we are in the process of
making an investigation relative to the shooting that happened last night. Before you answer any questions, it is my
duty to advise you of your rights. You have the right to
remain silent. Anything you say may be used against you.
You have the right to consult with your attorney before
making any statements or answering any questions. You
have the right to stop the questioning at any time."

Shea trembled slightly, and Cahill reached out a steadying
hand. "Don't worry," he whispered. "It's just form. They
read *Miranda* warnings anytime there's a shooting investigation."

"Officer Shea," Johnson said, "will you tell us what happened on New York Boulevard around five o'clock this
morning?"

"My brother officer and I recovered a 1970 Chevrolet,"
Shea answered. "The car had been stripped, motor and everything taken off. We were on our way to the station house
to make out the proper papers. At New York Boulevard and
112th Road, after they were brought to my attention by my
brother officer, I observed two male Negroes walking south.
They fit the description we recalled on an armed assault and
robbery. At this time my brother officer made a U-turn. I
stepped from the vehicle, shield and ID card in my left hand,

69

and yelled, 'Stop. Police officers.' Then the male in the yellow jacket and white hat said, 'Fuck you, you're not taking me,' and started running with the other male."

The police stenographer halted the questioning to insert a new tape in the Stenorette recorder. Then Johnson picked up again.

"Could you describe these two men?"

"One had a yellow waist-type jacket and floppy white hat. The other had a brown three-quarter-length leather jacket."

"How tall were they?"

"I don't recall."

"Were they tall, short?"

"I didn't pay attention to height. We had a report that these men robbed a cab."

"All right," Johnson said. "Go on with your story."

"I chased the two subjects into the lot. There's a chain-link fence in the middle of the area, and both males ran alongside the fence. At this time, the male with the yellow waist-type jacket reached in the vicinity of his front pocket and came up with a black metal revolver."

"How far were you from this person?"

"Ten or fifteen feet. At this point I fired three shots from my service revolver. The male in the yellow waist-type jacket gave the revolver to the male in the brown leather three-quarter-length jacket and fell. I stopped, checked the male in the yellow jacket, and yelled to my partner to go after the other male Negro."

"Where did the man in the brown jacket go?" Johnson asked.

"He ran forward along the fence past an old garage. Then I heard two more shots. I yelled to my partner, 'Are you all right?' but there was no response. Next I heard a car starting up and taking off. I kept yelling, and a short time later my partner came back to where I was and asked if I was all right. Then radio cars started coming into the area, and Patrolman

Tom Scott brought a male in a brown three-quarter jacket over to us. He was the other one."

Deputy Inspector Harold Tyson leaned forward to insert himself into the questioning. "What was the time element from the time you fired your shots at the son and Patrolman Tom Scott coming over with the father?"

"Five to ten minutes."

"Where did the younger one take the gun from?"

"I think it was his pocket. It came from where his pocket would be. It could have been his waistband. I don't know for sure, but I know I saw the gun. I saw the gun and, when he started to turn, I fired."

"It must have been fairly dark then," Tyson noted.

"No sir, a few minutes before daylight."

"All right," Johnson said. "Officer Shea, you are temporarily excused. We might want to talk with you again after we've spoken with your partner. Mr. Cahill and Mr. Peterson, you may remain to advise Patrolman Scott if you wish."

Shea left the room and went to a telephone to call his wife a second time. At 1:26 P.M. the interrogation of Walter Scott began.

"What is your name?" Johnson asked.

"Walter Scott."

"Shield number?"

"13777."

"When were you assigned to the 103rd Precinct?"

"March of last year."

As he had done with Shea, Johnson advised Scott of his constitutional rights. "Do you understand?" he asked when finished.

"Yes sir, I do."

"How old are you?"

"Twenty-five."

"At about five o'clock this morning where were you?"

"We were northbound on New York Boulevard between

71

112th Road and Mathias Avenue," Scott answered.

"Did you have occasion to stop anyone?"

"Yes sir, we did. We saw two male Negroes who fit the description of a past robbery with a gun on a taxicab. We made a U-turn and pulled abreast of the men. Patrolman Shea got out of the car with his shield showing and announced himself as a police officer. With this, the male Negro on the right turned and said, 'Fuck you, you're not going to take me.' "

"Is that what he actually said?" Johnson interrupted.

"Yes, at which time both defendants started to run. Patrolman Shea chased the two men into a wooded area, at which time I called for assistance and pulled my car onto 112th Road between Dillon and New York Boulevard. Then I exited from the car and came up behind Patrolman Shea in the wooded area. He was behind the two male Negroes, and I was behind Patrolman Shea. At this point the male wearing the yellow jacket and white floppy hat seemed to make a motion on his right side. Patrolman Shea fired his gun, and the smaller of the two perpetrators handed the taller of the two a gun. Then the smaller perpetrator fell by the fence. Patrolman Shea stayed there, and I chased the other perpetrator around a tree. He stopped, wheeled, and fired a shot. I returned the fire, at which time I ran back to my car on 112th Road and drove over to Dillon looking for the perpetrator, but I couldn't find him. Then I came back to Patrolman Shea by the fence, and he went out to get the radio cars that were responding."

Johnson looked questioningly at the witness. "Is that the whole story as you saw it?"

"That's it."

"You fired one shot?"

"One shot."

"Where?"

"I was behind a tree, maybe twenty feet from the garage outside the fence."

"Then what happened?"

"I couldn't catch him, so I ran back to my car on 112th Road. I figured I might get him at Dillon. I took my car from 112th Road around to Dillon where I jumped out, but I didn't see him so I came back to help Patrolman Shea."

For the first time in the proceedings, Glanvin Alveranga interrupted. "Scott, when was the first time you saw the gun?"

"After Patrolman Shea shot the smaller of the two and he handed it to the fellow with the leather coat."

"After Patrolman Shea fired, you saw the gun?"

"After he shot, the perpetrator stumbled and, as he stumbled, he handed the other defendant the gun."

"Can you describe the weapon?" Alveranga pressed.

"From what I saw, it was a Saturday night special."

"What color?"

"Black or blue-black."

"Was it a revolver?"

"Yes."

"You saw the barrel?"

"Yes."

Inspector John Wilson looked up from his notes. "How far was Shea behind the two of them when he fired the first shot?" Wilson asked.

"Roughly five to ten feet."

"How far behind Shea were you at the time?"

"Three to five feet, somewhere in that neighborhood."

Several of the brass present noted the distance on their pads. At such close quarters, there was no room for honest error on Scott's part. Either there had been a gun or he was lying.

"You're excused," Johnson told him. "We might want to talk with you again."

It was 1:40 P.M. Five minutes later Frank Damiani (the cabdriver whose robbery had preceded the shooting) was ushered into the room.

"You've seen Mr. Armstead," Johnson told him. "Were you asked to identify him?"

"Yes, twice."

"Was he one of the men who robbed you?"

"No."

Johnson stood up to leave.

"Where are you going?" Alveranga asked.

"To call the District Attorney."

"Let Harold Cannon do it," Alveranga said. "You and I have another job to do."

Al Farrell was getting annoyed. It was 2:00 P.M., and he had been on overtime for six and a half hours without a break. The previous day he had testified before a Queens County grand jury and got four hours' sleep. He wanted to go home. Instead, he and his partner were cooped up in the roll-call room of the 103rd Precinct with Add Armstead while police brass scurried by. Armstead wasn't even good company. Outside of thanking Farrell for a cup of coffee the cop had bought him, he hadn't said a word.

Stomach growling, Farrell rose from his chair and wandered toward the vending machines to examine the available supply of chocolate bars and peanut butter cookies. As he did, Robert Johnson and Glanvin Alveranga entered the room.

"Please come with us," Johnson said to Armstead.

"Where to?"

"Upstairs."

They walked from the room, leaving Farrell and Tom Scott behind.

On the second floor Alveranga opened the door to a small

office, and the three men stepped inside. Armstead looked around, then crossed to the window and stared out with his back to his captors. "You gonna tell me something?"

"Your boy is dead," Johnson said.

"I guess I knowed."

"How could you run away and leave him like that?" Alveranga asked softly.

"I ran 'cause I had money in my pocket and I thought they was fixing to rob me. He was just a boy. I didn't think they'd hurt him. I swear that. I never knowed they would hurt him."

7

APRIL 28, 1973— THE DAY ENDS

As the powers-that-be groped for the truth about Clifford Glover, an explosive situation was building. Shortly after noon, a group of reporters appeared at the Glover-Armstead home. Lost in the swirl of events, Eloise Glover stood dazed by the front door and sobbed, "Clifford went to school every day except when he stayed home to help me. He took good care of his two little sisters. His brother, Henry, was his best friend. Everybody loved him. When I took him to church as a baby, everyone wanted to hold him."

Within the hour her remarks had been broadcast throughout the city, and a group of angry South Jamaica residents led by State Assemblyman Guy Brewer began to gather outside the 103rd Precinct station house. The task of calming them fell to two men—Deputy Commissioner for Community Affairs Roosevelt Dunning and his chief assistant, William Johnson.

Born in Virginia, the son of an oyster shucker, Dunning had been raised by a foster family in New York. While on the force, he worked his way through college and law school, attending classes at night. In March 1973, at age forty-nine, he was named Deputy Commissioner for Community Affairs by outgoing Police Commissioner Patrick V. Murphy. Ironically, as a child, Dunning had attended P.S. 40 in South Jamaica—Clifford Glover's alma mater. Dunning was black.

William Johnson was born and brought up in Harlem. The son of a carpenter, he joined the force in 1955 and, like Dunning, worked his way through school at night. In 1961 he graduated first in his class from New York Law School and transferred to the Police Department's Legal Office. For six years Johnson served as a police lawyer. Then, on July 1, 1967, his father was murdered by a junkie on Lenox Avenue in Harlem. Hours after the funeral, Johnson walked into the office of Chief Inspector Sanford Garelik and asked for reassignment to the Manhattan North Homicide Unit. Mulling over the request, Garelik consented on one condition: "You have to promise me that, if you find the man who did it, you won't kill him." Eighty-eight days later William Johnson arrested the man who had murdered his father. Pursuant to a plea-bargaining arrangement, the killer received a ten-year sentence with opportunity for early parole.* Shaken by the experience, Johnson resigned from the force and opened a legal-services office in the Brownsville section of Brooklyn. In May 1969 he was named Director of Public Safety (police and fire) by Gary, Indiana, Mayor Richard Hatcher. Three years later he returned to New York to become Assistant Deputy Commissioner for Community Affairs. Like Dunning, William Johnson was black.

Called to the 103rd Precinct in midday, Dunning and

*Johnson's experience was typical of New York "justice." Only 10 to 15 percent of all persons arrested on felony charges in New York City are convicted or plead guilty to a major charge. The remainder have their cases dismissed, are acquitted at trial or, as is most often true, plead guilty to a misdemeanor. Almost 80 percent of all defendants accused of murder in New York City are allowed to plead guilty to a lesser charge and are sentenced to ten years in prison or less.

Johnson first met with the police officials on hand, then mounted the station-house steps to speak with Assemblyman Brewer and the crowd. "There will be no cover-up," Dunning pledged. "We promise you that. The decision-making process is under way, and we will be a part of that process. This matter will be handled fairly in accordance with the law."

"The white man's law?" someone shouted.

"*The* law," Dunning answered.

Slowly the crowd thinned. When the immediate crisis had passed, Johnson turned to his boss. "No matter what happens," he said, "I'm afraid we haven't heard the last of this one."

Meanwhile, inside the station house, the next stage of the investigation was about to begin. Moments after the questioning of Walter Scott ended, Harold Cannon had telephoned the Queens County District Attorney's Office and asked that someone be sent over to take formal statements from the shooting participants. Shortly before 3:00 P.M. Assistant District Attorney Martin Bracken answered the call.

A native of Queens, Bracken joined the DA's office after graduating from Fordham Law School in 1970. One of his grandfathers had been a Deputy Chief Inspector for the New York City Police Department. His uncle had been a police chaplain for twenty-five years. Bracken himself was named after a cop. From what little he knew about the Glover shooting, it was an assignment he did not relish.

At 3:25 P.M. Thomas Shea and James Cahill were summoned back to the conference room on the second floor. Of the persons present at Shea's first interrogation, only Hugo Masini remained. The previous stenographer had been replaced by a new one. Cottell, Alveranga, Flanagan, Braunstein, Wilson, Tyson, and Robert Johnson were gone. In their place, Captain Daniel O'Brien of the 16th Detective Division had been added. Bracken introduced himself, ad-

78

vised Shea of his constitutional rights, and began to question him.

"Patrolman Shea, what unit are you assigned to?"

"103rd Precinct Neighborhood Police Team, Anticrime."

"And you have been on the police force for how long?"

"Twelve years."

Sensing that Shea was more nervous than before, Cahill leaned over to assure him that the presence of an assistant district attorney was not uncommon. "If nothing else, it will take the heat off the cops when they drop the matter," he whispered.

"Your age?" Bracken continued.

"Thirty-six."

"Can you tell me what happened at approximately five A.M. this morning in the vicinity of New York Boulevard and 112th Road."

"Yes," Shea answered. "We were proceeding north along New York Boulevard when my partner drew my attention to two male Negroes who were walking south. They fit the description of a past armed robbery of a taxicab. My partner made a U-turn. I stepped from the vehicle with my shield and my ID card in my left hand and said, 'Stop. Police.' . . ."

For fifteen minutes Shea recounted his story. Shortly after 3:40 P.M. he was excused, and Bracken summoned Walter Scott to the room. Cahill remained. Bracken advised Scott of his constitutional rights and led him through the early stages of his narration. Then the focus turned to the moment of confrontation: "As Patrolman Shea identified himself, the suspects ran. I took my car and drove it to 112th Road between New York Boulevard and Dillon Street. About halfway down the block I jumped from my car and went into the woods. At a point in the woods I came upon Patrolman Shea, who was in pursuit of the two suspects. I was about five feet behind him, and I could observe the suspect in the white hat making a motion to his right side."

"Did the suspect have his back to you at this time?" Bracken interrupted.

"Yes," Scott answered. "Patrolman Shea then fired his service revolver, and the defendant began to stumble. As he stumbled, I saw the defendant hand the other suspect in the brown leather jacket a revolver."

"You saw the individual put his hand to his side?"

"Yes."

"Did he ever turn around?"

"He was making a turning motion."

"In which direction?"

"Towards Patrolman Shea."

"And he handed the other individual a revolver?"

"He handed the other suspect in the brown three-quarter-length jacket a revolver."

Masini looked thoughtfully at the witness. Bracken continued his questioning. "What happened then?"

"At this time I started pursuing the other defendant. I chased him around a tree and, when he was approximately twenty-five feet from me near a slight incline by an abandoned garage, he turned and fired a shot at me. I started to slow down and fired a shot in return."

"What did you do then?"

"The defendant had started to pull away from me, so I turned and went back to my car and drove it around to Dillon Street. I looked for the other perpetrator, but I couldn't find him."

"All right," Bracken said. "Thank you."

The interrogation over, Scott and Cahill left the room. "One more to go," Masini said. "Let's get Armstead."

Captain O'Brien rose to summon the witness. Almost as an afterthought, Masini realized that everyone in the room was white. "Why don't you ask Harold Cannon to sit in on this?" he suggested.

Cannon and Armstead entered the room together. Not

having been privy to the earlier questioning, Cannon was still under the impression that Armstead was the primary subject of investigation. The next thirty minutes were to disabuse him of that notion.

"Mr. Armstead," Bracken began, "where do you live?"

"109-50 New York Boulevard."

"Are you employed?"

"Yes sir."

"What do you do?"

"I'm a burner with a torch."

Bracken moved quickly through the preliminary stages of interrogation to the moment of confrontation.

"He got out of the car," Armstead said. "He said, 'You black son of a bitch,' and then he fired a gun."

"He fired the gun while you were on the street?" Bracken asked.

"Yes."

"How far away was he from you?"

Armstead looked around the room. "From here to that door."

"How much distance would you estimate that to be?"

"I don't know. I figure from here to that door."

"About fifteen feet?" Bracken pressed.

"I don't know."

Masini made a mental note of Armstead's refusal to guess at a number.

"Were you facing him when he fired the gun?" Bracken continued.

"I turned around. He said, 'You black son of a bitch,' and then I seen he had a small gun in his hand, and that's when I seen he fired."

"How long did you see him?"

"Just a second. He said, 'You black son of a bitch,' and I seen he had a gun."

"When he pointed the gun, what did you do?"

81

"I took off."

"Did your son run with you?"

"Yes."

"Did you see him fire the gun again?"

"No. I heard it."

"How far into the woods did you get when you heard another shot?"

"Maybe about ten feet, and I kept running. Then I fell down and, when I got up, I heard another shot."

"When you fell down, was your son behind you?"

"He was right in back of me."

"Did you see what happened to your son?"

"No. I got to Dillon Street and, when I turned around, my son wasn't there. And, when I was on Dillon Street, I saw a patrol car and I told them, 'My son is over there in the bushes. Somebody is shot.' "

"Did you mention anything about the shooting at that time?"

"Yes, I told them somebody is shot over there, and I told them my son is over there."

Pausing periodically to collect his thoughts, Bracken led Armstead through the remainder of the morning's events. "Do you own a gun?" he asked as the interrogation neared an end.

"No sir."

"Did you have a gun with you at that time?"

"No sir."

"Did your son have a gun with him?"

"Ten years old?" Armstead spat out. "No!"

"You don't have a gun for protection or anything at home?"

"No."

At 4:00 P.M. the interrogation ended. Armstead walked from the room with Cannon at his side and, at the detective's behest, seated himself on a bench in the corridor. Of all the cops he had dealt with in the past ten hours, Cannon was the one Armstead trusted most. The detective seemed more like him than the others.

"Look," Cannon said softly. "This is a stinking situation, and I want to clean it up. I'm going to ask you a question, and I want an honest answer. Do you own a gun?"

Armstead fidgeted with his hands. "Yes," he finally answered.

"Where is it?"

"Take me to my job, and I'll show you."

The second floor of the station house had come to resemble a political clubhouse on election night with new pieces of information pouring in. At 3:30 P.M. Captain Raymond Kenny of Emergency Services reported on a search of the lot and surrounding area by twenty men marching elbow to elbow with rakes and shovels. No gun had been found. The police laboratory advised Cottell that a neutron-activation test performed on Armstead earlier in the day showed no trace of weapon fire on the suspect's hands. Four policemen returned from a search of the Glover-Armstead home. All they had found was a blackjack in the top drawer of the bedroom dresser. There was no sign of a revolver. Armstead's police record was reviewed. In addition to the two convictions admitted under questioning, he had pleaded guilty to a charge of selling skimmed milk as whole in 1965.

Late in the afternoon Shea's personnel folder arrived from police headquarters in Manhattan. It showed 226 arrests in twelve years—twice the city-wide average. There was only one complaint against him on file with the Civilian Complaint Review Board—an unsubstantiated allegation of assault seven years earlier. But his record did reveal three previous shootings, one of which (Felix Tarrats), like the present incident, centered on a "missing" gun. Also on file was a summary of the alleged pistol-whipping of a fourteen-year-old boy.

Taking notes as they went, Cottell and Masini studied the folder. Toward the end of their review, they came upon several performance evaluation reports on Shea filed by previous commanding officers. In each instance his bosses had rated him among the "middle fifty percent" of their men. "Work quality good," one officer had written. "A good team worker, always willing to share load. Judgment usually sound but has tendency to act without realizing consequences."

"Patrolman Shea has an enormous amount of energy and drive," a second officer had written, "but he has a tendency to act without considering all the facts. If energy and drive are channeled in the proper direction, Officer Shea has the potential to become an outstanding patrolman."

"The energy and drive weren't properly channeled," Cottell observed ruefully.

"What were you doing out on the streets at five in the morning?"

Armstead and Cannon were in the front seat of the detective's car on their way to the Pilot Automotive Wrecking Company. He needed this case "like a hole in the head," Cannon told himself. In slightly more than a month, he would be eligible to retire on pension, and the last thing he wanted was a long, dirty investigation.

"I was going to work," Armstead answered.

"Do you always go to work at five in the morning?"

"No sir, but sometimes I do. We only work half a day Saturday, and I had to go in early to get the crane started. Then, when the others get in, it be ready."

"This gun we're going for," Cannon asked, "did you have it with you this morning?"

"No sir. No way I could have had it and it be at the yard now."

Shortly after 4:00 P.M. they arrived at the Pilot Automotive Wrecking Company. A rusting chain-link fence cordoned off the plot. Behind it, piles of worn tires and burned-out cars surrounded a small, dilapidated shop. Taking a key from his back pocket, Armstead opened the fence gate and led Cannon inside. A second key unlocked the shop. The building's interior resembled a small garage, with stacks of tools and car replacement parts strewn across the floor. Having threaded his way through the equipment, Armstead stopped beneath a shelf and pointed up. "There," he said.

Reaching up, Cannon pushed aside a pair of brake shoes and found a small metal box. Inside was a leather holster and a .38-caliber revolver. Checking the bullet chamber, the detective saw five live cartridges. "Where did you get this?" he asked.

"I found it under the front seat of a car."

"Do you have a permit?"

"No."

"It's against the law to have this. You know that, don't you?"

"Yes sir. I was going to bring it in, but somehow I never done it."

"Does your boss know you have this?"

"Yes. He lets me keep it. It's never been no trouble."

"It's trouble now," Cannon said.

At the station house, half a dozen reporters had gathered. Cahill telephoned his wife to tell her that he wouldn't be home for several more hours, then went out to the street and put another quarter in the parking meter by his car. Shea sat in a room off the reception area with Walter Scott at his side.

"Don't worry," Cahill said upon his return. "One of the rules of police investigations is that they drag on forever. It'll be all right."

Charlie Peterson joined the group. "I don't like it," he said. "There are too many bosses here. I'm worried about Ortolano."

Cahill nodded. Eight months earlier, a New York City policeman named Francis Ortolano had been on patrol-car duty when he spotted a stolen car occupied by three youths. After he instructed the occupants to halt, there ensued a high-speed chase, during which the fugitives ran a police roadblock, nearly killing a cop. Several blocks later they screeched to a halt and fled. Ortolano (who had never shot at a suspect in six previous years on the force) fired three times, killing one of the fugitives with a bullet in the back. The victim was twelve years old, unarmed, and black. A predominantly white upper-middle-class grand jury had refused to indict the officer. Thereafter the scuttlebutt among cops was that the police brass felt it would have been better for "community relations" if Ortolano had been indicted.

"I don't know what's happening in all these conferences that are going on here," Peterson said. "But I don't want Tom's future in the hands of this community."

"What's the worst that can happen?" Shea asked. "A reprimand?"

"A reprimand, or you could be transferred," Cahill told him, "at worst suspended."

"It's not fair," Shea grumbled. "I was only doing my job."

Cahill nodded as he had done before, but his mind was somewhere else. He was beginning to measure some of the cops who had made their way to the aging red-brick station house: Inspector Robert Johnson, son of a valet, black; Detective Harold Cannon, son of a laborer, black; Assistant Deputy Commissioner William Johnson, son of a carpenter, black; Captain Glanvin Alveranga, son of a cabdriver, black;

Deputy Commissioner Roosevelt Dunning, son of an oyster shucker, black.

"We might have a problem," Cahill said.

Upstairs, in a small conference room on the second floor of the South Jamaica station house, Thomas Shea's fate was being weighed by five men. As had been the case for most of the day, Chief of Detectives Louis Cottell was the guiding force behind their deliberations. With him were Hugo Masini, Roosevelt Dunning, William Johnson, and a fifth man—Special Legal Counsel to the Police Commissioner, Bertram Perkel. The remaining police who had journeyed to South Jamaica would have no further say in the decision-making process.

Perkel was the most recent addition to the group. Throughout the day Masini and Cottell had been in constant telephone communication with Police Commissioner Donald Cawley. As their doubts concerning Shea's story grew, Cawley had telephoned Perkel and asked him to join the deliberations.

Short, slightly built, with fine brown hair that stretched below the nape of his neck dangerously past the point of being "mod," Perkel had engaged in a profitable labor law practice for a number of years before taking the job as Special Counsel to the Commissioner "because police work seemed like fun." He had a lean face, prominent nose, and slightly hungry look. While many cops considered him to be far "too liberal," he did have a reputation as "a straight shooter." "If Perkel is going to fuck you," said one cop, "he'll tell you first. He's honest that way."

Speaking from notes taken during the day, Cottell reviewed what was known about the case. Shea and Scott, he felt, had been acting as good cops when they stopped to question Armstead and Glover. While not a complete match, the suspects' clothing had been similar to that worn by the taxi robbers. Also, it was unlikely that Shea had fired immediately after stepping from the car as claimed by Armstead. In all probability, he had shot after the suspects ran.

"But that," Cottell said "is where Shea's credibility ends. Walter Scott could not have driven around the corner and run into the lot in time to witness the shooting, as both cops now claim. The transfer of a gun from Glover to Armstead is implausible. Shea's entire story rests on the premise that a ten-year-old boy willingly engaged in a gun battle with two men who identified themselves as police. It just couldn't have happened that way," Cottell continued. "And according to Shea's personnel file, this isn't the first time a gun has disappeared."

One by one, the arguments on Shea's behalf were rebutted. The gun found by Harold Cannon at the Pilot Automotive Wrecking Company could not be the missing weapon. Armstead didn't have time to run to the shop and back before flagging down Al Farrell. Armstead and Glover were not the taxi robbers. Frank Damiani's testimony had established that. Moreover, Armstead's record, while that of a petty criminal, revealed no tendency toward violence.

"A gun is a defensive weapon," Cottell concluded. "And any cop who fires it for a purpose other than self-defense is acting as prosecutor, judge, and jury. Thomas Shea did not fire his weapon in self-defense. I think it's clear from the record before us that a crime has been committed."

No one responded. Cottell looked around the room, then focused on Perkel. "Some action has to be taken," the Chief of Detectives said. "But I want your assurance that the Commissioner will stand behind us."

"He will," Perkel responded. "What do you recommend?"

"We have to arrest him."

"I'm not so sure," Roosevelt Dunning interrupted. "There's a good community-relations argument to be made for an immediate arrest, but I'd rather wait until the case is presented to the grand jury. A summary arrest will make it hard to get cops to testify, and it will be even worse for Department morale."

"I agree," William Johnson seconded. "With the evidence as we know it, Shea can be arrested later as easily as now."

"That begs the issue," Cottell answered. "When a cop breaks the law, he should be arrested like anyone else. I don't believe in two classes of citizens when it comes to law enforcement."

Masini sided with Cottell. The vote stood at two even— two white cops in favor of a summary arrest, two black cops against it. All eyes were on Perkel. "I'll be back in a minute," the Special Counsel said, rising from his chair. "I want to call the Commissioner."

As the five cops caucused, Martin Bracken was in a quandary. At age twenty-seven, the young Assistant District At-torney simply didn't know what to do with the powder keg he had been handed, and there was nowhere to turn for guidance. Albert Gaudelli (Chief of the DA's Homicide Bureau) was on vacation. Thomas Demakos (Gaudelli's boss) was not at home. Thomas Mackell, the former District Attorney, had resigned on April 23, 1973, and the acting head of the Queens County District Attorney's Office (Frederick Ludwig) was nowhere to be found. Bracken wasn't even sure whether or not he had the power to arrest Shea if the cops wanted him to do so. Finally, after an hour of frantic inquiries, he traced Ludwig to a bar in Parkchester in the Bronx and conferred with him briefly on the telephone.

Then, Bracken returned to the second floor of the station house, where Harold Cannon and Glanvin Alveranga sat in a small office near the main conference room, awaiting further instructions. Shortly before 7:00 P.M. Cottell walked through the office door and approached Alveranga. "I've got a job for you," the Chief of Detectives said.

At 7:00 P.M. Thomas Shea, James Cahill, and Charlie Peterson were led to an office on the ground floor of the station house. The door was made of splintered wood painted green with an opaque glass insert. A small black plaque with the words "Commanding Officer, 103rd Precinct" in white letters was nailed to the frame.

The three men stepped inside, where Glanvin Alveranga sat waiting. Shea took a seat by the door, and Alveranga looked up from his desk. *"You're under arrest for the murder of Clifford Glover."*

Shea's cheeks reddened.

"Give me your guns," Alveranga said.

Shea didn't move.

"Give me your guns," the Captain repeated.

Shea reached for his service revolver, and Alveranga drew back. "Don't worry," Shea said. "It's not loaded."

Alveranga took the gun and placed it on the desk in front of him. "Now your off-duty revolver and police ID card."

Shea complied.

"And your badge."

Very slowly, Shea reached for the shield he had worn for twelve years—a small piece of nickel and copper alloy two and a half inches high and two inches wide. The crest of the City of New York was emblazoned on the center with a policeman and seventeenth-century Indian on either side. Above the figures were the words "City of New York, Police"; beneath them was the number 22737.

"Let's have it," Alveranga ordered.

Shea dropped the shield on the desk. "But I didn't do anything wrong," he said, his voice rising slightly. "I was out there doing my job, and now I'm being arrested."

Alveranga shrugged.

"Don't you hear what I'm saying to you, goddammit? I didn't do anything wrong."

Still there was no response.

"You son of a bitch," Charlie Peterson muttered, glaring at the Captain. "You're enjoying this. Don't you realize what you're doing to this man?"

"It's not the end of the world," Alveranga answered.

"Not the end of the world? Not the end of the world?" Peterson exploded. "Look! I don't care what your rank is. You—"

Cahill interrupted. "I'd like to talk with my client alone. Could we go outside for a minute?"

"I don't know," Alveranga answered. "He's a prisoner."

"He's also a cop. He's not running anywhere."

"All right. But make it quick."

The two men retreated to an adjoining office. "I didn't do anything wrong," Shea repeated. "He pulled a gun, and I was scared. I didn't want to be killed."

"I know," Cahill told him.

"I didn't do anything wrong. What about my family? What about my job?" His words were starting to mix with sobs. "Oh, Jesus! What am I going to do?"

"Look," Cahill said softly. "This is only the beginning of a long fight. Everything will work out all right in the end."

"That's what you told me all afternoon. They're going to lock me up in jail."

"Not if we can help it. There's no nice way to go through this, but we can try to get you out on bail tonight. Compose yourself so they won't know they've gotten to you. Then—"

Alveranga stuck his head into the room. "Let's go," he said.

Two detectives stepped forward and began to lead Shea away.

"Aren't you going to put cuffs on him?" the Captain asked.

"No way," one of the men answered. Almost apologetically they escorted their prisoner out a side door to the street where a patrol car waited.

It was 7:30 P.M.

"Where we going?" Add Armstead asked the two cops who stood over him in the roll-call room.

"We have to arrest you," one of them said. "You were in possession of a dangerous weapon. That gun you had hidden at work is against the law."

Silently the prisoner followed his captors to their car. At a court annex in central Queens, he was given a summons and desk-appearance ticket informing him that he had been charged with violation of Section 265.05-2 of the New York State Penal Code. "This means you have to appear in Part One-A of the Criminal Court on May seventeenth," the desk officer explained. "If you don't show, a warrant will be issued for your arrest."

Armstead nodded. The two cops hustled him back to their car. "Can I go home now?"

"Where do you live?"

"109-50 New York Boulevard."

"That's too far out of our way," the driver told him. "We'll drop you off at Jamaica Avenue and Queens Boulevard."

An hour later—frightened, weary, and cold—Add Armstead walked through the front door of his home. His children were asleep. In the living room Eloise Glover sat with several friends.

"I been to hell," Armstead said, walking toward Mrs. Glover. "But I didn't do nothing wrong. I swear it. I loved that boy like he was my own. I wouldn't have done nothing to hurt him."

"Add," someone said gently, pointing to a man standing

in the corner, "this is Henry Blackman, Clifford's father."

Armstead straightened up and walked toward the stranger. "All these years," he snarled, "more than ten years, you been walking around and never done nothing for that boy. There was a time he needed you, needed you bad. You didn't come see him once. Get out of my home, mister. There ain't nothing you can do for him now."

Central Booking was a blur, too many people doing too many things. Someone grabbed hold of Thomas Shea's hands and he was fingerprinted. Mug photos (full face and profile) were taken. James Cahill arrived and apologized for being late. He had been held up at the station house, trying to convince Walter Scott to go home rather than wait until his partner was released. Charlie Peterson telephoned to say that Bonnie Shea had been notified of the arrest by Art Monahan—a fellow cop, neighbor, and family friend.

Harold Cannon arrived and was handed a piece of paper headed "Criminal Court of the City of New York—Felony Complaint." After inserting the form in a battered typewriter, he began to type: "Detective Harold Cannon, Shield #1174, being duly sworn, says that on April 28, 1973, at about 5:00 A.M. at 112th Road and New York Boulevard, Queens, the defendant Thomas Shea did commit the offense of murder. . . ."

Shortly before 11:00 P.M. Shea was taken from Central Booking to the Queens County Criminal Court, where Cahill, Charlie Peterson, and Robert McKiernan (President of the Patrolmen's Benevolent Association) joined him.

"I came as soon as Charlie called," McKiernan said. "It's a terrible thing to take a life, but sometimes it can't be avoided. The PBA will stand behind you all the way."

A court attendant interrupted to inform Cahill that Judge Allen Moss was ready to hear the charges and set bail. Cannon's complaint was read, and Cahill rose before the court. Briefly, he cited Shea's family ties, financial resources, and long-standing employment as a cop. "Your Honor," he concluded, "there is no chance that the defendant will flee the jurisdiction of this court. I ask that he be released without bail on his own recognizance."

"I can't do that," Moss answered. "Bail is set at twenty-five thousand dollars."

McKiernan stepped forward and offered a check drawn on the PBA account.

"Your check is unacceptable," Moss told him. "The PBA might decide not to authorize this man's defense."

"But, Your Honor," Cahill protested, "it's impossible to find a bail bondsman at this hour."

"Then your client will have to be remanded."

Shea began to shake. "Your Honor," McKiernan interrupted, "I don't want this man in jail. I'll give you the deed to my home as collateral."

"I'm sorry," Moss said. "I need cash or a bond. That's the law."

Two correction officers seized the prisoner by the arms. Charlie Peterson reached out as if to intervene, then dropped his hands to his side. "This is the saddest moment of my life," he said.

"Around midnight," Thomas Shea remembers, "they took me to jail. All my life, all I'd ever wanted was to be a cop. All I had ever tried to do was my job. Never in my wildest dreams had I envisioned myself as a defendant in the criminal justice system. When they led me away, I kept asking myself over and over, 'Why?'

"We got to the Queens House of Detention, and they made me strip naked for a physical. I didn't want the doctor to touch me. His coat was filthy, and it looked like he hadn't

94

washed his hands. I guess that's the kind of doctor who works midnights in a jail. He checked me for lice and stuck a finger up my rectum. Then they took blood. I was afraid the needle wasn't sterile. After that they brought me to a cell that was empty except for a toilet and a wooden bunk. There was no mattress or sheets, just one blanket. The blanket was gray. The toilet was caked with excrement and completely exposed to the other prisoners. There was no way I was going to use it. All of a sudden I started imagining robbers and muggers and people I'd put in jail. I'd heard stories about cops who were sent to prison and what happened to them. I wondered if I was going to make it through the night."

As Shea stared through the iron bars, a fellow prisoner limped toward him and held out a second blanket. Shaking his head, the cop stepped away from the bars and began to pace, back and forth, back and forth. There was no room to move. His stomach ached. His mind was clogged. Inside his chest, something was building that would not subside. Choking off his emotions, Shea fought it as best he could, then slumped on the bunk in his cell and began to cry.

PART TWO

8

THE DAY AFTER

There were no windows to let in the sun. Only his watch told Thomas Shea that dawn had come. The cramps in his stomach were worse, but he refused to use the toilet. Motionless, he sat on the bunk in his cell.

A prison guard appeared and told him that bail had been posted. Wordlessly Shea followed his captor down the hall to the reception area, where Robert McKiernan stood waiting.

"I'm sorry it took so long," the PBA President said. "It's hard to find a bail bondsman who's open on Sunday."

Shea nodded his understanding. "I appreciate your being here. I'm pretty shook up."

"Don't worry," McKiernan told him. "The PBA will stand behind you one hundred percent on this. If you're railroaded, no cop in the city will be safe."

They walked to McKiernan's car, where, faceup on the front seat, page one of the *Daily News* screamed, in bold black headlines, BOY, 10, SLAIN BY PATROLMAN; COP IS CHARGED WITH MURDER. After tossing the paper aside, McKiernan drove to the 103rd Precinct station house. There

Shea used the toilet and emptied the personal belongings from his locker.

"Can you get home all right?" McKiernan asked.

"No problem. My Volkswagen is parked across the street."

"Okay. Try to get some sleep. We'll take care of you. I promise."

The ride home went slowly. Tired and numb, Shea had trouble keeping his eyes open. He hadn't slept for forty hours. Passing through Brentwood, he turned off the main road onto a quiet residential street marked Gibson Avenue and slowed to a halt in front of a large brown and yellow house shaded by trees. As he exited from the car, his wife Bonnie rushed toward him.

"Get in the house," Shea said, stopping her in her tracks.

"What?"

"Get inside. You don't know what kind of nut might have come out here to get me." He draped an arm across her shoulders. "Come on, let's go."

Together, they walked inside, where their two daughters (ages eleven and twelve) sat waiting. "Art Monahan told me what happened," Bonnie said. "The newspapers and television filled in the rest. You don't have to talk about it if you don't want to."

"Has anyone been bothering you?"

"A couple of reporters came by and asked for pictures of the kids. I told them no."

The telephone rang, and Shea picked up the receiver.

"This is Ace," a voice said. "I'm gonna get your mother-fuckin' ass. You're a dead man."

"Anytime you want to try," Shea snapped, "just come on out."

Slamming the receiver down, he looked at Bonnie. "Have there been many of those?"

"All morning," she answered.

"We'll get an unlisted number tomorrow. If the phone rings before then, I'll answer it."

Bonnie nodded, and Shea began stripping off his clothes. "Throw these out."

"I can wash them," she said.

"I don't want to see them again. Throw them out."

"Everything?"

"Everything but the shoes."

Bonnie looked down at the pile on the floor. "I can wash them, really."

"I'll throw them out myself," Shea said, gathering the clothes and crumpling them into a ball for deposit in the garbage.

"Do you want breakfast?"

"That would be good."

While Shea showered, Bonnie made fried eggs, toast, coffee, and orange juice. "Once you eat," she told him, "you should get some sleep."

Add Armstead stood on the porch of the small wood frame house at 109-50 New York Boulevard, accepting the condolences of neighbors and friends. Like Shea, he had cast aside his clothes of the previous day, vowing never to wear them again. Later he would decide to save the three-quarter-length brown leather jacket because he could not afford a new one.

As Armstead spoke, several reporters took notes. "Clifford and me was close. I loved him like a son, and he called me Daddy. He wasn't no angel, but he was coming around real good. He was a good boy."

Every so often one of the newsman sought to coax a statement from Eloise Glover, who stood silently at Armstead's side, her three children beside her. Finally, she spoke. "I never had nothing against the police, but they was wrong to shoot my boy. Clifford didn't do nothing wrong. He never

101

knowed what he was called for. There was no reason that boy had to be killed. They killed my boy in cold blood."

One of the children began to cry, and Armstead bent down. "You ain't going to bring him back by crying," he admonished. "You just gotta keep going."

Robert McKiernan sat behind the wheel of his car and rubbed his eyes. He had been without sleep for twenty-four hours, but several tasks still lay ahead.

Organized in 1844, the New York City Police Department was the oldest municipal peace-keeping force in the United States. To McKiernan's knowledge, this was the first time a New York City cop had ever been summarily arrested for shooting a suspect. The procedure smacked of "politics." If Shea had committed a crime, McKiernan felt, it was up to a grand jury to indict him. The Department had no business condemning one of its own men. And to call the shooting "murder" struck the PBA President as unconscionable. "Murder" connoted intent to kill. It was a wanton, unspeakable offense. The charge against Shea represented "a threat to every cop in the City of New York."

"It's the Commissioner's fault," McKiernan told himself. "His job is to protect every one of his men until they're proven guilty in a court of law." In fact, McKiernan planned to tell the Commissioner just that in a matter of moments. Sunday, April 29, was the day of the Department's annual communion breakfast. Very shortly the Commissioner would be addressing 2,000 New York City policemen. McKiernan planned to confront him on the dais and demand an explanation for Shea's arrest.

Normally McKiernan was a quiet man. Born and brought up in New York, he had fought in the European theater during World War II, where he saw action in the Battle of the Bulge. Two years after joining the Police Department, he became involved in PBA politics and served as a precinct delegate for twenty years. Having been elected President of the PBA in 1972, he quickly earned a reputation for thoughtful, fair-minded behavior. Indeed, some line cops had criticized him for being "too soft on the politicians and police brass." Now, for one of the few times in his career, McKiernan's gray eyes were blazing.

Unaware of McKiernan's approach, Donald Cawley stood before 2,000 angry cops at the communion breakfast. The situation was volatile, and the neophyte Commissioner knew it. Within hours of Shea's arrest, members of the 103rd Precinct had threatened to walk off the job. Only the determined all-night efforts of PBA Trustee Charlie Peterson and PBA Delegate Ron DeVito had stemmed the revolt. Again and again, Peterson had counseled, "Look, this will straighten out in the end. Thomas Shea will be fully exonerated and back in the precinct working alongside of you. Meanwhile, you're professionals. Do your job."

Grudgingly the cops had carried out their assignments but, across the city, dissent was spreading. Before dawn, fifty cops from other commands had arrived at the South Jamaica station house and begun to picket. In dozens of precincts the incident was discussed on police radio frequencies in direct violation of Department regulations, which forbade "nonofficial" communications. Always the comments were the same: "Shea was a cop doing his job in an area where a lot of people carry guns. . . . Most shoot-outs last only a second or two. If a cop hesitates, he can be killed. . . . Hey, that cop could have been me."

Speaking on an unrelated subject from a prepared text, Cawley was all but drowned out by catcalls from the communion audience. Finally, he set aside his notes and, in an apparent about-face from the previous day, told his audience,

"The charge of murder was wrong. I will have more to say on the subject later today. In the interim, I ask for responsible conduct from each of you. Thomas Shea will be treated fairly."

Then, gathering his notes, the Commissioner left moments before McKiernan's arrival. Several hours later, the following statement was broadcast to all New York City cops via police radio:

⤙ FROM THE OFFICE OF THE COMMISSIONER

As a result of the investigation into the killing of Clifford Glover, the District Attorney who conducted the investigation ordered the arrest of Police Officer Thomas Shea. . . . It is with outrage that I heard the actions of the police officer described as "murder." Murder clearly connotes a premeditated design to kill someone, and there is nothing in this investigation to my knowledge that substantiates such a characterization. I deplore and resent any suggestion that the dedicated police officers of this great department conscientiously abuse their sworn powers.

Martin Bracken arrived at work in midmorning. As the Assistant District Attorney "on call" for the weekend, he was required to spend all day Sunday in the DA's office, located in the Queens County Criminal Court Building.

The media reaction to Shea's arrest troubled Bracken greatly. Both the *New York Times* and *Daily News* had carried front-page stories stating that it had been "ordered" by him. In truth, he had neither ordered nor performed the arrest. The cops had done both. Indeed, Bracken could not have "ordered" it even if he had wanted to. To effect an arrest, the District Attorney's office must file a request with the Criminal Court, after which the court issues a bench warrant which is executed by the cops. All Bracken had done was announce the arrest to the press once it had taken place. "Someone has to tell them," Louis Cottell had said. "Why don't you do it?" Cognizant of his boss's command to "do whatever the cops tell you to do," Bracken had acceded to the request. Now he regretted his malleability.

Outside the courthouse, sixty cops under the leadership of PBA President Robert McKiernan were picketing in noisy protest. Dressed in the civilian clothes they had worn to the communion breakfast an hour earlier, they marched back and forth across the plaza, chanting slogans as a bevy of reporters and news cameramen looked on. Suddenly a car pulled up to the curb, and out stepped Frederick Ludwig, the Acting District Attorney for Queens County.

Ludwig's position was precarious. Fifty-nine years old, a former police captain who had been known to black cops as "The U-Boat Commander" during his tenure on the force, he had received a law degree from St. John's University and joined the Queens County District Attorney's office as Chief Assistant to DA Thomas Mackell. When Mackell resigned in April 1973 after being indicted on charges of obstructing justice, Ludwig was elevated *ex officio* to the role of Acting DA pending the appointment of Mackell's successor by New York Governor Nelson Rockefeller. Now, as Bracken listened in horror, the same man he had spoken with less than twenty-four hours earlier told the assembled crowd, "There was no need for the arrest of Thomas Shea. I never made this decision. I was not consulted by my assistants. Had I been notified, a different procedure would have been followed.

⅄ "Tomorrow," Ludwig continued, "I will seek to reduce the charges against Shea. From what I know of the case, the grand jury will either refuse to indict or charge the police officer with negligent homicide. Within a day or two," the Acting District Attorney closed, "I will make a decision about what to do with Martin Bracken, who handled the case. My decision could be to suspend or dismiss him."

Moments later Ludwig ascended the courthouse steps and instructed that Bracken be sent to his office. "Sit down," he said when the young assistant appeared.

Bracken did as ordered.

"Young man," Ludwig began, "you've caused quite a bit of trouble, and you might have to be fired. Perhaps it would be best for all concerned if you handed in your resignation."

"That's not fair," Bracken answered quietly. "I didn't order the arrest. You know that. Besides, I telephoned you yesterday, and you okayed everything that happened."

Ludwig leaned back in his chair. "I recall no such conversation."

Slowly Bracken felt his composure slipping. Somehow the tables had to be turned. "Listen, you son of a bitch," he snapped. "I called you, you okayed everything, and I can prove it. I taped our conversation yesterday and, if I get canned, I'm sending a copy to every newspaper in the city."*

Ludwig blanched. Both men sat silent.

"We shall forget the matter," the Acting District Attorney said at last. "I must have been tired when you called."

"You weren't tired," Bracken shot back. "You were drunk."

Patrolman Eddie Anderson disliked the morgue. He always had and always would, but police procedure required him to identify a body now lying in Manhattan as the person shot by Thomas Shea.

One day earlier Anderson had cradled Clifford Glover's head in his arms on the way to Mary Immaculate Hospital. Now the cop was alone, driving toward the office of the Chief Medical Examiner of the City of New York at 520 First Avenue.

*In fact, Bracken had not taped the telephone conversation.

Anderson had been born in South Carolina and reared in Brooklyn. A good-looking, gentle man, with a kind face and neatly cropped Afro, he joined the Police Department after several years with the United States Postal Service "because the city paid better." Through four ghetto assignments, he had never fired his gun.

"You're a cop," Anderson told himself again and again as he drove toward Manhattan. "Be professional. Get hold of your emotions."

Unaware of Anderson's impending visit, Dr. Yong Myun Rho (New York City's Deputy Chief Medical Examiner) had begun his daily work. His office was obligated by law to perform complete autopsies on all persons who died violent, accidental, or suspicious deaths. Two medical attendants placed the body of Clifford Glover on a stainless steel slab. Then, with several interns looking on, Rho began to cut, dictating to a stenographer as he probed the remains laid out on the table in front of him:

> The body is that of a young Negro male child appearing the stated age of ten years, well-developed, well-nourished, measuring five feet one-half inch in length and weighing ninety-eight pounds. Rigidity is complete, and a faint lividity mottles the posterior aspects of the body. The head is covered by abundant, short, black kinky hair. The conjunctivae are pale. The corneae are cloudy. The irides are brown. The ears and nose are not remarkable. Natural teeth are present. A bullet wound is present on the back.
>
> The entrance of the bullet wound is on the right side of the back just inside the lower angle of the scapula. It is a sharply outlined, circular hole surrounded by a narrow rim of excoriated skin measuring one-third inch in diameter. The track of this bullet wound is directed forward, upward and slightly to the left. The bullet has fractured the right seventh rib posterially and perforated the middle and upper lobe of the right lung. There is approximately two thousand cc. of

107

blood in the right pleural cavity. The bullet then fractured the right first rib anteriorly. The right subclavian artery above this rib has been torn. The bullet finally exited the skin over the superior clavicular region at a point one inch to the right of the anterior midline.

As the autopsy continued, Rho studied the victim's neck, cardiovascular system, respiratory tract, liver, spleen, urinary tract, genitalia, pancreas, gastrointestinal tract, head, and bone structure. Midway through the examination, Eddie Anderson entered the morgue to identify the body.

"Brace yourself," a medical attendant told him. "The autopsy isn't complete. The boy has been opened up, but we haven't had time to sew him back together again. All you can see are his insides and his face."

Several hours later, accompanied by a neighbor, Eloise Glover journeyed by subway to the morgue. There she viewed the body of her son for the first time.

"I'm sorry," Dr. Rho told her.

Without a sound, Mrs. Glover bent down and touched Clifford's forehead. Then she went home. That night she gathered most of her boy's belongings together and put them in a large carton so she wouldn't have to look at them again. Among the possessions packed away was a composition Clifford had written in school the previous Halloween:

What Am I?
They chose me from my brothers. "That's the nicest one,"
they said, and they carried me out a face and put a candle
in my head, and sat me on the doorstep. Oh, the night was
dark but, when they lit the candle, I smiled.

Clifford's teacher had praised the composition as excellent. "Creative" was the word she had used. Clifford had been very proud.

Fingering the paper, Eloise Glover shook her head. She wished she could read better than she did. Maybe then she would have been able to understand what it was that Clifford had been saying.

9

THE CITY REACTS

Sunday is a day of rest. The full brunt of the shooting was not felt until the workweek began.

Outraged by Frederick Ludwig's performance on the courthouse steps, several prominent South Jamaicans led by Assemblyman Guy Brewer visited the Acting District Attorney on Monday, April 30, and made their anger known. Following their departure, Ludwig summoned reporters to his office and announced a reversal of his decision to seek a reduction of charges against Thomas Shea. "The facts will be put in, and the grand jury will decide. I'm not recommending anything," the Acting DA said. However, the reversal of position was too little and too late. Fear of an official "whitewash" had already spread beyond controllable bounds.

By midafternoon several hundred demonstrators were marching outside the 103rd Precinct station house, carrying placards demanding that Shea be tried on a charge of murder. An anonymous telephone caller warned authorities that the Black Liberation Army would execute two policemen in retaliation for Glover's death. Twenty pickets appeared outside Shea's Brentwood, Long Island, home carrying signs reading "THOMAS SHEA—YOU WILL PAY." Four Suffolk County cops were assigned to a round-the-clock guard of Shea's family because of death threats against them. As dusk fell, 500 demonstrators gathered on Linden Road near the shooting site, and Queens Borough Commander Charles McCarthy ordered an end to routine police patrols along New York Boulevard. In addition, to guard against ambushes, McCarthy instructed all cops in South Jamaica to refrain from responding to calls for assistance unless accompanied by a backup unit.

On Tuesday, May 1, emotions escalated still further. Roy Wilkins, Executive Director of the NAACP, issued a statement calling Clifford Glover's death "a case of police murder." "Nothing," the nationally respected black leader said, "can excuse the killing of a ten-year-old boy who was not connected in any way with a crime. His only fault was that he was black."

Wilkins's words were echoed by National Urban League Director Livingston Wingate, who called a New York City press conference to denounce "impetuous police action against black youths." Victor Soloman (Associate National Director of the Congress of Racial Equality) urged Governor Nelson Rockefeller to appoint a special prosecutor to investigate the case.

Late in the day, tensions rose still further when Clifford Glover's body was placed on display at the McClester Funeral Home. From 6:00 to 9:00 P.M. hundreds of area residents stood on line outside the tiny pink stucco and stone building, waiting to pay their respects. Then, after viewing the boy's body, they filtered into the night, where demonstrations were rapidly turning to disorder. By 9:00 P.M. bands of youths were roaming the streets. An empty police van was firebombed, and the officers who extinguished the blaze were pelted with bricks and bottles. An angry window-smashing spree halted traffic on New York Boulevard. Desperate for

111

help, the police turned to a black cop named Howard Sheffey.

Sheffey had joined the force in 1956 and been promoted to sergeant in 1969. His influence lay in the fact that he was President of the Guardian Society.

Formed in 1949 as a fraternal organization for black policemen, the Guardians were a potent force within the Department. Initially, their mission had been to improve the lot of black policemen, who were confined to predominantly black precincts, disciplined more harshly than their white counterparts, and rarely promoted within the force. However, with the 1963 March on Washington, the urban riots, and growing black awareness of the 1960s, the Guardians came to assume a far more diverse role. By the time Sheffey was elected President in 1971, the organization was actively lobbying for more progressive police attitudes toward the black community.

To the Guardians, the death of Clifford Glover underscored the "white cop-black victim" formula which was all too familiar to each of them. Following Frederick Ludwig's pledge to seek a reduction of the charges against Shea, Sheffey had written to Governor Rockefeller, Mayor Lindsay, and Commissioner Cawley demanding a full investigation of the shooting. On the evening of Tuesday, May 1, Sheffey was at the Guardians' clubhouse in Brooklyn with forty fellow members when the 16th Division Command telephoned for help. The 103rd Precinct, Sheffey was told, desperately needed black policemen to ease the crisis.

At Sheffey's urging, three dozen members of the Guardians drove to South Jamaica. There, dressed in civilian clothes with shields pinned to their jackets, they labored for several hours to calm community members and keep the increasingly edgy white cops from losing perspective. By evening's end, order had been restored. Four policemen were injured; eight persons arrested. The Guardians had done their job well but, as Sheffey departed, he issued a word of warning: "This is the last time we come as a group to control our own people."

Wednesday, May 2, saw the crescendo of discontent continue. A community-affairs officer reported to Glanvin Alveranga that the Black Liberation Army had recruited several members of the Black Assassins street gang to kill policemen in retaliation for Glover's death. The Seven Crowns youth gang announced its intention to descend upon Public School 40 and "savagely beat" all white teachers. Flyers advocating a "People's Trial of Thomas Shea" were distributed throughout South Jamaica, proclaiming, "The 103rd Precinct has traditionally been known for harboring trigger-happy, head-knocking policemen." Several bomb threats were relayed to police headquarters. A reporter for the *Daily News* received a small box wrapped in brown paper in the morning mail. Inside was a .38-caliber bullet, a picture of Thomas Shea with a hole through the forehead, and a note which read, "We want an end to police brutality and mass murder in our black community. Shea must die."

By Wednesday evening the 103rd Precinct station house had come to resemble a fortress under siege. Heavy wood barricades cordoned off its entrance from the street. Two hundred tactical patrolmen had been bussed in from other precincts to deal with the ever-present crowds. In the hope of dispelling rumors, a special communications center was set up to allow area residents to telephone the police with questions and statements about the shooting. Police Commissioner Donald Cawley sent a letter of condolence to Eloise Glover, expressing deep regret over "the tragic incident which took the life of your son." Still, disorder continued. Roving bands of black youths hurled bottles and stones at storefront windows and passing cars along New

113

York Boulevard. Five persons were arrested; four more cops injured. "This is nothing," Alveranga told a subordinate as the night wore on. "The funeral is tomorrow."

The death of Clifford Glover had struck a responsive chord throughout New York. Millions of people had witnessed Add Armstead recite his tale of woe on television. The city's three major newspapers were saturated with blaring headlines and photographs of the dead boy. No segment of the populace had been left untouched.

"I know it's hard," a suburban housewife wrote to Eloise Glover, "but thank God that in 1963 a black child named Clifford Glover was *born.*"

"I'm a cop and would rather remain anonymous," another letter read, "but I'm truly sorry for what happened. As a policeman, I feel a special sense of loss."

Benjamin J. Malcolm, New York City's Commissioner of Corrections, wrote:

Dear Mrs. Glover,

I am acting as an agent for a group of inmates incarcerated in the Queens House of Detention for Men. These inmates, immersed in their own grief, are reaching out to you in light of the tragic loss of your son, Clifford, to express their sympathy.

I have enclosed for you the sum of $68.17 they have collected in his name for your family. They have truly given all they can. I can only add my own sympathy to their magnanimous gesture.

On Thursday, May 3, those who raged and those who mourned, the vitally interested and the merely curious gathered together for the funeral of Clifford Glover. Three hours before the scheduled noon ceremony, the pews in the Mount

Zion Baptist Church on 107th Avenue in South Jamaica began to fill. By eleven all seats had been taken and a crowd of 800 onlookers stood outside. Twenty minutes earlier than planned, Reverend John Mason stepped to the pulpit and welcomed the congregation.

Dressed in a black suit, white shirt, and silver tie, Add Armstead sat in the first row, staring at the white casket in front of him. Eloise Glover was at his side, her two-year-old daughter Patricia asleep in her arms. Behind the last row of pews, Captain Glanvin Alveranga stood alone—the only uniformed cop in attendance. Against the advice of staff members who feared for his safety, Alveranga had insisted on attending the ceremony.

Joining as one, the congregation sang "Jesus Keep Me Near the Cross" and "Trouble in My Way." Reverend Mason read several passages from the Bible, and two more hymns followed. Then Reverend Vaster Johnson stepped to the pulpit. Inside the crowded church, the temperature had risen well above eighty degrees. Ventilation was poor, and the air heavy.

"Clifford Glover was not so much the victim of a bullet as he was the victim of a vicious system," Johnson declaimed. "His sun went down long before noon. Is there any difference from a rope one hundred years ago in Alabama or a gun now in South Jamaica? I wonder if it was the price of being black standing before a gun with a white finger on the trigger."

The congregation seethed as Vaster Johnson concluded his oration. Fearful of what might follow, the Reverend Albert S. Johnson, who was to deliver the eulogy, strode to the pulpit. Speaking with a mastery that had come from years of dialogue, he calmed the crowd.

"This little boy is in the presence of the Lord," Albert Johnson cried.

"That's right," the congregation answered.

"He ain't here no more."

115

"That's right," they said.

"But if he was here," Johnson went on, "he'd ask his black friends to cool it. We don't believe in black and white. We're all brothers. There are only two groups of people where our Lord is concerned—those who are saved and those who are not. Anytime you walk the streets hating the white man, you're on the way to hell."

At 1:30 P.M., as rock star Stevie Wonder, who attended the service, sang "Were You There When They Crucified My Lord?" Clifford Glover's casket was carried from the church to a waiting hearse for transport to Plain Lawn Cemetery in Long Island. As the pallbearers moved through the crowd, most of whom had been standing in the hot sun for hours, an angry rustle stirred. Then a handful, followed by a dozen, and finally several hundred persons surged forward, brandishing upraised fists in a black power salute. "If the cops kick one black ass in South Jamaica tonight," Alveranga murmured, "this city will explode."

Fourteen blocks from the Mount Zion Baptist Church, the 103rd Precinct station house stood prepared to receive the funeralgoers. Barricades manned by tactical patrolmen surrounded the building. Inside and in buses several blocks away, one hundred additional policemen awaited instructions. In the distance, the voices of five hundred marchers could be heard.

"We want Shea," the crowd chanted. "We want Shea."

The cops at the barricades tensed and stood their ground. Their orders from Queens Borough Commander Charles McCarthy were specific. They were to hold ranks and make no arrests.

"We want Shea," the crowd chanted.

PBA Trustee Charlie Peterson looked apprehensively at the approaching mob.

COPS ARE PIGS, one placard read. MOMMA, MOMMA, HIDE YOUR CHILD, THE FILTHY COPS ARE RUNNING WILD, decreed another.

"We want Shea," the crowd chanted, surrounding the station house.

A bottle crashed behind the patrolmen manning the barricades, then another. Several rocks hurtled toward them.

"Hold ranks," a TPF supervisor shouted.

The rain of rocks and bottles continued.

"That's all," Peterson shouted, heading toward McCarthy. "I've had it. My men won't stand here like Kewpie dolls waiting to be hit. I forbid it. Either you let them make arrests or I'm pulling them off the job."

Several more rocks and bottles followed. "Okay," McCarthy said at last. "If they actually see someone in the act of assault, they can arrest him."

The cops moved forward and divided the crowd into several groups. Then the demonstrators remassed and retreated in the direction from which they had come. On New York Boulevard a group of youths pushed into a pizza parlor, scooped up slices of pizza, and ran on. Others smashed windows as storekeepers hurriedly lowered heavy iron gates to protect their wares. At Liberty Avenue, dozens of marchers began pounding on cars driven by whites. A sixty-year-old man was struck in the face by flying glass when a rock was hurled through the side window of his car. A young woman lost control of her vehicle when a brick flew through the windshield. Regaining control, she drove on, chased by a handful of people who shouted, "She just killed a black child. Stop her!"

On Brinkerhoff Avenue an appliance store was looted. On 109th Avenue two liquor stores and a supermarket were stripped. A car abandoned by a white driver was set aflame. Then the skies opened, and heavy rain began to fall. Slowly the crowd dispersed, carrying bottles of liquor, groceries, and cases of beer. By dusk, order had been restored. Seven civilians and four cops had been injured.

That night a fifty-three-year-old black man who, with his son, owned and operated a liquor store on 109th Avenue in South Jamaica inspected the ruins of his establishment. "Every dime we had was in this business," the man said. "Now we're wiped out. They took everything we had. The shooting was only an excuse. These vandals don't give a damn for anyone or anything. If they had any concern for the dead boy, they wouldn't have done what they did on the day he was buried."

As the community raged, so did the cops. Many policemen in the 103rd Precinct genuinely believed that Thomas Shea had fired in self-defense. Others had grave doubts concerning the veracity of his story but identified with him as "a man who was doing his job." Virtually all of them bitterly opposed the charge of murder.

In an effort to calm the men under his command, Glanvin Alveranga sought to address them each individually. "I know you're unhappy about the arrest," he said time and time again, "but I want you to put yourself in another pair of shoes. Imagine yourself coming home one night and your wife telling you that your ten-year-old son has been shot to death in the back by a policeman. What would your reaction be?"

The Captain's words had a calming effect on some, but the majority of cops continued to believe that Shea's arrest was "politically motivated." The presence of such "dignitaries" as Manhattan Borough President Percy Sutton at the Glover funeral reinforced their view, and the actions of Queens Borough President Donald Manes strengthened it still further.

Shortly after Glover's death, Manes (a white man) paid a condolence call on Add Armstead and Eloise Glover. Speaking stiffly before reporters (who had been notified in advance of his visit), Manes expressed "the shock shared by many people throughout the city" and pledged, "There will be justice." Then, holding a photograph of Clifford Glover in his hands, Manes announced the establishment of a "Clifford Glover Memorial Fund" to purchase athletic equipment for black children in South Jamaica. At the close of the festivities, Armstead thanked Manes for his "very thoughtful" gesture. Then, after the Borough President had gone, the embittered father turned to Eloise Glover and complained, "Basketballs! That's all they think we need. Ain't he ever heard of books?"

On Friday, May 4 (the day after the funeral), the rift between rank-and-file cops and "the politicians" grew even wider. Responding to pressure from the Mayor's office and the media, Police Commissioner Donald Cawley called a press conference at police headquarters in Manhattan to announce the creation of a special panel to screen out members of the Department who had shown "a chronic use of force in their work."

Speaking to newspaper, radio, and television reporters, Cawley declared, "To clear the air, I am releasing the record of Patrolman Shea's previous cases involving firearms." He then summarized each of Shea's previous shooting incidents and closed with a reference to the death of Clifford Glover. "I disagree with the charge of murder, but the officer clearly made a mistake and pulled the trigger when he shouldn't have."

Within hours, the Patrolmen's Benevolent Association reacted. Speaking at a hastily called press conference of his own, PBA President Robert McKiernan attacked the release of Shea's record as "despicable," adding that the treatment received by Shea had "upset other policemen and perhaps made them reluctant to perform their duties." Noting that Shea had made more than two hundred arrests and assisted in an additional three hundred, McKiernan angrily declared, "We wish the Commissioner would stop releasing statements to the press about Patrolman Shea until he has had his day in court. As a matter of fact, we demand it. If necessary, we will seek to have the judge in this matter call Cawley and order him to make no further statements regarding the case. Cowardly police administrators," McKiernan closed, "are robbing law-abiding citizens of the protection they pay for and deserve. The Patrolmen's Benevolent Association regretfully informs the general public that we are recommending to our men that they be extremely careful and cautious before taking any action against suspected criminals. Policemen have been sold out again by politicians, and this city slips still further towards anarchy."

With McKiernan's statement, polarization within the Department over the arrest of Thomas Shea reached new heights. The PBA was and remains a potent force in city life. As the union and collective bargaining agent for the police, with a membership roll that includes 99 percent of the city's patrolmen, it holds extraordinary influence over millions of New Yorkers. Indeed, if Cawley doubted the political strength of the PBA, he had only to look at the results of a 1966 referendum which decided the fate of New York's Civilian Complaint Review Board. The purpose of the Board had been to evaluate complaints of alleged police brutality. The referendum had pitted the PBA (which wanted the Board out of existence) against the panel's supporters (including New York City Mayor John Lindsay and Senators Robert Kennedy and Jacob Javits). The city electorate sided with the PBA by an overwhelming two-to-one margin.

Now, with rank-and-file cops voicing open opposition to their Commissioner, a near-intolerable situation existed. In precincts across the city, renewed rumblings of a police walkout were heard. Demands for Cawley's resignation sprouted. In South Jamaica the burden weighed heaviest on Glanvin

Alveranga who, as the first black precinct commander in Queens, had to lead his men in a manner consistent with his responsibilities as a police officer and his convictions as a man.

Four days after Clifford Glover's funeral, Alveranga posted a memorandum on the bulletin board of the roll-call room in the 103rd Precinct station house:

TO ALL MEMBERS OF THIS COMMAND
As commanding officer, I wish to take this opportunity to thank each member of this command for the high level of performance that has been maintained during the recent disorders. The level of professionalism, the intelligent, prompt response to emergencies and the forbearance displayed by you in dealing with the extreme provocations of recent days makes me proud to be in command of such a fine body of police officers.

Then, dressed in uniform, for several weeks Alveranga toured the churches of South Jamaica, speaking before Sunday congregations. In answer to a reporter's query, the police captain said, "I want to assure members of the community that they will have my complete assistance with any type of problem. I think Sunday is a good day to talk with them."

Reverend John Mason of the Mount Zion Baptist Church (where Clifford Glover's funeral had taken place) told reporters that Alveranga was "warmly received by my parishioners." Deputy Commissioner for Community Affairs Roosevelt Dunning said later that Alveranga's sensitivity was "a major contributing factor in the restoration of calm to South Jamaica." But throughout his travels, despite his mission of bringing peace to others, Alveranga found none for himself. One particular thought kept gnawing away at his insides.

Alveranga felt nothing but revulsion over the death of

Clifford Glover. Not once during his own tenure on the force had he fired his gun except for police training. He was convinced that Shea and Scott were lying about the shooting. But if the Shea-Scott story was false, then one very troubling question remained.

Thomas Shea wasn't the only cop who had fired a gun on the morning of April 28, 1973. By his own admission, Walter Scott had fired too. Scott claimed that he had shot at Armstead in self-defense after Glover had been struck by Shea's bullet and passed a "black revolver" to his stepfather. But if there had been no gun and Armstead was unarmed, then Scott was lying about the cause and timing of his own shot.

Everyone had come to assume that Thomas Shea shot and killed Clifford Glover. Alveranga wasn't sure they had arrested the right cop.

10

THE INVESTIGATION

As South Jamaica raged, an intensive police effort to find evidence justifying the death of Clifford Glover was under way. Under the direction of Captain John Curran and Sergeant Clarence Reichman, teams of Emergency Services patrolmen combed the shooting site for spent bullets, bullet holes, or anything else which might substantiate Shea's version of events. The searchers used rakes, shovels, metal detectors and magnets. Hundreds of area residents were interviewed with regard to what they had seen or heard on the night of the shooting. To supplement their efforts, a team of detectives patrolled the vicinity of the lot for several days from 4:00 to 6:00 A.M. in the hope that passersby might have been present during the predawn hours of April 28, 1973. No exculpatory evidence was found.

Every potentially helpful lead was followed. Two days after the shooting, a forty-five-year-old man informed police that he had been robbed in South Jamaica by a boy who resembled Clifford Glover. The informant was interviewed by detectives from the 16th Division Homicide-Assault Squad. Under questioning, he admitted that the robbery (which had not been previously reported) was eighteen months old and had been perpetrated by a youth approximately five feet eight inches tall and fifteen years of age.

Patrolmen from the 103rd Precinct reviewed files at the Queens County Narcotics Bureau in the hope of finding Add Armstead, Eloise Glover, or Clifford Glover mentioned as a suspect. When their efforts failed, they rechecked the files for references to two former boarders in the Glover home. Other policemen checked to ascertain whether Tony Minutello (Armstead's boss) had an arrest record or might be linked to the sale of stolen automobile parts. Minutello was "clean."

An anonymous source telephoned the 103rd Precinct and reported that "the real Clifford Glover" had died three days after birth. The boy shot by Shea, the caller said, was a child who had been shipped to New York by a cousin of Eloise Glover "for welfare purposes." Despite its irrelevance, the lead was pursued with negative results.

After a week of intensive investigation, only two pieces of potentially helpful evidence had been uncovered and these were virtually useless. On Sunday, April 29 (the day after the shooting), a retired policeman named Joseph McKeefery reported to police that he had found a plastic imitation pistol in a lot several blocks from the shooting site. A Good Humor salesman, who had been walking his dog at the time of his discovery, McKeefery told investigators that he had decided to stroll down New York Boulevard "after hearing about the Officer Shea incident." The gun was vouchered at the 103rd Precinct station house, and McKeefery thanked for his interest.

The second piece of evidence was more intriguing. On Monday, April 30, while draining a sewage catch basin on the northeast corner of Dillon Street and 112th Road, a three-man police team under the direction of Detective Henry Sephton found a metal starter's pistol in a pile of dredged-up silt. But as ballistics experts quickly noted, the

124

gun was incapable of firing live ammunition. And, in any event, it had been found in a sewer directly opposite the direction in which Armstead had fled according to Shea's own testimony.

"Keep trying," PBA Trustee Charlie Peterson urged when informed of the negative results. "There has to be something out there that will substantiate Shea's story." However, as dozens of policemen worked on Thomas Shea's behalf, a second, very different investigation was unfolding.

On Tuesday, May 1, Albert Gaudelli (Chief of the Queens County Homicide Bureau) returned to the District Attorney's office from a ten-day Caribbean vacation. Born and raised in Queens, a graduate of Manhattan College and New York Law School, Gaudelli had joined the DA's office in 1968 in the belief that it would be the quickest route to trial experience. Married, the father of three infant children, short and pudgy with a large nose bent slightly to the right, he wore gold-rimmed glasses and sported a thick black mustache. His hairline had receded prematurely, leaving him almost completely bald save for a thick fringe of curly black hair around the edges of his cranium. At age thirty-four, Gaudelli was both committed to his job and politically ambitious. Newsworthy cases seldom escaped his notice.

Gaudelli's first act upon returning to work and learning of the case was to telephone John Guido. Short and stocky with thinning gray hair, Guido had been on the force since 1946. A decent man, he also happened to be one of the most hated cops in New York. Since 1972 Guido had been Commanding Officer of the New York City Police Department's Internal Affairs Division, the sole function of which was to investigate allegations of police misconduct. In the wake of the Knapp Commission hearings on police corruption, the number of cops assigned to Internal Affairs had grown to more than two hundred.

"I need your help," Gaudelli told Guido three days after

the shooting. "I can't let regular cops from the 103rd Precinct handle this case for several reasons. One, it wouldn't be
fair to turn them loose on a brother officer who's their friend.
Two, no matter what happens, they'll be accused of covering
up. And three," Gaudelli paused, "the charge of covering up
might not be so far from the truth."

As he had done with so many other "dirty" cases, Guido
accepted the task. The following day he placed two subordi-
nates, James Skennian and Mark Frances, in charge of the
investigation.

Born and brought up in the Bronx, fifty-seven years old,
Skennian had been a cop for twenty-seven years. Before join-
ing Internal Affairs, he had commanded the city's 1st Divi-
sion Homicide Unit, where he served as point man in the
Department's investigation of the murder of mobster Joey
Gallo.

Frances was eleven years Skennian's junior but had served
on the force since 1947. Tall and heavyset with black hair
and brown eyes, he was among the most relentless and intense investigators on Guido's staff. "Mark Frances is like a
meat grinder," a colleague once said. "He's a machine."

Guido assigned Skennian to the case because the former
homicide commander "knew about murder." He chose
Frances because "Mark was a particularly aggressive investigator." Together, the three men conducted one of the most
thorough investigations in the history of Internal Affairs.
"Technically," Gaudelli remembers, "Frances was the junior
man on the case. But in reality, it was his baby. He was all
over the place."

Frances was driven by his belief that Shea and Scott were
lying. To prove it, he toiled like a man possessed. Working
nonstop ten-hour days, he gathered every scrap of information on the two men that existed within the Department. He
broke down Shea's arrest record by race and interviewed the
black suspects. Each of Shea's past partners was questioned

with regard to racial incidents they might have witnessed. Every bar in South Jamaica was checked to determine whether Shea or Scott had been drinking on the night of the shooting. Tapes of police radio transmissions on the morning of April 28, 1973, were transcribed and evaluated.

Next, Francis interviewed the police witnesses who had spoken with Shea on the day of the shooting. "Don't you think it's a little strange," Frances asked Sergeant Joseph Kennedy, "that Clifford Glover was shot square in the back?"

"I'm not here to analyze what happened," Kennedy answered. "I can only tell you the facts as I heard them."

"Do you really believe that Walter Scott could have driven around the block and run into the lot in time to see the shooting?"

Kennedy repeated his response, which was hardly surprising. Frances had expected little or no cooperation from Shea's brethren. "Let's face it," he told Gaudelli later in the investigation. "Right or wrong, most cops in this city identify with Shea. At the time of the shooting he wasn't drunk. He was on duty. He was a cop trying to do his job."

One week after the shooting, accompanied by eleven men from Emergency Services, Francis, Guido, and Skennian surveyed the increasingly infamous lot. Three days later they returned with Add Armstead and asked him to retrace the route he had taken on the day of the shooting. Then, keeping in mind the revolver that had been recovered at the Pilot Automotive Wrecking Company, Frances instructed Armstead to run from the lot to Pilot, enter the shop, go to the shelf where the gun had been kept, and run back to the spot on Dillon Street by the lot where he had flagged down the passing police cars. Armstead complied, and Frances ran beside him with a stopwatch in his hand. Midway through the experiment, Armstead collapsed from an attack of asthma and was unable to continue.

On the morning of May 15, 1973, Frances, Guido, and Skennian returned to the lot again. This time, they came with a videotaping crew and ten additional cops. As the cameras turned, four men playing the roles of Add Armstead, Clifford Glover, Walter Scott, and Thomas Shea reenacted the Shea-Scott version of the shooting. One patrolman, playing the role of Walter Scott, drove his car 240 feet down New York Boulevard and 100 feet up 112th Road, while Frances, imitating Shea, chased two suspects 150 feet into the lot. The first cop then jumped from his car and rushed 130 feet to a point near the chain-link fence where the shooting had occurred.

"It just doesn't work," Frances said when the re-creation was complete. "There's no way Scott could have seen the shooting."

"Scott couldn't have seen the shooting!" It was one thing to make the statement and another to prove it. The latter was the task of the Queens County District Attorney's Office, which, politely speaking, was in a "state of transition." Frederick Ludwig had instructed Gaudelli to move slowly on the case until a clear public consensus emerged. Meanwhile, black community leaders were clamoring for the appointment of a special prosecutor, and fed up with Ludwig's handling of the matter, PBA President Robert McKiernan had wired Governor Nelson Rockefeller suggesting that the Acting DA be removed from office. On May 9 Rockefeller responded by announcing the appointment of New York attorney Michael Armstrong as the new Queens County District Attorney.

Born in Manhattan, educated at Yale College and Harvard Law School, the forty-one-year-old Armstrong was a perfect choice. As an Assistant United States Attorney he had been a first-rate prosecutor. Five years of private practice on Wall Street had endowed him with a reputation as a topflight legal mind. But Armstrong's most important credential was his two-year tenure as Chief Counsel to the Knapp Commission investigating charges of police corruption. "I like cops," Armstrong once said. "There are very few things I'd rather do than sit down in a bar and have a drink with one." But the fact remained that, when warranted, Armstrong could be tough on cops, and the media knew it. Behind his light blue eyes, brown hair, and Tom Sawyer look-alike appeal was a man of integrity and iron resolve.

Taking command, Armstrong found the Queens County DA's office in chaos. "Most prosecutor's offices are underfinanced and understaffed," he told a colleague. "But things here are ridiculous." As Armstrong saw it, the root of the problem was that, under Thomas Mackell, staff members had been poorly selected and badly trained. Political affiliation had outweighed merit in the hiring process. Novice assistant DAs had been sent into court with inadequate supervision.

The statistics told the story. Throughout New York City, two-thirds of all persons actually tried on felony charges are convicted. In Queens, the total for 1972–1973 was hovering near 50 percent. Worse still, in cases where felony charges had been reduced to misdemeanors, the conviction percentage in Queens stood at 29.7—this is a county where most jurors were thought to be "law-and-order types" with a tendency to convict.

To counteract these deficiencies, Armstrong established a hiring review board whose members were forbidden to inquire into an applicant's political preference. Training seminars were set up for the office staff. But, most significant, Armstrong moved quickly to import or elevate capable attorneys to high-level positions. Two of these personnel changes were to have a direct bearing on the case of Thomas Shea. As his first act in office, Armstrong asked John Keenan

(Chief of Homicide in the Manhattan DA's office) to become his Chief Assistant. Born in New York, a graduate of Fordham Law School, the forty-three-year-old Keenan had been a prosecutor for seventeen years. He was, in Armstrong's words, "the best prosecuting attorney I've ever known."

Next, Armstrong elevated Joan Carey (a thirty-three-year-old Assistant District Attorney) to the post of Deputy Chief of Homicide. Tall and slender with shoulder-length blond hair, perfect teeth, and a nose like Candice Bergen's, Carey had graduated from New York Law School in 1968 and been hired by Mackell the following year. Aware of her status as a "token woman," she had nonetheless persevered and won respect from the office's seventy male lawyers as a first-rate attorney.*

As Armstrong took control of the District Attorney's office, the grand jury probe into Clifford Glover's death was already under way. In truth, Shea's arrest had been a largely symbolic act. Further prosecution of the case hinged on the willingness of the grand jury to indict. Starting on May 2, under the direction of Albert Gaudelli and his assistant, Alan Parente, the grand jurors heard evidence in the case. One by one, witnesses told their version of events. On May 17 Parente escorted the jurors to the lot to enable them to place the testimony in better perspective. Slowly the evidence was accumulating, but the crucial question remained: What will the District Attorney's office ask the grand jury to do? Without pressure from above, it was unlikely that the grand jury would indict.

As Gaudelli and Parente formally presented the case, the task of gathering facts for a final recommendation by Armstrong and his staff fell largely to Joan Carey. Escorted on

---

*John Keenan later became Special Prosecutor for the State of New York and, following that, Chairman of New York City's Off-Track Betting Corporation. Joan Carey is now a judge of the Criminal Court in Queens.

various occasions by John Keenan, Harold Cannon, and Mark Frances, she interviewed dozens of witnesses and visited the lot ten times.

Meanwhile, Internal Affairs continued its probe. The gun found by Add Armstead under the seat of an abandoned car and kept by him at the Pilot Automotive Wrecking Company was traced to a South Carolina employee of the United States Bureau of Sports and Wildlife, who said that it had been stolen from the glove compartment of his car several years earlier. On May 11, 1973, Detective Nat Laurendi of the New York County DA's Squad administered a polygraph examination to Armstead. Four key questions were asked:

1. Did you have possession of a gun when you left for work on Saturday morning, April 28, 1973?

2. Did one of the policemen call you a black son of a bitch?

3. Did Clifford Glover pass you a gun at any time that morning?

4. Were you going to work at the time of the shooting?

Armstead's answers were consistent with his earlier statements. Laurendi reported that, in his professional opinion, the witness was telling the truth. The results were not surprising. Prior to the police-administered examination, Gaudelli had secretly brought Armstead to a private lie-detection expert for similar questioning—just in case.

Searching for every possible clue, Michael Armstrong and his staff studied transcripts of the April 28, 1973, police radio transmissions and station-house interviews. Grand jury testimony was analyzed and evaluated. Finally, Armstrong, Keenan, Carey, Gaudelli, and Tom Duffy (the newly appointed head of the DA's Appeals Bureau) caucused on a final recommendation.

Community pressure for a murder indictment was enormous. Shortly after Armstrong had taken office, a group of black businessmen and elected officials had visited him to urge that Shea be dealt with harshly. "Remember," one of the men warned, "your appointment as District Attorney runs out in December. We'll be around for the fall election."

"That's nice," Armstrong answered, "but I won't be. I've already notified the four major parties that I won't be a candidate. I'm here to clean up the mess that's been left behind; that's all. This case will be prosecuted like every other. I'm not about to indict some cop for murder just to placate the black community."

Against this backdrop, the deliberations progressed. Clearly, several factors weighed in Shea's favor. The shooting had not been a cold-blooded, premeditated act. At five o'clock in the morning, he hadn't been cruising the streets of South Jamaica looking for someone innocent to kill. The clothing worn by Armstead and Glover resembled that of the taxi robbers. Also, contrary to Armstead's testimony, Armstrong and his staff considered it highly unlikely that Shea had exited from the car and fired his gun before the suspects ran.

However, these points were relatively minor compared with the evidence against Shea. Walter Scott's claim of having witnessed the shooting and gun transfer was implausible. Rather than act like a guilty man, Armstead had flagged down the first police car he saw following the incident. Shea had several other questionable incidents on his record. And, most important, Clifford Glover had been shot square in the back.

"Forget about Scott," Armstrong summed up. "Forget about Shea's past shootings. Forget about Add Armstead. That boy was shot in the back while he was running away. Shea engaged in the all-too-common police practice of shooting a fleeing black suspect from behind. If he had killed a

crook, he probably would have been awarded a merit cita-
tion. But it turned out to be a ten-year-old boy. He broke the
law and, if we make an example of him, it will deter other
policemen from doing the same thing. Under the New York
State Penal Code," Armstrong concluded, "Shea can be
charged with murder or manslaughter. We have to decide
which one."

As the District Attorney's office continued to deliberate, the
Patrolmen's Benevolent Association augmented its support
for Thomas Shea. On Tuesday, May 8, at the PBA's monthly
meeting, President Robert McKiernan addressed the 350-
member delegate body.

"We have a good legal program," McKiernan said. "Anytime a policeman is arrested for conduct in the line of duty,
we handle the defense. Normally our legal staff is equal to
the task, but this is a special case. Never before in the history
of New York has a cop been arrested for murder.*

"Jim Cahill is a good lawyer," McKiernan continued.
"But because of the importance of this case, he has suggested
that we go outside the PBA and retain expert counsel. A
motion has been made that the Patrolmen's Benevolent Association authorize retention of an attorney to represent
Thomas Shea. The cost will run somewhere in the neighborhood of ten thousand dollars. I ask each of you to do for
Thomas Shea what you would want done for yourself under
similar circumstances."

*Fourteen months after the death of Clifford Glover, it was discovered
that in 1924 a policeman named Robert McAllister had been indicted and
tried for murder in the killing of an unarmed suspect. Acquitted after
twenty-three minutes of jury deliberation, McAllister was subsequently
promoted to the rank of Deputy Inspector. However, during the time the
Shea case remained active, neither the media nor any of the participants
were aware of the McAllister matter.

The motion carried unanimously. Several days later a forty-eight-year-old trial lawyer named Jacob Robert Evseroff was retained as counsel.

Tall, good-looking, with a full head of black hair graying at the temples, Jack Evseroff had learned his trade as an Assistant District Attorney in Brooklyn. With ten years' experience as a prosecutor and twelve in private practice, he was an acknowledged master. Whatever the occasion, his mood was proper. Depending on the requisites of a given case and jury, he could be flamboyant, hard-hitting, deferential, mean, or utterly charming. "Jack Evseroff has lots of polish," one colleague said, "but it's been put on over a very hard exterior. When he hits, it's like being whacked on the head with a block of shiny marble."

Fast on his feet, blessed with a reddish complexion which gave him a perpetually healthy look, Evseroff somehow also managed to look Irish. "Jewish smarts and Irish charm," one cop noted. "It's an unbeatable combination."

Evseroff's clients had run the gamut. Early in his career he represented a six-foot six-inch Black Muslim who appeared in court dressed in a black cap and flowing gown to defend against a charge of narcotics possession. Mobster Joseph Colombo and Colombo's reputed successor, Vincent Aloi, were also clients, as was basketball fixer Jack Molinas. But Evseroff had made his reputation by defending cops.

On April 19, 1971, distraught over the breakup of his marriage, a policeman named Jack Guarino wrote a suicide note before killing his wife: "Bury us together. We had a Camelot. It's got to end as Camelot did in destruction." Guarino, by his own admission, then shot his wife six times on a public street, reloaded, fired five shots into a witness, carried his wife's body to their car, drove home, placed the corpse on a bed, and went to sleep beside it. An all-male jury returned a verdict of not guilty by reason of insanity after an impassioned defense by Evseroff.

Peter Droner was a retired police sergeant. On an evening walk through Times Square, he became embroiled in an argument with a street peddler and kicked aside the man's wares. When the peddler retaliated with his fists, Droner pulled a gun, fired three shots, and killed the man instantly. After four hours' deliberation, a jury found Droner not guilty.

Time after time Evseroff had successfully defended policemen accused of wrongdoing. But in none of his cases had he represented a client as notorious as Thomas Shea. And none of his previous clients had killed a ten-year-old boy.

In the second week of May, Evseroff and Shea met for the first time. In truth, the attorney was less concerned with his client's problems than with his own. Several months earlier, Evseroff's second wife had left him, taking his two sons to Florida. Since then, by his own admission, the attorney had "lived on martinis and Valium." Then, on the night of Friday, April 27 (hours before Clifford Glover was shot), Evseroff returned home from work to be met by armed robbers, who ransacked his house and left him bound with wire, stuffed in a closet. Now, in a strange way, Jacob Robert Evseroff and Thomas Shea represented salvation for each other. Shea's plight gave Evseroff a much-needed mission, something to work for. And Evseroff promised Shea a defense.

"My name is Jack Evseroff," the attorney said when the two men were introduced. "My father immigrated to the United States from Russia. I fought in Europe during World War Two. I've been a criminal lawyer for twenty-two years. I want you to tell me about the case, and then we'll decide whether we like each other enough to work together."

"What do you want to know?" Shea asked.

135

"Why don't you tell me a little about yourself?"

"There's not much to tell," Shea answered. "I'm a cop. I've been on the force for twelve years. Once I thought I might want to be a sergeant or a lieutenant, but you have to pass a written exam for promotion. Some people have the ability to take tests; others don't. I don't."

"Are you married?"

"Yes."

"Children?"

"Two daughters."

The two men spoke for several hours. At day's end a bargain was struck.

"I'd like to represent you if you'll have me," Evseroff said.

"I'd rather have you than F. Lee Bailey," Shea answered.

On the afternoon of June 12, 1973, the inevitable occurred. Evseroff received a telephone call from John Keenan, Chief Assistant to the Queens County District Attorney.

"I understand that you represent Thomas Shea," Keenan said. "Michael Armstrong and I would appreciate it if you could drop by our office later today."

Evseroff went quickly, alone. Armstrong and Keenan spoke with him briefly.

"The grand jury has returned an indictment against your client," Armstrong said. "There will be an arraignment tomorrow. Obviously the press will be out in full force. We have an extremely volatile situation in South Jamaica, and I'd like to avoid a scene which might anger the community or the cops. We think the best way to accomplish this is to see that the case is accurately reported. Towards that end we're planning a press conference for tomorrow. It will be short and to the point. I'm hoping you'll limit any statement you make to the facts. If we don't all cooperate to keep this professional, there's no telling what might happen."

"What's the charge?" Evseroff asked.

"Murder."

At noon on June 13, 1973, Michael Armstrong announced the indictment of Patrolman Thomas Shea on a charge of murder. "This case," the District Attorney pledged after reading the indictment, "will be decided in the courts, not in the press or on the streets. Anyone interested should understand that it's going to be tried in court. It will not be helpful for anyone, no matter whom, to try to bring pressures to bear because this can only harm a fair adjudication."

"What about Shea's partner?" a reporter asked.

Since the day following the shooting, Walter Scott had been assigned to clerical duty at Queens Borough Headquarters.

"Walter Scott has not been indicted," Armstrong answered. "However, he is suspended from the force as of noon today."

As Armstrong answered questions, Shea moved to the arraignment part of the Queens County Supreme Court Building, where he pleaded "not guilty" to the charge of murder. Then, with Evseroff at his side, the patrolman headed for a side door.

"Wait a minute," Evseroff challenged. "Where do you think you're going?"

"Out the back," Shea told him. "There are a million reporters on the courthouse steps."

"That's right," Evseroff said, "and you're going to show them all right now that you don't have horns. Those photographers want a picture, and they'll get it one way or another. You can be on the front page of the *Daily News* with your

137

hand over your face looking like a thug, or you can walk out front, hold your head high, and let people see you're a human being."

"Okay," Shea said. "You win."

Slowly the two men pushed their way through the throng on the courthouse steps.

"Mr. Evseroff," a reporter asked, "what do you think of the way the District Attorney's office has handled the case?"

"I have every confidence that Mr. Armstrong and the people of Queens will give us a fair trial."

"Do you think your client will receive special treatment because he's a cop?"

"All we seek is a fair trial free of political pressure or racial bias."

"That's what you say," another reporter pressed, "but isn't this really a racial case?"

"Mister," Evseroff shot back, "it's only a racial case if people like you make it one."

"But isn't it true that, if this incident had occurred in Scarsdale, there wouldn't have been any shooting?"

"If this incident had occurred in Scarsdale, the boy wouldn't have had a gun."

Reaching the edge of the crowd, Evseroff and Shea climbed into a PBA car and disappeared down Queens Boulevard. Their primary source of news gone, the reporters rushed to the home of Add Armstead and Eloise Glover. Armstead was at work, but Mrs. Glover was there to meet them. "I just want justice to be done," she said. "I feel the grand jury did the right thing by indicting him. My son was innocent. He was shot down in the street.

"I don't feel strong anymore," Mrs. Glover added. "My son's gone, and I miss him."

11

PREPARATION
FOR TRIAL

On June 15, 1973, departmental charges were filed against Thomas Shea. Four days later, a similar action was instituted against Walter Scott. These proceedings were administrative in nature. In them, the Police Department alleged that Shea and Scott had violated police regulations on April 28, 1973. The charges would be heard regardless of the outcome of Shea's trial, but in deference to the murder indictment the administrative hearing was indefinitely postponed.*

On June 27, 1973, James Cahill appeared in New York State Supreme Court on Scott's behalf and demanded that his client be restored to active duty pending a full hearing of the departmental charges against him. "It's not fair for this man to remain under suspension," Cahill argued. "He has not been charged with the commission of a crime. It might take years for this case to be resolved." One month later, the court ordered Scott restored to active duty. He

---

*Full consideration of departmental charges against Shea in connection with the alleged pistol-whipping of a 14-year-old boy in March, 1972, was also deferred.

was assigned to a clerical post in Brooklyn.

Scott's return to uniform was particularly annoying to Armstrong and his staff. Despite intense pressure to change his story, Shea's partner had simply refused to bend. On three occasions he had met with Gaudelli, and each time the Chief of Homicide had hammered away at the implausibility of the Shea-Scott tale. Yet each time Scott had held firm. The irony of the situation was that, in Armstrong's view, Scott's testimony actually weakened Shea's case. By claiming that he had seen the shooting after driving around the block, Scott cast severe doubts on the credibility of Shea's entire story.

"Who knows?" Armstrong mused. "Maybe right after the shooting Scott ran into the lot, and Shea said, 'The kid had a gun; he flipped it to the other guy; you've got to back me up.'" The District Attorney pondered his scenario, then voiced another thought: "I'd love to know when and where Scott fired. Maybe he shot into the air afterwards to make it look as though he and Armstead had been in a shoot-out. Or maybe he fired the first shot when the suspects ran."

Summer passed without further incident. In late August, Evseroff filed a motion for the right to inspect all police records relevant to the case. One week later several procedural matters were aired in court. Each of the motions was tabled for subsequent resolution. If the dog days of summer were significant at all, it was for what did not occur. Throughout June, July, and August, Deputy Commissioner for Community Affairs Roosevelt Dunning and his staff labored to keep South Jamaica calm. Aided by the fact of Shea's indictment, they succeeded.

In mid-September, Dunning journeyed to upstate New York for several days of relaxation. Each year, at summer's end, the Patrolmen's Benevolent Association holds a three-

day convention at the Police Recreational Camp in Tannersville. Without fail, 1,200 persons, including PBA delegates,
police brass, New York State politicians, and honored guests,
are in attendance. Most black cops who are eligible choose
not to attend. "I went to a PBA convention once," Glanvin
Alveranga remembers. "I stayed for about three hours. Too
many policemen were drinking heavily. They were more
open about their feelings than might otherwise have been the
case. I found the disorderly situation very upsetting, so I
left."

On the final night of the convention, with Dunning in
attendance, PBA President Robert McKiernan hosted a
farewell banquet. One by one, various public luminaries were
introduced. Then McKiernan cleared his throat for the
grand finale: "Gentlemen, I'd like to introduce a dear friend
—Thomas Shea."

Twelve hundred cops stood in unison and roared. "They
cheered and cheered," Dunning remembers. "Maybe five of
us—Howard Sheffey, Louis Cottell, Hugo Masini, Donald
Cawley, and I—remained seated. The rest gave him an ova-
tion that lasted for five minutes. Midway through it, Shea
was lifted on top a table so everyone could see him better. All
I could think of was: 'Hey, why cheer for him? The only
thing this guy ever did was gun down a ten-year-old boy.' "

In truth, the reality of Thomas Shea's life was vastly different
from the Tannersville reception. Problems, both personal
and financial, were weighing heavily on him.

On the day of his arrest, Shea's salary had been discon-
tinued. For two months the Patrolmen's Benevolent Association reimbursed him out of "special funds"—the first time in
history that the PBA had paid the salary of a suspended cop.
But the payments were expensive and, at the end of June,
they ceased. Thereafter PBA delegates posted memoranda

141

on bulletin boards in precinct houses across the city asking
for contributions to Shea's salary. Biweekly raffles were conducted, with cops paying a dollar each for the chance to win
a "bottle of cheer." The fund-raising effort was only partially
successful. By summer's end it was a thing of the past.

Meanwhile, Shea and his family were living in constant
fear. Threatening letters arrived in the mail daily. One blood-
stained missive pledged that both of Bonnie Shea's legs
would be broken. Another reported that a group of black
businessmen had taken out a $10,000 contract on Shea's life.
Shea's daughters were withdrawn from school because of
death threats, and the Shea family home was put under a
twenty-four-hour-a-day police guard. Finally, in late August,
the children were sent to live with relatives in New Mexico
so they could attend school in the fall. Bonnie stayed behind
so as not to leave her husband, but the strain on their marriage was evident.

Marital problems are endemic to police work. Most wives
resent their husband's disruptive schedule, absence from
family events, and holidays spent alone. In addition, many
cops find that, after several years on the force, their feelings
harden as a defense mechanism against what they see on the
streets. On several occasions before the Glover shooting,
Bonnie had suffered from severe depression and anxiety "because Tom was never home." Now, under suspension and
unable to find a job, he was home a lot, but marital tensions
were fast mounting. "Tom was a good father and good husband," Bonnie told a friend, "but this thing has changed him
completely. Things aren't so good between us anymore."

Later Bonnie would look back on 1973 with more detach-
ment. "When you have bills pouring in and no money to pay
them, you get bitter. At least I did." But summer 1973 was
not a time which lent itself to calm observation. "If I'd
known we were going to go through this," Bonnie told her
husband, "I'd never have married you." In early September,

she moved to New Mexico to be with the children. Thomas
Shea sold the house and moved in with his sister.

It is extremely rare for a major case to be swiftly resolved,
and the case of Thomas Shea was no exception. Michael
Armstrong had hoped the matter would be tried before he
left office on December 31, 1973, but circumstances would
not permit it. Judge Peter T. Farrell, who had been assigned
the case, claimed a full court calendar until early 1974. Armstrong's disappointment was shared by John Keenan and
Joan Carey, who had been expected to try the case jointly
under the interim DA's direction. Albert Gaudelli was less
disappointed. As Chief of Homicide he anticipated being
assigned the case by incoming District Attorney Nicholas
Ferraro in January 1974.*

Even more pleased by the delay were Jack Evseroff and
Thomas Shea. It is a general rule of criminal litigation that
time is on the side of the defendant. Passions cool, memories
fade, witnesses move to other parts of the country or die—
occurrences most likely to benefit the defense. However,
while Evseroff did nothing to push his client's case to trial,
neither he nor Shea was idle. Rather, many long hours were
spent at Evseroff's office in Brooklyn preparing a defense.

Even if he had been so inclined, there was nothing Evseroff
could do to change his client's version of events. The Shea-
Scott testimony had been memorialized in transcripts of interviews with Robert Johnson and Martin Bracken on the
day of the shooting. Nothing could alter these remarks.
Thus, Evseroff concentrated on the points he hoped to make
at trial within the framework of what was already on the
record.

*A second personnel shift which occurred in January 1974 was the
replacement of Police Commissioner Donald Cawley by Michael Codd.

"I want the jury to see you as a cop," he told Shea. "The type of cop I knew back in the early 1950s. A gung-ho over-the-fence guy. On the day of the shooting you were doing your job. You could have driven right by Armstead and Glover and gone on to eat dinner. No one would have known the difference. Instead, you stopped.

"There was no way you could have known Clifford Glover was ten years old," Evseroff continued. "You didn't have time to ask for a birth certificate. With heels on his shoes, the boy was five feet two inches tall. Armstead is only five feet six. Everything is relative. And we have to make the jury understand that you're not trigger-happy. You only fired your gun four times in twelve years on the force, and most of your time was spent in high-crime precincts.

"Plus we have to do a job on Armstead. Unless the DA has something up his sleeve, he'll be the only real witness against you. I want the jury to see him as a two-bit petty thief and liar. Bookies use little kids as numbers runners. If a kid is caught, he's too young to go to jail. Maybe Armstead used Glover the same way to carry a revolver. Also, Armstead works for an automobile wrecking company. Maybe we can tie him in with the car-parts theft ring.

"Let's make sure the jury knows that Armstead had a couple of minutes after the shooting to get rid of the gun. And most important, even if the jury doesn't believe you and Walter, I don't see how they can possibly believe Armstead when he says you fired before he and the boy turned and ran. That doesn't make sense at all."

A lawyer doesn't have to like his client to do his job, but it helps. In a very short period of time, an unusually strong bond of friendship and trust had developed between Jack Evseroff and Thomas Shea. Both personally and professionally, they had become extremely fond of each other. "You know," Evseroff told his client in a moment of reflection, "there are two things about this case which make it difficult:

I wish the boy hadn't been ten, and I wish he hadn't been shot in the back."

"I wish he hadn't been shot at all," Shea answered.

In early 1974 the Shea case was reassigned to Justice Bernard Dubin, who announced his intention to hold a spring trial. May 8 was scheduled as the date for final pretrial motions, and both sides geared up for the proceeding.

For Albert Gaudelli, the case represented a unique opportunity. One of Gaudelli's prized possessions was a huge scrapbook filled with newspaper and magazine clippings which mentioned his name in connection with various investigations and prosecutions. In addition, the Chief of Homicide was planning to leave his job in the near future and run for a seat in the New York State Assembly. The benefits inherent in his prosecuting the Shea case were obvious but, in early May, his hopes were dealt a crushing blow. In an eleventh-hour move, Queens County District Attorney Nicholas Ferraro reassigned the case to Thomas Demakos. Gaudelli was relegated to the role of trial assistant.

Fifty years old, married, with two teenage sons, Demakos was Chief of the District Attorney's Supreme Court Trial Bureau. Most observers considered him the premier trial attorney in the office. A native New Yorker, he had worked as a certified public accountant for seven years, then enrolled in law school at NYU at age thirty-one "because I hated my job." After graduation he engaged in private practice until 1962, when he joined the District Attorney's office. In eleven years Demakos had never lost a case. Among the defendants he successfully prosecuted was a Queens housewife named Alice Crimmins tried on a charge of murdering her infant daughter and son.

Tall and pleasant-looking with graying black hair, a dark complexion, and decidedly Greek nose, Demakos was a nice man. Always well dressed in neatly kept but not-too-expensive suits, he had none of the brazenness usually associated with criminal prosecutors. Rather, he tended toward being soft-spoken and shy, so much so that reporters sometimes complained that he was "not very quotable."

"You want something interesting to write about me," Thomas Demakos once said. "I read *Anatomy of a Murder* twice. It was the best trial book I ever read."

Informed of the last-minute reassignment, Demakos balked at taking the Shea case on. One reason was that he had not been involved in the earlier investigation. "The key to successful prosecution," he told a colleague, "is careful preparation. I haven't done it. I know virtually nothing about the case." But equally important, Demakos didn't like the idea of prosecuting a cop. "Most of them are pretty decent guys," he said. Besides, once the Shea case was over, Demakos would have to work with cops again on a daily basis, and few policemen would look kindly on his role as the prosecutor of Thomas Shea.

Under normal circumstances, the new District Attorney might have bowed to Demakos's wishes, but very little about the Shea case was normal. Nicholas Ferraro knew that the media would focus on Shea's trial, and he could not risk a charge that he had led with less than his best. "I'm sorry," he told his number one assistant. "You have to do it. That's an order."

On Wednesday, May 8, 1974, the parties convened for a final hearing on pretrial motions. Jack Evseroff and PBA attorney James Cahill were present on behalf of Thomas Shea. Thomas Demakos and Albert Gaudelli represented the state. "The trial starts Monday," Justice Dubin told them when the last procedural matter had been resolved. "Ten o'clock sharp."

The weekend ahead would be active for all concerned. Demakos had only a few days to prepare his case, and Gaudelli's assistance would be needed on a round-the-clock basis. Justice Dubin had to clear his calendar to devote full time to the matter, and Shea had been instructed to find "character witnesses" to bolster his defense. But it was Jack Evseroff who had the most difficult task. Several months earlier he had arranged for his client to take a privately administered lie-detector test. The results had not been good. Now it was Evseroff's responsibility to prepare for any eventuality which might occur at the trial, and he was by no means completely confident of success.

One item was particularly troubling. On April 28, 1973 (the day Clifford Glover was shot by Thomas Shea), a tape had been made of all police radio transmissions. Subsequently the tape had been transcribed and forwarded to the District Attorney's office. Reports filtering back to Evseroff indicated that there was something horrible on the tape—something he could not afford let go to the jury.

PART THREE

12

THE JURY IS CHOSEN

Jack Evseroff sat at a table by the back wall of Ann's Café and waited for his client. Rather than meet in court, the defense team had agreed to start each day in a small diner across the street from the Queens County Criminal Courthouse.

As Evseroff sipped a cup of coffee, James Cahill joined him and ordered a Coke. The two men had met for the first time years earlier, when Cahill was an Assistant District Attorney and Evseroff was trying cases against him. For the next month, Cahill would be on loan from the PBA to Evseroff as a trial assistant.

As Cahill and Evseroff chatted, Thomas Shea entered the diner, accompanied by two men. For almost a year Shea had been guarded by New York City cops on a rotating basis. Each time he appeared in court, two different patrolmen had been assigned to go with him. However, as trial approached, the Commissioner's office felt that steady bodyguards would provide better protection, and volunteers were solicited. Eventually Mike Hinchy and Hugh Curtin were chosen.

Until a verdict was reached, Shea would go nowhere within the city of New York without them.

Hinchy and Curtin had been partners in the 103rd Precinct for two years. A seven-year veteran of the force, Hinchy was six feet three inches tall with an aquiline nose, bright blue eyes, and light brown hair streaked with gray. Rugged-looking, with the build of a man who worked to stay in shape, he had fired his gun at a suspect only once—April 13, 1971 (the day before he got married). Among his other assets, Hinchy was a genuinely funny man who delighted in telling anecdotes in a soft New York–accented voice. One of his favorites concerned a murder investigation launched in the South Bronx by two patrolmen who found the nude body of what appeared to be a huge decapitated male black. Twenty-four hours after their discovery, the cops were informed by a morgue official that they were investigating the death of a three-hundred-pound skinned gorilla. "There was," Hinchy delighted in adding, "a hot dog processing plant one block from the spot where they found the body."

Hugh Curtin had been a cop for fifteen years, ten of them in the 103rd Precinct. In many ways, he was the antithesis of his partner. Short and dumpy with dark brown hair, Curtin was less a leader than a follower. But he had a ready smile and was a good audience for Hinchy's humor. And there was a special motivating factor in Curtin's volunteering for the Shea assignment. From 1963 through 1971, Curtin had been partners with Patrolman Kenneth Nugent, whose name was now inscribed on the plaque hanging in the reception room of the 103rd Precinct station house. They had been on patrol-car duty together on the afternoon of August 21, 1971, when Nugent hesitated before firing in self-defense at an armed robber and was killed instantly by a bullet in the head.

In many respects, the task of guarding Shea would be thankless. Long hours, including late-night strategy sessions, were required. Moreover, by dictate of Glanvin Alveranga, no overtime would be paid. But Hinchy and Curtin both wanted the job. They felt that Shea was "a good cop who had been shafted."

Motioning for the new arrivals to sit, Evseroff outlined the day ahead. "This morning we start picking a jury," he told Shea. "It will be slow and should take several days. The most important thing for you to remember is that jurors don't like shows of righteousness from a defendant. If someone says something you don't like, ignore it and look straight ahead. If a performance is called for, I'll provide it."

Shea nodded. Whatever Evseroff instructed would be done. Evseroff had told him to get a haircut prior to trial, and his locks were trimmed. "Clothes are important," the lawyer had said. Shea was wearing his only suit—a dark brown polyester model.

"Justice Dubin is a kitchen-sink judge," Evseroff continued. "He'll allow both sides to put just about anything they want into evidence and then let the jury decide. He won't try to influence their verdict. All things considered, I think the trial will be fair."

Shea nodded again. In less than an hour he would enter a courtroom to be tried on a charge of murder, and he was scared. The only bright spot in an otherwise-frightening day was that Bonnie had come back from New Mexico to be with him. At his insistence, she would refrain from coming to court. He didn't want her to risk being recognized and assaulted. But every night, at least for the duration of the trial, they would be together at his sister's home on Long Island. If anything good were to come of this entire horror, maybe it would be that they could patch up the cracks in their marriage—cracks that had become gaping chasms in the past year.

"Let's go," Evseroff said. "It's almost ten o'clock. We don't want to keep the Judge waiting."

The date was Monday, May 13, 1974. The trial of Patrolman Thomas Shea was about to begin.

Queens Boulevard is a busy two-way thoroughfare with four lanes of fast-moving traffic separated by a center divider. The buildings which front it are lifeless and drab; the Queens County Criminal Courthouse is one of them. An ugly squat concrete structure eight stories high, it has all the charm of a gray cinder block. Even its lawn, well manicured and green, is rendered dull by unimaginative shrubbery planted and cut in straight lines.

Crossing Queens Boulevard with his bodyguards and counsel, Shea stared at the courthouse steps. About twenty picketers, mostly white, marched back and forth carrying placards. A BADGE IS NOT A LICENSE TO MURDER, read one. JAIL THE RACIST KILLER, demanded another.

"Ignore them," Evseroff instructed. "We have more important things to worry about."

Without breaking stride, the defense team entered the courthouse lobby, where they took an elevator to the third floor. Security precautions were unusually heavy. The normal complement of guards for a criminal trial is four. The Shea case had been assigned eighteen. A sign by the courtroom door read: ALL PERSONS ENTERING MUST SUBMIT TO A PERSONAL SEARCH. In addition, Evseroff noted, the courtroom was located away from the main corridors and would be relatively easy to secure in the event of trouble.

Inside, the courtroom seemed strangely divorced from reality. Richly paneled walls and towering ceilings contrasted markedly with the building's boxlike outer shell. Soundproof walls and the absence of windows further promoted the aura of a world alone. Six rounded air vents in the ceiling regulated temperature. The floor was covered with black linoleum tile. In back, five rows of wooden spectator pews stretched from wall to wall.

The front half of the courtroom was set like a stage. Facing the audience, the Judge's bench was at rear center on a raised platform with an American flag standing to the left behind it. To the right, at a ninety-degree angle with the bench, sixteen green leather chairs stood in two rows of eight. From them, twelve regular and four alternate jurors would weigh the testimony of witnesses sitting on the raised stand midway between the judge and jury. Directly in front of the Judge's bench was a small stenographer's table. Facing the bench, two larger tables were reserved for counsel. Thomas Demakos and Albert Gaudelli were already seated at the counsel table closest to the jury box. Evseroff, Cahill, and Shea settled behind the second table, with Hinchy and Curtin taking seats in the first row of pews behind them. Facing forward, Shea saw the words "In God We Trust" inscribed in gold letters on the courtroom wall.

Shortly after 10:00 A.M. Justice Bernard Dubin entered the room. Sixty-three years old with a lined face, large bulbous nose, pudgy hands, and full head of silver hair, he looked more like a kindly grandfather than a judge. Overweight and out of shape, he benefited enormously from the black judicial robe he wore. Without it, Dubin's appearance would have been altogether lacking in majesty.

Like most New York judges, Dubin was politically astute. A native of New Jersey, he had moved to Queens during the Depression and been admitted to the bar in 1935. Thereafter he served in private practice and as an Assistant District Attorney before campaigning successfully in 1954 for a seat in the New York State Assembly. Then, after four years as a legislator, he was elected to the New York City Criminal Court. In 1968 he was elevated to the New York State Supreme Court, thus gaining responsibility for trying major cases.

Dubin was an average jurist in virtually every respect. Few celebrated cases had been tried before him. He was not a legal scholar. If there was any respect in which Dubin excelled, it was in his ability to refrain from interjecting himself into a case so as to influence the jury. A raised eyebrow, a harsh tone of voice, a look of disbelief—any such gesture communicates to a jury the idea that the man in the black robe has an opinion on the question of guilt or innocence. Dubin genuinely tried to be fair, and he generally succeeded. His view of justice was that twelve jurors were less likely to be wrong than one judge, and he did his best to split every case down the middle. Only once had he notably failed. At the arraignment of Winston Mosely (the confessed killer of a New York woman named Kitty Genovese), Dubin took issue with the retraction of Mosely's confession and declared, "I can only say you're lucky that our system provides a trial for a monster like you. What you've done makes me want to vomit."

As Dubin entered the courtroom, Demakos rose to his feet. "Your Honor, the People move the trial of Thomas Shea under indictment 1719–73."

"The defendant is ready," Evseroff responded.

Clearing his throat, Dubin ordered that a panel of prospective jurors be brought in and instructed the reporters and spectators present to clear several rows of seats to make room for them. Minutes later, sixty-six would-be jurors were led inside. Fifty-nine were white. Only one was a woman.* Cards bearing the names of twelve prospective jurors were drawn at random from a wooden drum, and those twelve ushered to the jury box. Then the voir dire examination began.

Theoretically, the purpose of voir dire questioning is to find twelve impartial jurors who will fairly hear a given case.

---

*At the time of the Shea trial, women, if they so chose, were exempt from jury duty in criminal cases under New York law.

In reality, neither side wants any such thing. A lawyer's job is to win, and toward that end a biased jury can be extremely helpful. Evseroff was under no illusions about the type of jury he wanted. "Twelve Archie Bunkers," he told Cahill. "Twelve hard hats with American flag pins sticking out of their lapels." Demakos, by contrast, would have preferred ten Black Panthers, with two members of a radical Puerto Rican nationalist sect thrown in for good measure.

When the prospective jurors were seated, Dubin announced that the case involved a charge of murder against a policeman who had killed a young boy and would take between three and four weeks to try. Then Demakos and Evseroff interrogated the jurors, with regard to their attitudes toward race and crime. At the close of questioning, eight of the first twelve prospective jurors requested that they be excused for personal, medical, or financial reasons. Among them were two blacks, both of whom admitted that they would be unable to hear the case without prejudice. Eight more names were drawn from the drum, after which the questioning resumed. By midafternoon twelve jurors willing to serve had been selected, and the time had come for peremptory challenges.

Under New York law, both the prosecution and defense in a murder case may strike up to twenty prospective jurors for any reason. As Shea looked on, the court clerk passed a rack of cards bearing the names of each willing panel member to Demakos. Conferring briefly with Gaudelli, the Assistant DA excluded six of the chosen twelve—an Italian cemetery worker, an Irish gas station manager, an Italian Transit Authority worker, an Irish mechanic, a German bookbinder, and an Irish subway motorman. Next, Evseroff exercised two challenges, striking a Jewish textile company manager and the lone Puerto Rican on the jury panel. Then a ninth juror raised his hand and told the Judge that his religious convictions might preclude him from voting guilty no matter what the evidence. He was excused by court order.

The process had taken an entire day. Only three jurors had been chosen, but Evseroff had achieved a decided tactical gain. The prosecution had used six of its peremptory challenges; the defense, only two.

Tuesday, May 14, began with the routine which would be followed throughout trial. Thomas and Bonnie Shea awoke early and drove to Hugh Curtin's home, where Mike Hinchy joined them. Then, leaving Bonnie with Mrs. Curtin, the three men drove to Ann's Café, caucused with Cahill and Evseroff, and went to court. There any hope that a jury would be swiftly chosen was soon forgotten. Before a single name could be added to those already selected, two of the three jurors previously approved asked to speak with the Judge. One of them (a retired post office manager) told Dubin that a sudden illness in the family would make it impossible for him to serve. The other (a Transit Authority supervisor) explained that he feared retaliation from white or black co-workers after the trial ended, depending on which way the verdict went. Both men were dropped from the jury, leaving a retired textile company manager named William Seplowe as the single sworn juror.

"We're going backwards," Dubin wailed, throwing his hands in the air.

Fifteen more prospects were excused by the Judge before the box was filled again. Then Demakos exercised peremptory challenges against an Irish army clerk, an Italian truck driver, an Italian sheet metal worker, a German frozen food salesman, and an Italian sanitation worker. Evseroff followed by striking a black postal clerk, a Scandinavian computer programmer, a Jewish insurance salesman, a bearded electrician, and a bearded Jewish accountant. Then the last remaining new juror requested that he be excused for personal reasons. More names were called, and the initial panel of sixty-six prospects exhausted. As the trial broke for lunch, William Seplowe remained the only sworn juror.

Early Tuesday afternoon fifty-three more prospective jurors appeared in court. Only two members of this second panel were black. Six persons were excused by Dubin before the jury box was filled again. Demakos then exercised his twelfth and thirteenth peremptory challenges to strike an Irish telephone installer and a German data processor. Evseroff excused a Jewish typewriter repairman, a black subway motorman, a bearded transit dispatcher, and a black sanitation worker. By day's end a total of five more jurors had been chosen. The following morning, one of them (a paper company employee named Dominick Consalvo) asked to speak privately with the Judge.

"I was nervous yesterday," Consalvo said when he and Dubin were out of earshot of the other jurors. "When I went home last night, my wife asked if I told you everything, and I said, 'No, I forgot about our cousin.' "

"What about your cousin?" Dubin inquired.

"He shot a guy in a bar and, when he was running out, a cop shot him in the head."

"And because of that you couldn't be fair to the defendant?"

"I couldn't be fair," Consalvo answered. "No sense in lying."

Consalvo was excused, after which William Seplowe, the original juror, approached the judge. "Your Honor," Seplowe said, "I'm suffering from emphysema. That's why I had to retire from work. I thought I would be able to handle the job but now, with all this notoriety I've been getting in the papers, the tension has been building up in me. I can't breathe properly, and I can't concentrate. My name is in the newspaper every day."

Seplowe too was dismissed, leaving four sworn jurors. In

the hours that followed, Demakos struck an Irish welder, a German postal employee, an Irish bank guard, an Irish United Parcel Service employee, and an Irish bank clerk. Evseroff dismissed a long-haired Jewish motorcycle mechanic, an engineer, a "hippie" telephone company employee, a bearded Jewish social worker, a black electrician, and a professional magician.

By Wednesday night, nine jurors had been chosen and the second panel of prospective jurors fully depleted. Thursday morning thirty more prospects were ushered into court. Demakos dismissed an Irish Internal Revenue Service examiner and a miniskirted divorcée who was dating a cop. Evseroff ousted a female social worker, after which a tenth juror was chosen. Then all eyes focused on prospective juror number eleven—Ederica Campbell. The jury, as presently constituted, was all male and all white. Mrs. Campbell was a supervisor for the New York City Probation Department, the wife of a postal worker, *and black.*

"I'd be happier without her," Evseroff whispered to Shea. "But she's the best black juror we've seen so far. If we strike her, there will be two seats to fill, and we'll have only one challenge left."

Shea looked back at the remaining prospective jurors. Three of them were black. "Okay," he said. "You're the boss."

Mrs. Campbell was sworn in as juror number eleven. A twelfth juror was added shortly thereafter. Following lunch, four alternates were chosen. The process of selecting a jury had consumed the better part of four days. Thomas Shea's fate would be decided by the following twelve people:

1. Sidney Horn, a department store sales manager
2. William Meehan, an investigator for the State Department of Labor and the father of two cops.

3. Gordon Peck, a letter carrier.

4. George Stell, a retired restaurant owner.

5. Frank Gedgard, a retired telephone company employee.

6. William Heller, a retired liquor store owner.

7. Daniel Ehring, a billing clerk.

8. Angelo Sigurella, a textile clerk

9. Martin O'Brien, a gas company foreman, the brother-in-law of a cop.

10. Dennis Connolly, a telephone company cable splicer.

11. Ederica Campbell, a probation supervisor and the only black and only woman on the jury.

12. George Rieckehoff, a retired garage attendant.

In the ensuing weeks these eleven men and one woman would be all but forgotten by the media, which would focus attention on the more dramatic events of trial. But in the end, the power of decision would rest in their hands. Knowing full well the scope of their duty, Justice Dubin turned to address them. "An indictment is merely a means of bringing a case to trial," he cautioned after advising them of the charges against Shea. "It has no probative value whatsoever as to innocence or guilt."

Then he advised the jurors as to what lay ahead. "The District Attorney must open up and tell you what he intends to prove. The attorney for the defendant may or may not open. It's entirely up to him. After that you will hear the witnesses, and I want you to pay attention to every question and answer. They are all part of the trial. After the witnesses are heard, there will be summations. The lawyers will tell you what they think the evidence showed and make certain statements to you. Then I will charge you as to the law.

"Bear in mind," Dubin went on, "that what the attorneys say to you is not evidence. If you agree with them, fine. If you disagree, that's fine too. Even if I say anything about the evidence or testimony given, it's not what I say, it's what you heard and what you think that matters. You are not to discuss this case amongst each other, or at home, or with anyone else. You are not to follow any newspaper, television, or radio accounts of it. You are to keep an open mind until all the evidence is in and you go into the jury room to deliberate."

The hour was growing late, and Dubin sensed that it was time to bring his remarks to a close: "All we are looking for is a fair trial. We are in an American courtroom. We are all the same color, the same religion, the same nationality, and the same background for purposes of this trial. What you do when you leave this court and are not sitting on this case is your business but, while you are here, that's the way it has to be. I appreciate the fact that you have taken time from your everyday lives to sit on this jury. It's the most important service a citizen can render in time of peace."

As the jurors filed out of the courtroom, Evseroff was euphoric. "Look at them," he told Shea. "Eleven of them are people just like you."

"Yeah! But what about the twelfth?"

"Don't worry," the lawyer assured him. "In the end she'll go along with the others. Unless the prosecution has something special up its sleeve, this case boils down to the word of Add Armstead against two cops. There's no way that jury will convict."

13

THE PROSECUTION
BEGINS

Murder is the most feared of all criminal acts. Once perpetrated, there can be no compensation, no revocation, no undoing of the crime. Murder trials are viewed by the public with particular fascination, and the Shea case, as described by one courtroom buff, was "a hell of a thriller." Yet in contrast with the drama which would soon unfold, the first day of testimony, Friday, May 17, began slowly.

Bowing to the sensitivities of his assistant, Thomas Demakos permitted Albert Gaudelli to make the prosecution's opening statement. Rising to his feet, the junior attorney addressed the jury: "Ladies and Gentlemen, we have now reached the second stage of the proceedings. An opening is to tell you what the People intend to prove in this case. The defendant, Thomas Shea, stands before you charged with the crime of murder. . . ."

For the next fifteen minutes Gaudelli outlined the events of April 28, 1973. Reaching the crucial moments before the shooting, he declared, "When Add Armstead heard the car come alongside, he turned. He saw a man get out of the car, and he heard the man say, 'You black son of a bitch.' At this

163

point Add Armstead heard a shot and, when he heard the shot, he turned to his right and started to run into the lot. His boy was running behind him. He heard more shots, ran through the lot, and exited on Mathias Avenue. Then he ran through a yard and came out onto Dillon Street, where he flagged down a police car and shouted, 'They're shooting at my son.' When the police returned to the lot with Armstead, they saw the body of Clifford Glover lying on the ground mortally wounded. The boy died at seven A.M. that morning from the bullet wound inflicted on him by Thomas Shea."

Overall, Evseroff was relieved by Gaudelli's opening statement. Nothing could change the fact that a ten-year-old boy had been killed, but the prosecution was assuming a far heavier burden of proof than expected. It was one thing to show that Thomas Shea had improperly fired at a fleeing suspect whom he mistakenly believed to be a taxi robber, and quite another to prove that Shea had exited from his car shouting racial epithets with his gun blazing. If Add Armstead was claiming the latter (and it appeared he was), Evseroff planned on having a field day with cross-examination. As for his own opening statement, it would be short and to the point:

"Madam and Gentlemen of the jury! On behalf of Patrolman Thomas Shea, I choose to tell you what the good, credible, believable evidence in this case will be." Speaking softly at first, Evseroff recounted the nature of Shea's Anticrime assignment, followed by the report of the taxi robbery and Shea's sighting of Armstead and Glover: "Shea jumped out on the curb. He had his ID card and shield in his left hand, and he said, 'Stop. Police.' And one of the two looked at him and said, 'Fuck you! You're not going to take me.'

"With that," Evseroff continued, moving closer to the jury, "they began to run into this big lot and Shea went after them. They zigzagged back and forth through the lot, back and forth with this policeman chasing them. And there came a time when Clifford Glover reached in the direction of his pocket, took out a black gun, and began to turn. And this policeman fired at him. Glover stumbled and handed the gun to Armstead—not his father, his stepfather—and Armstead continued to run."

The groundwork laid, Evseroff raised his voice to a level just below shouting: "Mr. Armstead was to be arrested for attempted murder together with Glover, who was still alive. And then things began to happen at the station house. Groups came in from the community and began to protest. They spoke to many members of the Police Department, and there came a time when these leaders of the community spoke to an Inspector in charge of community affairs, and the whole picture changed. At that time it was decided that Patrolman Shea was it, and he was arrested for murder. That's what this case is all about."

At the conclusion of Evseroff's opening statement, a brief recess was called. Then the first prosecution witness, dressed in civilian clothes with a police badge pinned to his shirt pocket, took the stand.

"Raise your right hand," the court clerk intoned.

The witness complied.

"Do you swear to tell the truth, the whole truth, and nothing but the truth, so help you God?"

"I do."

"State your name and shield number."

"Charles Fox; Shield Number 14107."

The formalities completed, Demakos took over the questioning. "Officer Fox, how long have you been a member of the New York City Police Department?"

"A little over ten years."

"On April 28, 1973, were you assigned to the photo section?"

"I was."

"And what were you duties?"

"I did crime-scene sketches."

"And how long had you been doing that?"

"About seven years."

Standing before the witness, Demakos elicited his credentials—formal training at the Delehanty Institute in drafting, hundreds of maps and sketches drawn for police investigations. "Did there come a time," the prosecutor asked, "When you were given an assignment to make a sketch in the vicinity of New York Boulevard and 112th Road?"

"Yes."

"Do you recall when?"

"The week of May 12, 1973."

"How many times did you go there?"

"Seven."

"Will you tell the jury what you did when you went?"

"I was with a partner. We had a wheel that calibrates feet and inches, and we made sketches of features—houses, sewers, lampposts—in that location."

"Did there come a time when you put those measurements on a particular drawing?"

"Yes."

With the jury looking on, Demakos unfolded a large map drawn on a sheet of heavy off-white paper three by four feet in size. Drafted on a scale of one inch for every twenty feet, it depicted the lot, surrounding streets, sewers, buildings, trees, fences, and other features.

"Officer Fox," Demakos asked, "will you tell us what this is?"

"A crime-scene layout."

"This is the sketch you made as a result of the work you did in May 1973."

"Correct."

At the prosecutor's request, the map was marked as Exhibit 1 and received into evidence. Evseroff cross-examined the witness briefly with regard to the fact that the exhibit portrayed some but not all of the underbrush in the lot, after which Fox was excused.

Two more prosecution witnesses quickly followed. Detective Robert Willis of the Queens Forensic Unit testified that, on April 28, 1973, from 8:40 A.M. till noon, he had photographed the shooting site. Five of his photos were admitted into evidence despite Evseroff's objection that Willis's use of a wide-angle camera lens had produced distortion. Then Patrolman Heinz Graumann of the Police Department Aviation Unit recounted taking a series of aerial photos the same day. Six of Graumann's pictures were shown to the jury. Throughout the proceedings, Evseroff doodled on a lined yellow legal pad with a black felt-tipped pen. Shea looked straight ahead.

After lunch Demakos put six more photographs into evidence through the testimony of Detective Arthur Savarese, a police field technician who had visited the lot nine days after the shooting. Then court was adjourned, and the jury excused for the weekend. During the day the temperature outside had risen to an unseasonably warm ninety-two degrees—five degrees higher than the previous New York City record for May 17.

"Don't discuss this case with each other or at home with anyone," Dubin cautioned as the jurors were excused. "Don't listen to any radio or television reports. Don't read any newspaper accounts. Don't go to the scene. Just forget about the case and go swimming over the weekend. It's very hot out."

"Have a good weekend," Evseroff told Shea as they left the courthouse. "Try to relax and don't worry. All the prosecution did today was show the jury a map and seventeen photographs. Maybe it will give them a visual image of the lot; maybe not. Either way it proves nothing."

On the courthouse steps a reporter joined them. "Have you visited the shooting site?" he asked Evseroff.

"What are you, crazy?" the attorney answered. "A man could get killed in that neighborhood."

On Saturday, May 18, while the defense team rested, Demakos planned for the week ahead. Assistant District Attorneys try scores of cases each year, often with little or no preparation. Legal memoranda are seldom written. One case blurs with another. It is not uncommon for a prosecutor to glance self-consciously at his notes during cross-examination to check the name of the witness in front of him. But the Shea case was different from most trials. It was a *cause célèbre*, and Demakos was not about to "wing it." Even though the case had been handed to him on last-minute notice, he was determined that it would be meticulously prepared.

The previous weekend Demakos had spoken personally with virtually every police witness he planned to call at trial. Sitting in his office on the fourth floor of the Queens County Criminal Court Building, he met first with Harold Cannon, then with the other cops in groups of three or four each. "Look," he told them, "I don't like this case any more than you do. But police camaraderie and brotherhood go too far when they become disrespect for the law. You don't have to put yourself out for this trial. All I'm asking is that you tell the truth. Just tell the judge and jury what you heard and saw."

By and large, the cops were favorably impressed. Most of them had testified at the earlier grand jury proceeding and had been annoyed by what they perceived as Gaudelli's over-aggressiveness. The junior prosecutor had seemed to want more from them than they were willing or abie to provide. By contrast, the low-key manner in which Demakos addressed them was more to their liking, and they pledged honest if not enthusiastic cooperation. Now, one week later, the prosecutor was readying to meet with his key witness—Add Armstead.

On the morning of Saturday, May 18, settled in his office, Demakos leafed through a transcript of the trial's first week. Three stenographers working in shifts were responsible for recording every word formally uttered in court. The attorneys had ordered "daily copy," which meant that the morning after each day's proceedings a typed transcript was available to them.

Finding nothing in the material which had previously escaped his notice, Demakos turned to a stack of papers on his desk. At Mark Frances's request, Eloise Glover had forwarded a wealth of personal information to police investigators. Then Gaudelli had subpoenaed all Family Court records pertaining to the Armstead-Glover union. The story that emerged was not pretty, but Demakos knew it might come out at trial and he had to be prepared for any eventuality.

On April 4, 1967, a welfare worker named Sigrid Nambar had filed a neglect petition against Eloise Glover with the Queens County Family Court. In relevant part, the petition read: "The respondent mismanages the funds she receives from the Department of Welfare, and the children are not properly clothed or fed. . . . The respondent uses excessive force in the discipline of the children in that she strikes them with a belt strap." Eight weeks after the petition was filed, Judge Peter Donoghue ruled that Clifford, Henry, and Darlene Glover were "neglected children" within the meaning of the law and ordered Mrs. Glover placed under one year's supervision by the Queens County Department of Probation.

Flipping through the pages, Demakos read on. On May 4, 1967, and then again on December 23, 1970, Eloise Glover had filed paternity suits against Armstead. The first suit was brought in connection with the 1967 birth of her daughter, Darlene. Armstead admitted fatherhood and had been ordered to pay eight dollars a week support money out of his fifty-six-dollar weekly salary. The second suit, filed while Mrs. Glover was pregnant with Patricia Ann, resulted in an additional ten-dollar weekly judgment.

Clifford's elementary-school report cards were next. They painted the picture of a child average in ability but having difficulty in learning to cope with emotional problems. "Clifford is trying hard and is beginning to improve in reading and math," his second-grade teacher wrote. "But he needs to improve his self-control when excited or upset." One grading period later, the same teacher warned, "Clifford has been tearing up his work when angered. He must learn to control his anger rather than destroy when he's unhappy." The final trimester showed considerable gain. "Clifford," the teacher observed, "is learning how to control his anger. He is proud of his school work. This is helping him to progress slowly."

Turning the pages, Demakos saw an $871 bill from the McClester Funeral Home, which had been paid by a group of New York City civic leaders known as the One Hundred Black Men. A $184 bill from Mary Immaculate Hospital for blood, emergency-room treatment, and laboratory services had been ignored despite several demands for payment.

Shortly before 11:00 A.M. Harold Cannon arrived at Demakos's office with Add Armstead. The prosecutor would have preferred to call his chief witness the previous afternoon, which would have enabled the jurors to ponder his testimony over the weekend. Unfortunately there simply hadn't been time to prepare him. The next best thing though, would be to lead off with Armstead on Monday, when the jury would be attentive and fresh.

Sitting at a small conference table in the Assistant District Attorney's office, Demakos and Armstead reviewed the Fox map and photographs of the lot which had been admitted into evidence. Then Armstead recounted his version of the shooting. In every respect, it was consistent with his earlier statements to Martin Bracken and Robert Johnson at the

103rd Precinct station house as well as his grand jury testimony.

"Are you certain that Shea fired a shot before you turned and ran?" Demakos asked.

"Yes sir."

"That will be awfully hard for the jury to swallow," the prosecutor pressed. "Isn't it possible that you telescoped the shooting in your mind and that you ran before Shea shot because you were frightened?"

"No sir. He shot first. That's the way it happened."

By day's end Demakos was satisfied with Armstead's candor but worried about his effectiveness as a witness. Despite being a decent hardworking man, Armstead was uneducated bordering on ignorant. If he preached or rambled in front of the jury, it would be a disaster.

"I want you to listen to me very carefully," the prosecutor instructed, "because what I'm about to tell you is important. When we go into court on Monday, you'll be asked a lot of questions—some by me, a few by the Judge, and a lot by a man named Jack Evseroff, who will be after your hide. You're going to be nervous; most witnesses are. But there are a few simple rules I want you to follow.

"Listen very carefully to every question. If you don't understand a question, ask that it be repeated or explained. Don't volunteer information. Answer only the question asked and, if you don't know the answer, say so. Sometimes 'I don't remember' is the only honest answer. Don't argue with anyone. Just be honest and polite. Do you understand?"

"Yes sir."

The two men shook hands. "I'll see you in court on Monday," Demakos told him.

Monday morning, May 20, was reserved by Justice Dubin for personal matters. The trial resumed at 2:00 P.M. Entering the courtroom, Evseroff and Shea saw a dozen reporters. Every seat was taken. Cops in plain clothes, elderly courtroom buffs, South Jamaica community leaders—all were present. An unusual number of black courthouse employees—clerks, floor scrubbers, and washroom attendants—sat unobtrusively in the back row. Despite being locked in a heated campaign for reelection as PBA President, Robert McKiernan was also in attendance, as he would be throughout the trial. "This is where I belong," McKiernan told a reporter. "Every cop in this city is behind Thomas Shea."

Shortly before 2:00 P.M. Court Clerk James Higgins ushered the jurors to their chairs and readied himself to call the roll. One by one, as their names were called, the jurors answered, "Here." Then Higgins exited out the door behind the Judge's bench, reappeared moments later, and proclaimed, "Hear ye! Hear ye! Anybody having business before this part of the Supreme Court of the State of New York, County of Queens, step forward and you shall be heard, the Honorable Bernard Dubin presiding."

On that note, Dubin entered the room. Once he was seated, everyone who had risen for his entrance did likewise.

"The People call Add Armstead as their next witness," Demakos said.

"This is it," Evseroff whispered to his client. "If he stumbles, they have nothing at all."

As the hushed spectators looked on, Armstead walked slowly to the witness stand. He was wearing dark slacks and a light shirt open at the collar. In his left hand, he carried a peaked cap.

"Remember," Evseroff told Shea, "no matter what he says, just look straight ahead."

Armstead raised his right hand, and Higgins administered the oath.

Jesus, Shea thought. I'm on trial for murder.

Demakos ran into trouble at the very start of his questioning. "Mr. Armstead," he began, "you said you live at 109-50 New York Boulevard; is that correct?"

"Yes."

"And did you live there on April 28, 1973?"

"Yes."

"And how long before April 28, 1973, did you live at that address?"

"April 11th."

"Of what year?"

"1973."

Demakos shook his head. "No! Before April 28, 1973, how long did you live there?"

"I wasn't living there . . ." Armstead began slowly. "Oh! I'm sorry. I see. I moved there right after April 1971. I don't know what month exactly."

Evseroff relaxed. The witness didn't even know one year from the next. No jury would ever convict a cop on his testimony.

Undaunted, Demakos pressed on. "So you were living there from 1971 until April 28, 1973?"

"Yes."

"And you are still living there; is that correct?"

"Yes."

"Now on April 28, 1973, with whom did you live?"

"Eloise Glover."

"Were you married to Eloise Glover at that time?"

"No."

"Were you living common law?"

"Common law."

"Who else did you live with?"

"Clifford Glover, Henry Glover, Darlene Glover, and Patricia Glover."

"And how old was Clifford Glover on April 28, 1973?"

"Ten years old."

Shea shifted uneasily. Evseroff glanced toward the jurors

to gauge their reaction to the mention of Glover's age, but their faces were inscrutable.

Demakos went on. "How old was Henry?"

"He was eight years old."

"And the other two children, how old were they?"

"Darlene was seven; Patricia, three."

"Who was the father of the last two children?"

"Add Armstead," the witness answered proudly.

Slowly, with short simple questions, Demakos elicited bits and pieces of Armstead's past. "Had you been married before you went to live with Eloise Glover?"

"Yes."

"And was your wife living at the time you went to live with Eloise Glover?"

"No."

Rising to his feet, Evseroff objected to the question as "irrelevant." In truth, his main concern was that Demakos would elicit sympathy from the jury and thus erase the stigma which might otherwise attach to Add Armstead and Eloise Glover living together without being married. The objection was overruled by Justice Dubin, and Demakos continued.

"Do you have any children by your former wife?"

"Yes."

"How many?"

"Nine."

"What are the ages of these nine children?"

"I don't know, but from sixteen to thirty."

Proceeding in low-key fashion, Demakos next sought to defuse the issue of Armstead's arrest record by raising it before Evseroff could. "Have you ever been convicted of a crime?"

"Yes."

"When?"

174

"1965."

"What crime were you convicted of?"

"Statutory rape."

"Did you get any time for that?"

"Yes."

"How much?"

"Six months."

"Have you been convicted of any other crime?"

"Yes."

"What?"

"Having an unregistered vehicle with no insurance."

"When was that?"

"1965."

"Do you recall what punishment you received for the unregistered, uninsured vehicle?"

"One hundred twenty-five dollars or twenty-three days."

"Did you do the time or pay the money?"

"The twenty-three days."

The "problem areas" done with, Demakos moved to establish Armstead as a hardworking, gainfully employed man.

"Are you employed now?"

"Yes."

"And where do you work?"

"115-05 New York Boulevard."

"What kind of place is it?"

"It's a wrecking yard."

"And what do you do there?"

"I'm a burner."

"And as a burner, what do you mean; what do you do?"

"I cut motors out of cars."

"How long have you been working at this particular place?"

"Since 1963."

"What days of the week do you work?"

"Five and a half days; half a day on Saturdays."

"How far is this place of business where you worked from the place where you live?"

"Six blocks."

The stage was set for April 28, 1973. Raising his voice almost imperceptibly, Demakos forged ahead. "Was April 28, 1973, a Saturday?"

"Yes."

"Did you start to go to work that day?"

"Yes."

"What time was it that you left your house to go to work?"

"Ten minutes to five."

"And did anybody leave your house with you?"

"Yes."

"Who?"

"Clifford Glover."

After pausing to let the name sink in, Demakos continued. "Had Clifford Glover been going to work with you before on Saturdays?"

"Yes."

"On how many Saturdays prior to April 28, 1973, had he gone to work with you?"

"In the summertime, in the spring, he go every Saturday."

Hoping to break Armstead's concentration, Evseroff objected to the entire line of questioning as "leading and suggestive." Again he was overruled by the Judge.

"On April 28, 1973," Demakos continued, "you said that you and Clifford Glover left your house about ten minutes to five; is that correct?"

"Yes."

"And you proceeded to go to work; is that correct?"

"Yes."

"By what means of transportation?"

"We walked."

"Along New York Boulevard?"

"Yes."

So far, so good, Demakos thought. The crucial moment was now at hand.

"Did there come a time when you reached a lot between 112th Road and Mathias Avenue?"

"Yes."

"All right. Now, Mr. Armstead, in your own words, tell this jury what happened on April 28, 1973, at the point when you reached the lot that was on New York Boulevard between Mathias Avenue and 112th Road?"

All eyes were on the witness. "I was walking," Armstead began. "I was walking, and I heard a car pull up to the curb. So I turned to my left, and I seen a man getting out of the car. He had his hand like this."

"Like what?" Dubin interrupted.

Armstead lifted his right hand in a clenched fist.

"Go on," Demakos instructed.

"He said, 'You black son of a bitch.' I whirled to my right. I heard a gunshot, and I ran into the lot. About ten foot into the lot, I heard another shot."

Evseroff began jotting notes on his yellow legal pad. Demakos paused to let the jury reflect on the testimony, then resumed.

"At the point you ran into the lot, where was Clifford?"

"In back of me."

"What was he doing?"

"Running."

"What happened after that?"

"I ran for the fence crossing the lot and fell. Clifford fell on my leg. Then I dragged up and ran outside across a street and into some bushes. A patrol car was coming and I stopped it. They drove up and the officer on the passenger side got out and searched me."

"And then they picked you up; is that correct?"

"Yes."

"Where did they take you?"

"Back to the lot."

"What did you see at that time?"

"I seen my son lying on the ground."

Evseroff objected to the characterization of Clifford Glover as Armstead's "son," prompting Justice Dubin to address the witness: "By your son, who do you mean?"

"My stepson," Armstead answered.

"Who do you mean?" Dubin pressed. "What's his name?"

"Clifford," Armstead spat out. "Clifford Glover—laying on the ground."

For the next twenty minutes Demakos led the witness through the remainder of the fatal day. "Mr. Armstead," he asked in closing, "when you left your home on April 28, 1973, at about ten minutes to five, did you have a gun?"

"No."

"Did you have a gun when you reached the lot on New York Boulevard?"

"No."

"Did your son hand you a gun after he fell?"

"No."

"Did you say anything to the man who got out of the car on New York Boulevard?"

"No."

"Did your son say anything to him?"

"No."

"Did your son say to him, 'Fuck you, you're not going to take me'?"

"No."

"Your Honor," Demakos announced, "I have no further questions."

Then, as required by law, the prosecutor handed Evseroff a copy of Armstead's grand jury testimony and a transcript of the witness's question-and-answer sessions with Martin Bracken and Inspector Robert Johnson. Because grand jury sessions are conducted in absolute secrecy, the defense team had not previously seen the grand jury notes. However, copies of the Bracken and Johnson interrogations had been "leaked" to Evseroff.

"We'll take a brief recess while defense counsel reads the material," Dubin said. "Be ready to resume in fifteen minutes."

A trial lawyer's job is to win. There are certain rules he is expected to follow, but it is not required that he be "fair." Rather, his obligation to his client requires that, wherever legally permissible, he slant issues, appeal to prejudices, and suppress damaging facts to further his client's cause. Whether working for the Legal Aid Society or in private practice, he is a "hired gun" paid to distort a case while protesting that his every act is motivated by "the interests of justice."

Jack Evseroff was familiar with the rules of the game. He knew that, after a shaky start, Add Armstead's testimony had been extremely damaging. Now it was up to Evseroff to discredit the witness in any way possible.

Normally one of the best strategies available to a defense attorney in a murder case is to prosecute the deceased. "Dead men tell no tales," goes the adage. In addition, dead men are unable to speak on their own behalf at trial. If a lawyer is successful in labeling the deceased a junkie, a rapist, or a Mafia hit man, the jury will come to believe that perhaps the killing wasn't such a tragedy after all. Sympathy for the defendant inevitably follows. But the death of Clifford Glover offered no such opportunity. Outside of the Shea-Scott testimony concerning the alleged "black gun," there was little to be said against the ten-year-old victim. Accordingly, Evseroff chose the next best strategy—villifying the victim's father, who also happened to be the chief prosecution witness against his client.

Cross-examination is considered by many trial attorneys to be their most challenging task. It requires mastery of the facts, yet must be spontaneously based on the just-completed testimony of an adverse witness. While Add Armstead was on the stand, Evseroff had noted the significant points of his testimony on a lined legal pad. Then, working feverishly, the attorney had underlined the points he wanted to attack, either because they were particularly damaging or because they could be easily destroyed. Now he was ready to launch an assault, starting with the notion that Armstead and Clifford Glover had no business being out on the streets at five o'clock in the morning—that, contrary to the assertion of the witness, they were *not* going to work.

"Tell me this, Mr. Armstead," Evseroff began. "You go to work five and a half days a week; is that correct?"

"Yes."

"And you work a half day on Saturday; is that correct?"

"Yes."

"Now isn't it a fact that it was customary for you to open up this place at about seven-thirty on Saturday mornings?"

"Sometimes."

"Is it a fact that it was your usual practice to open up this place on Saturdays between seven and seven-thirty in the morning."

"Sometimes."

"Did anybody tell you to be at the place at five o'clock in the morning on April 28, 1973?"

"I told the boss I do that."

"You told him you would be there at five?"

"I told him I come in early on Saturday morning."

"But," Evseroff pressed, "it was your practice on other Saturdays to open the place between seven and seven-thirty; is that correct?"

"Yes."

The colloquy was hardly earthshaking, but Evseroff hoped it had planted a seed of doubt in the jury's collective mind. Next, he dredged up Armstead's criminal past, focusing on the charge of statutory rape, which the witness testified had earned him six months in prison.

"Now, you testified on direct examination, I believe, that you had been convicted of statutory rape?"

"Yes."

"And I think you testified in answer to a question Mr. Demakos asked you, that you received six months in jail; is that correct?"

"Yes."

"Did you serve six months in jail, or was it four?"

"Four months."

"So that when you answered on direct examination that you received six months, that was incorrect?"

"They gave me six months," Armstead answered. "I got two months off for good time."

"He didn't give you four months, did he?"

"No, he said six months."

Evseroff's questions were not designed to ascertain the length of Armstead's sentence (which he already knew), but rather to remind the jury that the chief prosecution witness had been convicted of statutory rape. Firing inquiries in rapid sequence, he pursued the matter for several minutes, frequently omitting the word "statutory" from his questions.

"Did I understand you to testify that, with respect to the rape case, you were given six months but in fact you only did four months; is that correct?"

"Right."

"And you were in fact only given four months?"

"No, he told me six months."

"Tell me this. Did you get six months or did you get four months for the rape? Which is it?"

"I put in four months."

"Did the judge give you six months or did he give you four months?"

"When I was in the room with the judge, he said six months."

Having milked the issue for all it was worth, Evseroff next moved toward the shooting, but only after another gratuitous swipe at the witness. "Now there came a time as you were walking along New York Boulevard with Clifford Glover—incidentally, you are not his father, are you?"

"No."

"You live with his mother, don't you?"

"Yes."

"And had you ever adopted him?"

"No."

"Did you ever marry his mother?"

"No."

Letting the exchange sink in, Evseroff moved back to the shooting. "As you were walking down the street, what happened?"

"I heard a car pull up behind me," Armstead answered, "so I turned around and looked back."

"And what did you see?"

Armstead clenched his fist as he had done when questioned by Demakos. "I seen a man getting out of the car with his hand like this."

"And, when he got out of the car, what did he do?"

"He say, 'You black son of a bitch.' "

"And what did you do?"

"I whirled to my right."

"And, when you whirled to your right, what did you do then?"

"I started to run."

"Did you see a gun in his hand at any time?"

"No."

182

"Did you ever see him fire a gun?"
"I didn't see it, but I heard it."

Demakos winced. Armstead now appeared to be saying that he had started to run *before* the shot. But, even more important, he was testifying under oath that he *never saw the gun.* No sooner were the words out of the witness's mouth than Evseroff reached for his transcript of the April 28, 1973, Bracken-Armstead question-and-answer session. Holding the pages aloft, he boomed, "Mr. Armstead, do you remember being questioned by Assistant District Attorney Bracken at the station house on April 28, 1973?"

"I don't remember."

Turning to page two of the transcript, Evseroff paused dramatically for effect, then began to read:

QUESTION: Were you facing him when he fired the gun?

ANSWER: I turned around. He said, 'You black son of a bitch,' and then *I seen he had a small gun in his hand. That's when I seen that he fired.*

"Did you see this man with a gun in his hand?" Evseroff demanded.

"No."
"When he got out of the car and he had his hand clenched, did he have anything in his hand?"
"I don't know."

Several spectators exchanged glances. The point of the questioning was clear. Evseroff was pushing the idea that Shea had gotten out of the car with his shield and ID card, not a revolver, clenched in his hand. And Armstead was waffling, contradicting his earlier statement that he had seen a gun.

"Did he show you a shield?"
"No."

"An ID card?"

"No."

"Did you see a gun in his hand?" Evseroff boomed a third time, his voice reverberating off the courtroom walls.

"No."

Pressing the attack, Evseroff turned to the witness's "abandonment" of his "son."

"When you turned around and you started to run, what did Clifford do?"

"He be in back of me."

"Did you say anything to Clifford?"

"No."

"Did you jump in between Clifford and this man?"

"No."

"Did you make any effort to protect him?"

"No."

"After you ran into the lot, did you turn around and see what happened to him?"

"No."

"Did you make any effort after you heard the second shot to turn around and see what happened to Clifford?"

"No."

"As you were running through the lot, there came a time when you fell; is that correct?"

"Yes."

"What happened to Clifford when you fell?"

"He be in back of me. He fell on my leg."

"And, when he stumbled, you got up and ran away?"

"Yes."

"You didn't go over and help him, did you?" Evseroff thundered.

"No."

"You didn't stay there and protect him?"

"No."

"You got up and ran; is that correct?"

"Yes."

"You never looked back?"

"No."

"Did you make any effort in any way, manner, shape, or kind to help him?"

"No."

"Did you ever stop on the street or in the lot to see what happened to him?"

"No."

"Did you know he was shot?" Evseroff roared.

"No."

Again, the lawyer reached for his copy of Armstead's question-and-answer session with Martin Bracken. After reading a portion of the interrogation which recounted Armstead's flagging down Patrolmen Al Farrell and Tom Scott, Evseroff boomed:

QUESTION: Did you mention anything about the shooting at that time?

ANSWER: Yes, *I told them somebody is shot over there.*

"And," Evseroff continued, "do you remember this question being asked of you in a statement made to Inspector Robert Johnson on April 28, 1973:

QUESTION: Where were you?

ANSWER: I was on Dillon. They came up, and *I told them my son is shot.* They said get in the car."

"I don't remember," Armstead answered quietly.

Again, the inconsistency was clear. On April 28, 1973, Armstead had advised both Bracken and Johnson that he told the two cops Clifford had been shot. Now, possibly because he was ashamed to admit abandoning his son, Arm-

185

stead was denying that he had known of the injury at the time he flagged the policemen down.

One of Evseroff's best weapons as a lawyer was his voice. Speaking skills can be developed, but unless a person is born with the "basic equipment," his oratorical prowess will never be truly great. Evseroff had the equipment. When he wanted it so, his voice rang loud and clear. Now he lowered it dramatically.

"You loved that boy didn't you, Mr. Armstead?"

"Yes."

"I have no further questions, Your Honor."

The questioning of Add Armstead had lasted for three hours. At 5:00 P.M. court was adjourned. Evseroff was jubilant. "I don't see how anyone can prosecute, let alone convict, a policeman based on testimony like that," he told Cahill as they left the court. "It's unbelievable. Add Armstead is nothing but an ignorant, uneducated, petty criminal. If it weren't for the media, there would never have been an indictment."

Cahill nodded. "It looks like we've got a winner."

Inside the courtroom though, a different scene was unfolding. "At first, I didn't want to try this case," Demakos told Gaudelli as the two men gathered their papers. "Now I believe in it as much as any case I've ever tried. That son of a bitch killed an innocent ten-year-old boy."

14

COPS ON
THE STAND

On Tuesday, May 21, the day after Add Armstead's testimony, Demakos presented six police witnesses in an effort to bolster his case.

Patrolman John Higgins was the first to testify. Speaking in soft measured tones, he told of responding to the lot, carrying Clifford Glover to his car, and rushing the boy to Mary Immaculate Hospital. Next, the prosecution called Eddie Anderson, who corroborated Higgins's testimony.

"How long did it take you to get from 112th Road and New York Boulevard to the hospital?" Demakos asked.

"I'd say between ten and twelve minutes," Anderson replied.

"Did you or your partner speak to the boy?"

"I spoke to him."

"Did the boy speak back?"

"He did not."

"Did any sounds come out of him?"

"He was groaning."

Cops generally make good witnesses. Having appeared

regularly at grand jury proceedings, evidentiary hearings, and trials, they understand legal jargon and are at home in court. For this reason, and perhaps also because they had promised Demakos their cooperation, the day went smoothly.

Following Anderson's testimony, Patrolmen Ralph Panico and Francis Alvy took the stand and told of responding to the shooting site. "Did there come a time," Demakos asked Panico, "when you arrived in the vicinity of 112th Road and New York Boulevard?"

"Yes."

"Did you see anything?"

"No."

"What did you do?"

"We went to Dillon Street and started to pass Mathias."

"Did you see anybody or anything at Dillon and Mathias?"

"Yes."

"Who or what did you see?"

"There was a man standing in the middle of the street, waving."

"Who was he waving at?"

"He was just waving," Panico answered, "and he was shouting something like 'shooting.' "

"Did you later learn who he was?" Demakos pressed.

"Yes."

"Who?"

"Add Armstead."

Francis Alvy, the prosecution's next witness, explained that he and Panico passed Armstead by because they thought a brother officer was in danger. Demakos did not quarrel with their motives. He had the testimony he wanted. Add Armstead had sought to flag down the first police car he saw after the shooting. It was hardly the act of a guilty man.

Following a break for lunch, Patrolman Thomas Scott was

sworn as the day's fifth witness. He told of responding to the lot with his partner, Al Farrell. "We proceeded to the corner of Dillon and 112th Road, and then we observed a man coming down Dillon Street towards us."

"Was he black or white?"

"Black."

"Was he running, walking, what was he doing?"

"He was like walking fast towards us, waving his hands."

"Show us how," the prosecutor urged.

Scott raised both arms above his head and swept them back and forth in a huge arc. "Like this. He was coming towards us to get our attention."

"And what did you do?"

"We pulled the radio car up to him, and my partner and I both got out. I didn't know who he was or anything like that, so I had my gun out. He was speaking very rapidly and excited."

"And what did he say to you at that time?" Demakos pressed.

"He was speaking very fast, saying, 'They're shooting in the backyard. . . . My son shot in the backyard."

"Did he say anything to you with respect to where to go?"

"He just kept saying, 'In the lot.' "

On cross-examination, Evseroff sought to negate the fact that Armstead had flagged down two police cars by reviving a collateral issue that had emerged during Armstead's cross-examination. "Patrolman Scott, you spoke with Mr. Armstead, did you not?"

"Yes."

"You had a conversation with him in your police car going to the station house?"

"Right."

"Did he tell you that, as he and his son were on the street, somebody stopped behind them?"

"Yes."

"Did he say to you that he then turned around and there was a man with a gun?"

"Yes."

"He told you that the man had a gun, that's for sure?"

"Right."

"I have no further questions."

The last witness of the day was Al Farrell, whose testimony was largely duplicative of what had been earlier said. As the session wore on, Justice Dubin leaned back in his chair, sometimes following the testimony closely, sometimes giving the appearance of less-than-total attention. The jurors' eyes seldom left the witnesses. They were a captivated as well as a captive audience.

"That's good," Demakos told Gaudelli at day's end. "I want that jury to listen carefully, so they understand what this case is all about."

Wednesday, May 22, the questioning of police witnesses resumed. Sergeant Joseph Kennedy testified to arriving at the lot, sighting Shea, and walking with him to Clifford Glover's body.

"What, if anything, did he say to you at that particular time?" Demakos asked.

"He told me he had to shoot someone back in the lot, that he [and his partner] were coming down New York Boulevard and observed two males fitting the description of a previous taxi robbery. When they got out of the car and identified themselves as police officers, the two males started running through the lot."

"Continue," Demakos instructed. "What else did he say?"

"Patrolman Shea said he was chasing them through the lot when one of them reached into his pocket and turned around with a gun. That's when he fired."

"Did you ask Shea if he recovered the gun?"

"Yes."

"What did Shea say?"

"He said he didn't recover the gun. He said that, when the one he shot fell, he *tossed* the gun to the other perpetrator."

"He told you he *tossed* the gun to the other person?" Demakos pressed.

"Yes," Kennedy answered.

"In that conversation, did Shea say anything to you about the boy saying, 'Fuck you, you're not taking me'?"

"I don't recall such a statement."

Demakos had elicited the testimony he wanted. Next, he called Sergeant Donald Bromberg to the stand and zeroed in on Bromberg's interview with Shea at the station house shortly after the shooting. "Tell us, what did Shea say to you in that conversation?"

"He stated that one of the men turned around, pulled a gun from his pocket, pointed it in his direction, and the officer fired. The second man *bent down,* took the gun from the first man who had fallen, and ran off."

The contradiction in Shea's statements was apparent. In talking with Kennedy, he had claimed that Glover "tossed" the gun to Armstead. Yet he told Bromberg that Armstead "bent down" to take it. Also, he had not told either man about Glover allegedly saying, "Fuck you, you're not taking me."

"Did Patrolman Shea tell you that one of these two people, Glover or Armstead, said to him, 'You won't take me'?"

"Not to my knowledge," Bromberg answered.

"Do you have any recollection of it?"

"No."

Rising to cross-examine the witness, Evseroff sensed the problem and decided to fire one of his big guns—the idea that Armstead would never have run in the first place if he hadn't done something wrong. "Sergeant Bromberg, did there come a time when you saw Add Armstead?"

"Yes sir, in the precinct station house at approximately eight-fifteen A.M."

"Did you speak with him?"

"Yes."

"Did he say that two white men jumped out of a car, and his son and he started to run?"

"Yes."

"Isn't it a fact," Evseroff boomed, "that you didn't ask him, nor did he tell you, why it was that he ran?"

The strategy backfired.

"He was frightened," Bromberg answered. "That's the impression he gave me."

It had not been a good morning for the defense and, as lunch neared, the possibility existed that things would get much worse. The next scheduled witness was Patrolman James McArdle.

"I know him," Shea told Evseroff. "He and I used to moonlight together as chauffeurs for the Carey Limousine Service."

"What else do you know about him?"

"He's in the Communications Division," Shea said. "He works with tapes."

At the close of Bromberg's testimony, James McArdle took the stand. To Evseroff's surprise, it was Gaudelli rather than Demakos who rose to question him. "Officer McArdle, how long have you been a member of the New York City Police Department?"

"Sixteen and a half years."

"And in April 1973 where were you assigned?"

"To the Communications Division as an audiotape technician."

"What were your duties at that time?"

"To make reproductions and transcripts of calls that came in on our radio frequencies."

"In the course of your duties, can you approximate how many reproductions you have made of official Police Department recordings?"

"About twenty-five hundred."

With McArdle's credentials as an "expert" established, Gaudelli shifted to the shooting date. "Did there come a time, Officer, when you removed from Police Department records the 103rd Precinct radio transmissions which occurred between eleven P.M. on April 27, 1973, and eleven A.M. on April 28, 1973?"

"Yes."

"And do you have that master tape with you?"

"Yes, I do."

Shea shifted uneasily.

"I show you this tape recording," Gaudelli continued, offering the witness one of two tightly wound reels resting on the stand in front of him. "And I ask if you recognize it."

"This is a reproduction I made of the master tape beginning at four hours, four minutes, and ten seconds of April 28, 1973, and concluding at five hours and thirty minutes of that day. There is an electronic impulse imprinted on the tape every five seconds."

"And the purpose of that is so, when the tape is replayed, you can tell the exact time of each radio transmission; is that correct?"

"That is correct."

"After you made the reproduction," Gaudelli continued, "what did you do with it?"

"It was delivered to the Queens County District Attorney's Office."

Gaudelli turned to the Judge. "At this time, Your Honor, I make an offer of the tape recording into evidence."

Immediately Evseroff was on his feet. "If Your Honor please, I respectfully object to the offer on grounds that it's not relevant, it's not material, and it's prejudicial to the defendant."

Gaudelli was quick to respond: "I submit to the Court that this matter is probative, relevant, and admissible."

A heated colloquy followed. After both sides had voiced their views, Dubin turned to the jury. "Go to lunch," he said. "Don't discuss this case, and don't listen to any radio or read any newspaper reports about it. Come back at two o'clock. I'll reserve decision until after lunch."

The proceedings resumed at 2:00 P.M. "The Court has gone over the tape transcript," Dubin announced. "That part of the transcript which pertains to this case is admissible, but the court orders the redaction [editing out] of everything in the tape that has nothing to do with the case."

"Your Honor," Gaudelli said with obvious joy, "I would like to actually play the tape for the jury's benefit. I have an audio technician here and, once we set up, he can operate the machine so as to only broadcast the admissible portion. If Your Honor will give me a moment or two, we'll set up."

"Let me ask a question," Dubin responded. "In the interest of time, are there any other witnesses we can put on while he's working on it?"

"I'll put another witness on." Demakos volunteered. "The defense calls Sergeant Thomas Donohue."

Donohue's recitation of events, including his postshooting conversation with Shea and Walter Scott, added little to the previous two days' testimony.

"Do you have another witness?" Dubin inquired when the questioning closed.

"No, Your Honor," Demakos answered. "I prefer that, before we put anybody else on, the tape be played."

"You said that before; where is it?"

"It should be here shortly."

The Judge shook his head, then turned to the jury. "Ladies and Gentlemen, there will be a short recess until the tape is ready."

Forty-five minutes later, court was reconvened. "I have some news," Dubin announced. "Evidently it will be another hour before they get the tape in order. It's after four now and, rather than keep you here doing nothing, we are going to adjourn. I don't want to make a career of this trial, but I guess it's one of those things. Have a nice evening. I'll see you tomorrow morning at ten o'clock."

As the day ended, Thomas Shea's fate appeared to be dangling on a string. Or, to be more precise, on a reel of tape.

The following morning, Thursday, May 23, Patrolman James McArdle was recalled as a witness, and Gaudelli handed him a sheaf of papers. "Officer McArdle, I show you this transcript and ask if you recognize it?"

"I do."

"Is it a transcript containing all transmissions for April 28, 1973, concerning a shooting in the area of 112th Road and New York Boulevard?"

"Yes."

"Do you have a tape of all the material contained in that transcript?"

"Yes."

"And do you have that tape with you?"

"Yes."

"At this time," Gaudelli announced, turning toward Dubin, "I offer the tape and transcript into evidence."

"Your Honor," Evseroff interrupted, "may we approach the side bar?"

"All right," the Judge answered, exasperation clearly present in his voice.

The two lawyers moved forward, and Dubin motioned for

McArdle to join them. Speaking in hushed tones so the jury could not listen in, Evseroff pointed to a line on the transcript: "This remark here isn't relevant, and it's clearly prejudicial."

"Is this still on the tape?" Dubin demanded.

"Yes, it is," McArdle told him.

"Well, it shouldn't be. That's got to be redacted."

Evseroff breathed a sign of relief.

"If I'm going to have to redact this," Gaudelli began, "I couldn't do it. You should have ordered it yesterday."

"Don't tell me what I should have done. I'm not the DA on this case," Dubin snapped. "If I were, I'd be down there prosecuting. Utter, sheer nonsense. A nonsensical statement that was. We will have another witness."

On that note, McArdle was temporarily banished and Captain Leonard Flanagan took the witness stand. Gaudelli led him through his chores as "on-duty Captain" for Queens on the day of the shooting, then focused on Flanagan's conversation with Shea and Walter Scott.

"Upon arriving at the 103rd Precinct, did there come a time when you spoke with Officer Shea?"

"Yes."

"Was anyone else present?"

"Patrolman Scott."

"What did you say to Shea, and what did he say to you?"

"Well," Flanagan began, "I told him I wanted more details, and he started telling me what happened. He said that him and Scott was in pursuit of two perpetrators. When they got to the beginning of the wooded area, Scott returned to his car, drove it around to 112th Road, and came into the area. I drew a rough diagram, and Shea indicated how they came in. I couldn't figure out how Scott—"

"Your Honor," Evseroff interrupted, "I move to strike anything which is the conclusion and operation of the witness's mind."

"I will allow the statement," Dubin said.

"I asked them how they came in," Flanagan continued, "and they drew a line on the diagram. I told them I didn't see how it was possible that Scott could get around and be there the same time Shea was before Shea discharged the gun."

"Tell us what Shea said," Gaudelli pressed.

"Shea said the line they drew was not exactly the right line. It should have been more of a curved line that would give Scott time to get in there."

"That line was supposed to indicate the path of the chase; is that correct?" Gaudelli asked.

"Yes."

"And you didn't think it was reasonable, did you?"

"No."

"You didn't think it was feasible that the two policemen could be where they said they were in terms of the line they drew; is that correct?"

"That's right."

At the close of Flanagan's testimony, there was a brief recess. "Five minutes, not fifteen," the Judge reminded everyone. When court resumed, James McArdle took the stand for the third time, and the much-ballyhooed tape was played. Having been further edited, it seemed anticlimactic. The tape, Evseroff hoped, was now a dead issue.

After lunch, Inspector Robert Johnson and Assistant District Attorney Martin Bracken testified with regard to the interviews they had conducted with Shea and Scott on the day of the shooting. Evseroff's cross-examination of both men was brief, and the session ended with Patrolman William Anthony, the 103rd Precinct station-house clerk, vouching for the authenticity of several clerical forms filled out by Shea on the morning of April 28, 1973.

"Not a bad day," Evseroff remarked as the defense team filed out of court. "Flanagan was the only witness who hurt."

"You know something," Cahill said. "Leonard Flanagan will be a captain for a long time. The job is civil service, so they can't take it away from him, and anything higher is by appointment based on merit."

The prosecution was proceeding on schedule. Its first four "visual witnesses" had provided a map and photographs of the shooting site. Then Add Armstead testified to the shooting itself, after which a dozen cops and Martin Bracken had recounted their postshooting conversations with Thomas Shea. On the morning of Friday, May 24, Demakos played his next few cards. Ten cops were called to the witness stand in an effort to prove that there had been no "black gun."

Detective Richard Gray (who had been Sergeant Joseph Kennedy's driver on April 28, 1973) testified that a brief search conducted by officers responding to Walter Scott's "ten-thirteen" call for assistance had been futile. Patrolman John McCabe (Sergeant Thomas Donohue's driver) stated that he saw no civilian in the vicinity of the lot who might have picked up the weapon. Detective Henry Sephton confirmed that a search of sewer catch basins in the area unearthed a metal starter's pistol, nothing more. Patrolmen Edward Zajc and Thomas Brophy of Emergency Services testified that they arrived at the lot forty minutes after the shooting and searched for a weapon without success.

Captain Raymond Kenny of Emergency Services was the day's sixth witness. He told of arriving at the lot at 1:30 P.M. and ordering the most thorough search possible.

"How many members of the Police Department were present and conducting the search at that time?" Gaudelli asked.

"About twenty."

"Were any tools used?"

"We used rakes, shovels, and our hands."

"And could you tell us the manner in which your men proceeded across the lot?"

"They were practically elbow to elbow," Kenny answered.

Next, Captain John Curran of Emergency Services confirmed Kenny's testimony. "First we searched the vacant lot with rakes and shovels. Then we searched east and west on Dillon Street between 111th and 112th Road. We searched open areas, driveways, lawns, gutters, everything. We searched Mathias Avenue between Dillon and New York Boulevard. We searched Claude Avenue, which is the next block over; all in the same manner."

"Was any weapon recovered?" Gaudelli asked.

"Not in the search that I conducted."

Sergeants Edward Leighs, John Segreto, and Clarence Reichman (all of Emergency Services) told of similarly futile efforts. The impact of their testimony was clear. The policemen searching the lot had been doing their best to find a weapon and thus exonerate a brother officer of wrongdoing. Now the thoroughness of their efforts had backfired. More and more it appeared as though there had been no gun.

Shortly after 3:00 P.M. the prosecution called Joseph McKeefery—the retired policeman who claimed to have found a black plastic pistol in a nearby lot on New York Boulevard one day after the shooting. Showing the toy to the jury, Demakos offered it into evidence. Under no circumstances could it have been the alleged black gun. It was not capable of firing (which Walter Scott claimed Armstead had done), and it had been found several blocks from the shooting site. Nonetheless, the prosecutor wanted the record to show that he had withheld nothing that remotely resembled exculpatory evidence.

The "weapon" (stamped "Auto Pop, Made in Hong Kong") was passed from juror to juror, after which court was adjourned for the Memorial Day weekend. "I wish you all a happy holiday," Dubin said in parting. "Forget about this case; have fun. I'll see you Tuesday."

"You know something," Cahill observed, turning to Shea when the jury had departed. "Most of these witnesses haven't wanted to testify against you. They'd all be happier if they'd been off duty the day Clifford Glover was shot."

"They aren't the only ones," Shea responded. "I wish I'd been off duty, too." He paused to reflect on the week ahead, then turned to Evseroff. "Who do you think the prosecution will call next?"

"Your guess is as good as mine," the lawyer answered.

The guessing game ended Monday night, when Cahill received a telephone call from Walter Scott. "Bad news," the cop reported. "I've been ordered by the Department to appear in court tomorrow morning."

"I guess that means we're still not finished with the tape," Cahill said.

15

THE TESTIMONY OF
WALTER SCOTT

When a good lawyer tries a case, his involvement is total. He
eats it, thinks it, and wakes up in the middle of the night to
jot down notes about it. While shaving in the morning, he is
likely to stop in mid-stroke, his face lathered with shaving
cream, to compose a paragraph for use in front of the jury.
In court even more is demanded of him. For sixty minutes
an hour, he must concentrate on every question asked and
every answer given. Then, when the day's proceedings are
done, he must prepare for the next set of witnesses to be
called the following morning.

As the trial of Patrolman Thomas Shea entered its third
week, Thomas Demakos and Albert Gaudelli were exhausted. Neither man had taken a day off since early May.
Both had worked nightly until midnight. Now they were
preparing for a major gamble—calling Shea's partner, Walter Scott, as a witness for the prosecution.

Clearly, Scott would be uncooperative. Subsequent to the
shooting, he had been unwilling to testify before the grand
jury until given a grant of immunity. Then, when Demakos
sought to discuss the case with him on the Saturday prior to

trial, the cop had refused. In all probability, his courtroom testimony would back Shea to the hilt. Nonetheless, Demakos was determined that he be called to testify.

In part the prosecutor's resolve stemmed from his method of trying cases. He believed in putting everything before the jury. "Scott says he was there," Demakos told Gaudelli. "I'll call anyone who claims he saw what happened." Then too, the prosecutor reasoned the jury might hold it against him if he failed to call Shea's partner as a witness. It would look as though the DA's office had something to hide. But most compelling, Demakos wanted to show Walter Scott up as a liar. He had read the cop's prior testimony and thought he could break him in front of the jury.

On Tuesday, May 28, the trial resumed. Almost immediately, Demakos called Scott to the stand.

"Raise your right hand," Court Clerk James Higgins instructed.

The witness complied.

"Do you swear to tell the truth, the whole truth, and nothing but the truth, so help you God?"

"I do."

Sitting at the counsel table with Cahill and Evseroff, Shea cast a worried look toward the jurors. There was no way to tell how they were leaning. Doubtless, many of them were aware that their names had appeared in the newspapers. They couldn't be happy about that, especially the jurors with young children. Still, they remained inscrutable.

The ill will between Demakos and Scott was obvious from the start. After a few preliminary questions, the prosecutor got to the heart of the matter. "Mr. Scott, were you on duty on April 28, 1973?"

"Yes."

"What hours?"

"From eleven P.M. on April 27 to eight A.M. on April 28."

"Did you have a partner with you?"

"Yes sir."

"Who?"

"Police Officer Thomas Shea."

"Were you in an automobile?"

"Yes."

"Were you the driver?"

"Yes."

Glancing at the outline of questions he had prepared for the occasion, the prosecutor continued. "Did there come a time on April 28, 1973, when you were proceeding up New York Boulevard approaching 112th Road and Mathias Avenue?"

"We were."

"And as you approached 112th Road, did you see anything?"

"It was Mathias we were approaching," Scott answered. "I observed two black males, one wearing a white floppy hat and a gold jacket and the other wearing a three-quarter-length brown coat."

"What did you do as you made this observation?"

"I nudged Patrolman Shea, and I said to him, 'There are the two guys from the taxicab stickup.' "

"What happened after that?" Demakos pressed.

"We made a U-turn and pulled up alongside. Patrolman Shea exited from the car and said, 'Stop. Police.' "

"Did he have a gun in his hand?" Demakos asked, moving closer to the witness.

"I don't believe so. I was getting out of the car at the same time."

"Did you have your gun in your hand?" Demakos pressed, his voice growing louder.

"Yes sir."

"If Your Honor please," Evseroff interrupted, "I respectfully object to Mr. Demakos raising his voice to this witness, and I ask for a direction that the District Attorney be instructed to stand back from the witness while examining."

"Keep your voice low," Dubin ordered.

"All right, Judge," the prosecutor answered. "I'll try." Then, standing his ground directly in front of the witness, Demakos continued. "What happened after the defendant Shea said, 'Stop. Police'?"

"The one in the white floppy hat and gold jacket yelled out, 'Fuck you, you're not going to take us.' We started chasing them, and they ran south on New York Boulevard into the lot."

"Then what happened?"

"As we were pursuing them, Tom yelled back to me, 'Get the car and head them off.' "

"How many steps had you taken in pursuit?" Demakos queried.

"I don't know. I wasn't counting."

"You took a few steps?" the prosecutor pressed.

"That's correct."

"And then you ran back and got the car?"

"Correct. I got back in the car, and I started going around to 112th Road. Halfway up 112th Road, I got out of the car and ran into the lot."

"What did you see when you ran into the lot?"

"I saw Armstead, Clifford Glover, and Police Officer Shea running."

"Where was Shea?"

"He was behind them."

"How far behind them?"

"Ten feet, maybe."

Tension in the courtroom was reaching new heights. "How far away were you from them?" Demakos pressed.

"Fifteen feet maybe."

"What happened then?"

"The one in the white hat made a turning motion and I heard shots."

"How many?"

"Three."

"What happened after you heard the shots?"

"The one in the white hat staggered forward with his hands outstretched, and the father *took a gun* from his left hand."

"When did you first see the gun?" Demakos demanded.

The witness pushed both arms forward. "When Clifford Glover went like this with it."

The prosecutor nodded with satisfaction. First Shea had told Sergeant Joseph Kennedy that Clifford Glover "tossed" the gun to Armstead. Then Shea told Sergeant Donald Bromberg that Armstead had "bent down" to pick it up. Now Walter Scott was testifying that Clifford Glover reached out and handed the gun to his father—three different versions of the same event.

"Will you describe the gun?" Demakos pressed.

"It was black metal."

"Was it a revolver?"

"I believe it was."

"How far away from the father were you at the time he took the gun from the boy?"

"About ten feet."

"What happened after that?"

"I started pursuing the father."

"Where?"

"He ran north around a fence and two big trees. There's an incline there, and he turned and fired at me."

"Did you have your gun out at that time?"

"Yes sir."

Breaking off his questions, Demakos reached for the map drawn by Patrolman Charles Fox and placed it on an easel in front of the jurors. "Would you step down here, please," he asked the witness, "and indicate to the jury the route the father took as you pursued him?"

Scott complied, sketching a narrow line on the exhibit. Then Demakos resumed his interrogation.

"How far behind Armstead were you when he fired at you?"

"About fifteen feet."

"What did you do?"

"I returned fire."

"Then what happened?"

"He was fleeing again."

"And what did you do?"

"I turned around and went back to 112th Road."

"You ran back to your car?" Demakos asked incredulously.

"That's correct."

"How far in front of you was he?"

"Maybe twenty feet."

The scorn in the prosecutor's voice was obvious. "Although you were only twenty feet behind Armstead, you ran all the way back to your car parked on 112th Road?"

"Yes."

"Then what happened?" Demakos asked, still shaking his head.

"I drove it around to Dillon Street, got out, and looked around for Armstead."

"Did you see anything?"

"No sir."

Walter Scott was sticking to his story, but Demakos had elicited the testimony he wanted. It was Scott's claim that after chasing Armstead and Glover for several yards, he had run back to his car, driven 340 feet around the block to 112th Road, jumped out of the car, and run 130 feet more into the lot in time to see Clifford Glover make a turning motion toward Thomas Shea. Moreover, Scott's story rested on the claim that Armstead and Glover had run so slowly as to enable the cop to drive around the block, run into the lot, and witness the shooting, but that Armstead had thereafter run so swiftly as to elude capture.

"What did you do after Armstead got away?" the prosecutor asked.

"I started back toward Patrolman Shea."

"Where was he when you saw him again?"

"In back by the fence where the kid was."

Once again, Demakos edged toward the critical portion of the tape, which he had been unable to play for the jury. "Did the boy say anything to you?"

"Yes sir."

"Were you standing over him?"

"I believe I was."

"And the boy said?"

"He said, 'Don't shoot; don't shoot.' "

"Did you say anything in return?"

"No sir."

"Did you curse at him?"

"I did not."

"Did you tell him—"

"Your Honor," Evseroff roared, drowning out the prosecutor's words, "this is the highest form of prosecutorial misconduct. I am trying to defend a client with the grossest type of prejudice."

"You don't have to yell and scream like that," Dubin admonished. "It's uncalled for."

"If Your Honor please," Evseroff persisted, "I object to him saying anything further about this in the presence of the jury."

"Judge," Demakos interrupted, "I'm going to request that the tape be played here with this witness on the stand to determine whether or not he said a few things."

"I object to that proposed practice," Evseroff shouted, his face red with anger.

Once again, Justice Dubin deferred decision. "We're not

going to do it now. It's a quarter to five, and I'm going to adjourn. I will decide tomorrow."

The jury was excused. Then Dubin admonished the lawyers before him. "Now both of you listen. One thing I want in this court is an orderly trial. I don't want any yelling or screaming. I don't want any play acting. I don't want any histrionics. And I don't want to be in a position where I have to yell to make myself heard. Is that understood?"

Both sides responded in the affirmative. On that note the day ended.

At the start of proceedings on Wednesday, May 28, Demakos renewed his request. "Your Honor, my application is to bring the tape into the courtroom and play it as I am questioning the witness Scott."

"If Your Honor please," Evseroff entreated, "I move at this time on behalf of Patrolman Thomas Shea that the District Attorney be precluded from asking any further questions of the witness with respect to the tape. In the posture of this case, I'm hard pressed to see anything more prejudicial to the defendant. It's collateral, it's irrelevant, it's immaterial, and it's highly prejudicial."

Dubin threw his hands in the air. "The Court has heard the same arguments before. The District Attorney has a right to test the witness's credibility. I will allow the tape."

When the jurors were seated, Demakos recalled Walter Scott to the stand. Then, focusing his questions on the spot where Clifford Glover had fallen, the prosecutor began. "Where was it that you saw the boy stagger after you heard the three shots?"

Scott pointed to a spot on the Fox map, indicating a location in the middle of the lot.

"Did you go by the boy when you chased the father?"

"I imagine I would have."

"The jury doesn't want your imagination," Demakos snapped. "Did you see the boy when you ran after the father?"

"No."

"There came a time when you were standing over the boy; is that correct?"

"Yes."

"And where was the defendant Shea at that time?"

"He had gone out to get some help on New York Boulevard."

"So there were no other police officers at the scene near the boy except yourself; is that correct?"

"I can't answer that question."

Scott's evasiveness was futile.

"You testified that the defendant Shea went out to get help," Demakos persisted. "Is that correct?"

"That's correct."

"If there were police officers standing with you, why would the defendant Shea go out for help?"

Evseroff objected to the question as "argumentative," but Demakos had proved his point. Walter Scott had stood alone over the body of Clifford Glover.

The crucial moment was now at hand. "Judge," Demakos urged, "I request that the tape be set up."

"All right," Dubin told him. "I will allow it."

On signal from Demakos, Albert Gaudelli distributed a new transcript to each juror. Then the tape was played.

"Ten-thirteen," the jurors heard Walter Scott cry. "112th and New York Boulevard."

"Ten-thirteen," the dispatcher sounded. "112th and New York Boulevard; 112th and New York Boulevard. Ten-thirteen."

"Three Charlie on the way," a radio car responded.

209

The jurors pulled closer.

"We got one of the two guys from the taxicab robbery," Scott said.

"What is your location now?" the dispatcher asked.

"Back street on Dillon, the garage."

"Central," a police team radioed forty seconds later, "where's the unit for the ten-thirteen?"

"Anticrime," the dispatcher asked, "what's your location on that ten-thirteen?"

"The backyard."

"Location? What address?"

"We're on Dillon Street," Scott shouted.

"We just passed there," another car called. "We don't see nothing."

"The backyard," Scott cried. "Come over to Dillon Street. You'll see a green Javelin or something."

The time was four minutes and forty-five seconds past 5:00 A.M. on the morning of April 28, 1973. Walter Scott was standing over the body of a mortally wounded ten-year-old boy.

The jurors listened intently.

✝ *"Die, you little fuck,"* Scott said.

When the furor subsided, Evseroff rose to examine the witness. Somehow, despite what the jury had just heard, he had to rehabilitate Scott as a credible figure.

"Patrolman Scott," the defense attorney began, "how old are you?"

"Twenty-six."

"Are you married or single?"

"Married."

"Do you have any children?"

"Yes sir, I have a baby."

"How old?"

"One month."

Nothing could be gained by further delay. The tape had to be confronted directly. The colloquy about to occur had been rehearsed several times. "Patrolman Scott, there came a time, did there not, when certain things were played for you —this tape you heard just now?"

"Yes sir."

"Isn't it a fact that, on the morning of the occurrence, you were not the only policeman in Queens with a walkie-talkie?"

"That's correct."

"Were there other units transmitting?"

"Yes sir."

"For instance," the attorney continued, "you will observe something on the transcript which says, 'We are responding to 112th and New York Boulevard.' That wasn't you talking, was it?"

"No sir."

"Would you say that this was some other police officer making that communication on a walkie-talkie?"

"A walkie-talkie or a car radio."

The big denial was at hand.

"Was that your voice, the epithet that was hurled?"

"No sir," Scott answered softly.

"Did you hear that on the tape?"

"Yes sir."

"Was that you speaking?"

"No."

For the first time since the trial began, open disbelief registered on the faces of several jurors. They had heard the tape. The voice was Scott's. Evseroff, who had done the best he could, paused briefly, then moved on, asking the witness to recount his sessions with Inspector Robert Johnson, Assistant DA Martin Bracken, and the Queens County grand jury. In each instance the attorney pushed the notion that, unlike Armstead, Walter Scott had never changed his story.

211

"Did there come a time," Evseroff pressed, "when you went to the District Attorney's office?"

"Yes sir."

"Who questioned you?"

"Mr. Gaudelli."

"Would you tell us what happened in the course of that interrogation?"

"Yes sir," Scott answered. "Mr. Gaudelli told me that, if I didn't tell them what they wanted to hear, they were going to fire me and seek an indictment against me for perjury and hinderance of prosecution."

"Did you change your story?"

"No sir, I did not."

Walter Scott—the honorable man who stood firm in the face of overwhelming pressure. Others, Evseroff wanted the jury to believe, were not so principled. As proof thereof, the attorney next raised the issue of community pressure as the motivating force behind Shea's indictment. "Did there come a time on April 28, 1973, when you saw some members of the community at the 103rd Precinct station house?"

"Yes sir," Scott answered.

"How many?"

"About three or four."

"Were these civilians?"

"Yes."

"What did you observe with respect to these people?"

"One of them came out of a meeting with the superior officers and said, 'If something isn't done about this, Jamaica is going to burn.' "

The attorney paused to let the answer sink in. "Was it thereafter that Patrolman Shea was placed under arrest?" he finally asked.

"I believe it was."

Two additional points for the defense followed: the first, that Shea and Scott had not known Clifford Glover was a ten-year-old boy; the second, that Shea and Scott genuinely believed they were apprehending two taxicab robbers. "A description had come over the radio with respect to the clothing of two perpetrators of a taxicab stickup; is that correct?"

"Yes sir."

"Is it a fact that the transmission indicated one of the two was wearing a white hat?"

"Yes sir."

"And was Clifford Glover wearing a white hat?"

"He was."

"Did the transmission indicate that the other perpetrator was wearing a brown three-quarter-length jacket?"

"Yes sir."

"And was Armstead wearing such a jacket?"

"Yes sir."

"Did you believe that these two were the perpetrators of that stickup?"

"Yes sir."

"Was it your intention to take them into custody?"

"Yes."

Evseroff was now ready to pose the question which, to his way of thinking, epitomized the entire case. *"Patrolman Scott, were you doing your job as a policeman?"*

"Yes sir, I was."

"I have no further questions."

Quickly Demakos was on his feet. "If Your Honor please, I have several additional inquiries."

"Go ahead," Dubin instructed.

His voice dripping with contempt, Demakos approached the witness. "Mr. Scott, you are a trained police officer; is that correct?"

"I believe so," Scott answered.

"And as a trained police officer, are you required to note the height of possible perpetrators?"

"Yes."

"And as a trained police officer, are you required to note the ages of possible perpetrators?"

"Yes."

"And as a trained police officer, are you required to note the weight of possible perpetrators?"

"Yes."

As Evseroff had done several times earlier in the day, the prosecutor paused for effect. "You are a trained police officer, are you not?"

"I'm still a human being," Scott answered.

"So you are," Demakos murmured. "I have no further questions."

The testimony of Walter Scott had come to an end. Moments later the jury was excused until 2:00 P.M. "We picked up points," Demakos told Gaudelli as the two men gathered their papers prior to lunch. "Scott's testimony is crucial to Shea's defense, and we made a liar out of him."

"Does the jury know that?" Gaudelli asked.

"I think so. They heard the tape. I'm just sorry we couldn't do more to shake the son of a bitch. He's unflappable."

A courtroom security guard approached the prosecutors. "I just thought you'd like to know," the guard said, "Walter Scott is in the men's room puking."

16

THE PEOPLE'S
CASE ENDS

The case against Thomas Shea was proceeding apace. When court resumed on the afternoon of Wednesday, May 29, the prosecution called Harold Cannon to the stand. Under questioning by Gaudelli, the detective recounted his trip with Add Armstead to the Pilot Automotive Wrecking Company.

"I show you this," Gaudelli said, handing Cannon a revolver, "and ask if you recognize it."

"I do."

"Is this the gun and holster together with the ammunition that you recovered from Add Armstead's place of business on April 28, 1973?"

"It is."

With Dubin's permission, Gaudelli introduced the weapon into evidence and passed it to the jurors. As could be readily seen, it was silver, not black.

Like a majority of the previous thirty-one witnesses, Cannon was generally helpful to the prosecution, but one major problem remained: No one had directly corroborated Add Armstead's version of the shooting itself. Thus, beginning on the afternoon of Wednesday, May 29, and continuing through the following day, Demakos gambled. Not fully confident of their ability to withstand cross-examination, he called as witnesses eight members of the South Jamaica community (all of them black), who claimed to have seen or heard events directly related to the death of Clifford Glover.

Doris Lyons of New York Boulevard testified to looking out her bedroom window and seeing Shea fire his gun the moment he stepped from the car. Jane Boolds (a bookkeeper driving home from a dance at 5:00 A.M. on April 28, 1973) claimed she saw Shea jump from his car and chase two blacks into the lot while Scott continued driving around the block without ever emerging from the vehicle. Elaine Fryer of 112th Road recounted hearing shots, looking out a bedroom window, and seeing Shea stand over the body of Clifford Glover. Marie Young of Mathias Avenue told of coming home from her job as a barmaid and getting ready for bed when she heard shots, looked out the window, and saw Armstead running across the street. Albert Robinson of Mathias testified to hearing the same shots and seeing Armstead run into some bushes. Robinson's daughter, Wanda, described hearing shots, seeing Armstead run into the same bushes, and then hearing one more shot fired. Helen Kelly of Dillon Street testified to seeing Armstead flag down the first police car that passed after the shooting. An eighth community witness, Katie Robinson of New York Boulevard, appeared senile and disoriented on the stand. Her testimony was at odds with that of every other witness and included improbable dialogue as well as the statement, contradicted by all other accounts, that ten minutes elapsed between the first and last shots fired.

Four of the community witnesses—Elaine Fryer, Marie Young, Albert Robinson, and Helen Kelly—added nothing to the prosecution's case. Evseroff was willing to concede that Shea had stood over Clifford Glover immediately after the shooting to ascertain the boy's condition and that Armstead had crossed Mathias Avenue before flagging down the police. Nor did the defense attorney tarry with Katie Robinson, who was such a pathetic figure on the stand that her testimony fell of its own weight. However, the other three community witnesses were potentially dangerous—until Evseroff emasculated each of them on cross-examination.

Doris Lyons claimed to have seen Shea fire his gun the moment he stepped from the car. However, she was extremely vague about what had caused her to rise from bed to look out the window before the shooting started. Then Evseroff dug into his case file and produced a signed statement which Mrs. Lyons had given police investigators on April 28, 1973. The statement contained no mention of her having witnessed the shooting. Indeed, to the contrary, Lyons had told police detectives that she neither saw nor heard it because "I went to get a bathrobe."

Wanda Robinson's testimony was also potentially damaging to Shea because the timing of shots she allegedly heard conflicted with Walter Scott's claim of having fired in self-defense. Scott had said the last two shots—one by him and one by Armstead—were fired in rapid succession. Wanda Robinson claimed that there was only one shot at the end and that it came after Armstead had fled the lot. Evseroff discredited her testimony by forcing the admission that she had never told anyone (including her father) about witnessing the incident until just prior to trial.

That left Jane Boolds. If her testimony that Walter Scott never stepped from his car prior to the shooting were allowed to stand, Scott's credibility would drop to sub-zero.

"Miss Boolds," Evseroff began, cross-examining the witness, "when did you come forth and tell anybody about this?"

"The day of the incident I reported it to the police."

"I see. And did anybody interview you?"

"Yes."

The defense attorney was floundering.

"And did you ever speak to anybody in the District Attorney's office about this?"

"Mr. Demakos."

Sitting in the front row of spectator seats, Shea's bodyguard Hugh Curtin began scribbling furiously on a sheet of paper.

"Did you speak to Mr. Gaudelli or any other assistant?" Evseroff pressed.

"No, just Mr. Demakos."

Curtin handed the paper to Cahill, who waved to Evseroff. Briefly the two lawyers caucused. The defense had a new lease on life.

"Miss Boolds," Evseroff asked, returning to the witness, "did you ever hear of Patrolman Timothy Hurley?"

"Yes."

"What do you know about him?"

"Objection," Demakos interrupted.

"Oh, no!" Evseroff thundered. "No!"

"Counselor," Justice Dubin intervened, "do you have a specific question?"

"Yes, I have a specific question," the defense attorney roared. "Isn't it a fact, Miss Boolds, that your brother is under arrest for killing Patrolman Hurley?"

"Yes."

"I have no further questions," Evseroff snapped. Then, shaking his head, he returned to his seat. "Woodwork witnesses," he muttered to Shea. "Woodwork witnesses, every one of them."

The "woodwork witnesses" had been a failure, and on Friday, May 31, Demakos returned to safer ground. Patrolman Edward Keegen, a police ballistics expert, testified that the starter's pistol found by Detective Henry Sephton in the sewer on Dillon Street was incapable of propelling a projectile. Next, Patrolman Stephen Egger of the Manhattan Forensic Unit described dusting the starter's pistol for fingerprints. None had been found, indicating that it had been in the sewer long before April 28, 1973. Together, the two men made it clear that the starter's pistol was not the "black gun" allegedly passed from Glover to Armstead.

After Egger, the prosecution called Detective Frank Guigliano of the Manhattan Ballistics Unit to confirm what the jurors could see with their own eyes—that the revolver found by Harold Cannon at the Pilot Automotive Wrecking Company was not "black." "This is stainless steel," Guigliano stated, inspecting the weapon. "It has a whitish finish." Following Guigliano's testimony, Detective Albert Birtley of the 15th Burglary and Larceny Squad recounted combing the lot with three other officers for evidence of the bullet allegedly fired by Add Armstead. "Did you find any?" Birtley was asked.

"No sir," he answered. "We didn't."

Inexorably the prosecution's case was drawing to a close. However, several loose ends remained—among them the extremely important legal technicality that no one had testified from direct knowledge that Clifford Glover was dead. On the afternoon of Friday, May 31, Eloise Glover took the stand.

"Mrs. Glover," Demakos asked, "did you have a son by the name of Clifford?"

"Yes, I did."

"And was his name Clifford Glover?"

"Yes," she answered softly.

"And will you tell me when he was born?"

"November 16, 1962."

"I'm sorry," Demakos said, straining to hear her. "You'll have to speak louder."

"November 16, 1962."

In the span of a year, Eloise Glover's world had collapsed

around her. Her oldest child was dead. Her second son, Henry, was suffering from an extreme emotional disorder, fueled by his inability to cope with Clifford's death. For long periods of time, Henry would sit alone in the rain. Once, looking at a tub of bacon scraps in a meat market, he had told the butcher, "That's my brother Clifford all cut up in his coffin."

"Mrs. Glover," Demakos asked, "did there come a time on April 29, 1973, when you went to the Medical Examiner's office in Manhattan?"

"Yes."

"And did there come a time at the Medical Examiner's office when you viewed a body?"

"Yes."

"Was that the body of your son Clifford?"

"Yes sir."

"And did you identify your son's body that day?"

"Yes."

The prosecutor's examination of the witness took less than two minutes. Following her departure, Dr. Yong Myun Rho (who had performed the autopsy on Clifford Glover's body) was called to the stand. One item in the pathologist's testimony was of particular note. The victim had been struck down by a bullet which entered his body one and a half inches from the center of his back.

Following a weekend recess, testimony resumed. On Monday, June 3, a police laboratory technician named Charles Pompa told the court that a spectographic analysis of the starter's pistol found in the Dillon Street sewer indicated that the gun could have been underwater for months. Then, at Evseroff's request, Add Armstead was recalled as a witness.

"This gun right here," Evseroff boomed, waving the revolver found at the Pilot Automotive Wrecking Company. "Do you recognize it?"

"Yes," Armstead answered.

"How long did you have this gun at the yard?"

"I guess about three or four months."

"You found it originally, is that right?"

"Yes."

"Where?"

"Under the seat of a car."

Evseroff's strategy was clear. Despite its silver color, he would play the gun for all it was worth.

"Tell me, Mr. Armstead, what kind of car was it?"

"I don't know."

"What make of car was it?"

"I don't know."

"What year car was it?"

"I don't know."

"What was the color of the car?"

"I don't remember."

"When you found this gun," Evseroff pressed, "did you show it to your boss?"

"Yes sir, he seen it."

"Did you ever fire this gun, Mr. Armstead?"

"No."

A crucial question was at hand. "Did you ever bring this gun home with you?"

"Yes," the witness answered.

Evseroff paused dramatically and looked toward the jurors, letting the fact sink in. Add Armstead was a man who had carried a gun to and from work.

"When did you bring this gun home with you?" the attorney asked at last.

"I don't know. Three or four times."

"Was there any special reason?"

"No reason."

"Just brought it home?" Evseroff demanded.

"Just brought it home."

Then, as he had done two weeks earlier, the defense attorney led Armstead through the day of the shooting, seeking additional contradictions in the witness's testimony.

"Why were you going to your place of business at five o'clock in the morning?"

"Sometimes the crane don't start so good. It takes a long time to start the crane."

"Did you tell Patrolman Thomas Scott that, when you turned around, you saw a man with a gun?"

"I don't remember," Armstead answered. "I was scared. I might have told him that, but I didn't see no gun."

Demakos held his breath. The witness was doing a good job. He was following his instructions, answering only the questions asked, not overextending himself. Evseroff was getting nowhere trying to break him.

With great flair, the defense attorney pointed to the map of the shooting site drawn by Patrolman Charles Fox. Perhaps, if pushed hard enough, Armstead would trace a route at odds with the one he had testified to earlier.

"Mr. Armstead," Evseroff coaxed, "would you care to come to the map, please, and show the jury where it was that you ran?"

The witness hesitated.

"Would you do that, please?" the lawyer urged.

"I can't read a map very good."

"You can't read a map?" Evseroff scoffed. "Can't you read at all?"

"No."

There was little to be gained from further interrogation. Moments later Evseroff's questions ceased. Then, shortly before noon on Monday, June 3, its case complete, the prosecution rested. After three weeks of testimony from forty-seven witnesses, the initiative was about to pass to the defense.

"It's our ball," Evseroff said, turning to Shea and Cahill. "Let's play with it."

17

THE DEFENDANT'S CASE

In many respects, a criminal trial is like a game of chess. Each side is perpetually maneuvering for position. An attorney who stays on the defensive for too long will find that he has lost the capacity to attack. The boldest offensive thrust can be undermined by a slight strategic error. Each move must be plotted with consummate care.

Thomas Demakos had built his case well. First four police witnesses provided a visual image of the lot. Then the prosecution had played its strongest piece, Add Armstead, placing him squarely in the center of the board. The community witnesses were a failure; but Eloise Glover had earned valuable sympathy points, and more than three dozen police witnesses had strengthened Armstead's testimony.

By contrast, Jack Evseroff had been forced into battle with an arsenal that was limited at best. His most valuable corroborative witness, Walter Scott, had been wiped from the board. The gun allegedly passed from Clifford Glover to Add Armstead had never been found. If the defense were to succeed, its strongest piece would have to be played immediately. As soon as court resumed on the afternoon of Monday,

June 3, Evseroff rose and announced, "If Your Honor please, the defense calls Thomas Shea."

The atmosphere was electric. One of the oddities in criminal litigation is that the defendant tends to be forgotten. Witnesses testify, lawyers pontificate, the Judge rules, and all the while the defendant sits and watches. For three weeks Thomas Shea had been obscured by a haze of legal proceedings. Few people had seen him standing in the courthouse corridor, gazing out the window during recess at pickets demanding his incarceration. Reporters had not been by his side when spectators pushed forward in the elevator, threatening, "We're going to get you when your bodyguards are gone." No courtroom observer had fully gauged Shea's fear or the embarrassment inflicted by the snide observation of a *Daily News* reporter that the defendant had worn the same suit to court every day for three weeks. "I don't have ten suits," Shea complained to Evseroff that night. "I have one. That's no crime."

Court Clerk James Higgins administered the oath to the witness, and Evseroff began his questions on safe ground. "Mr. Shea, how old are you?"

"Thirty-seven."

"Are you married or single?"

"I'm married."

"Do you have any children?"

"Yes, two girls, fourteen and twelve."

"And what is your occupation?"

"I'm a police officer," Shea answered proudly.

"Have you ever been convicted of a crime?"

"No sir."

"Have you served in the armed forces?"

"Yes, in the United States Air Force."

"How long did you serve?"

"Four years."

Having introduced his client as a family man and Air

224

Force veteran, Evseroff next moved to establish Shea's credentials as a cop. "Officer Shea, how long have you been a member of the Police Department of the City of New York?"

"Thirteen years."

"In how many arrests have you participated?"

"Anywhere from seven hundred to one thousand."

"How many arrests have you yourself made?"

"Conservatively speaking, approximately two hundred fifty to three hundred."

"On the morning of April 28, 1973, to what unit were you assigned?"

"The 103rd Precinct Neighborhood Police Team, Anticrime."

"Were you assigned with another officer?"

"Yes sir, Patrolman Walter Scott."

"And were you in uniform or plain clothes?"

"Civilian clothes, sir."

"Were you in a regular Police Department car or a private car?"

"A private car."

Evseroff paused momentarily. The stage was set for Thomas Shea to tell the jury his version of events surrounding the death of Clifford Glover.

"Patrolman Shea," the attorney urged, "if you would, I would like you, slowly, clearly, to relate to this court and this jury the incidents immediately preceding five A.M. on April 28, 1973. Tell us in your own words what happened."

As had been the case with those critical moments earlier in the trial—most notably the testimony of Add Armstead and Walter Scott—the courtroom spectators were absolutely silent. Speaking in a strong, clear voice, Shea began. "Well, at approximately five A.M., I was proceeding to the station house to continue an investigation on a car that had parts taken from the front but hadn't been reported stolen yet. I was the passenger; Patrolman Scott was driving. In the vicin-

225

ity of 112th Road and Mathias Avenue my partner pointed
to two black males proceeding southbound and said, 'Those
are the two from the taxicab stickup.' "

"Did you look in the direction in which he was pointing?"
Evseroff interrupted.

"Yes sir."

"And what did you see?"

"I saw two black males, one wearing a brown three-quarter-length leather jacket, the other wearing a yellow jacket
and a white floppy-type hat."

"As you looked at these individuals, did you ascertain
their ages?"

"No sir."

"Did you know that one of them was ten years old?"

"Definitely not."

Demakos and Gaudelli sat side by side, taking notes as the
witness spoke. Evseroff forged ahead. "What is the next thing
that happened?"

"I reached into my pocket and took out my shield and ID
card. We pulled abreast of the individuals, and I started to
exit from the car with my shield and card in my left hand.
I said, 'Stop. Police,' and the individual on the right said,
'Fuck you, you're not taking me.' "

"Do you know the identity of that individual?"

"Yes sir, Clifford Glover."

"What is the next thing that happened?"

"The two individuals started to run, and I chased them
into a lot."

"Had you taken your gun out?"

"Yes," Shea answered. "After the individual said, 'Fuck
you, you're not taking me,' I drew my revolver."

The most important moment of the trial was at hand.
Thomas Shea's fate would rest on whether or not the jurors
believed his answers to the next half dozen questions.

"When they went into the lot," Evseroff pressed, "did they take any particular direction?"

"They ran in more or less a zigzag fashion."

"As you were pursuing them, what happened?"

Shea took a deep breath. "The individual in the white hat and the yellow jacket slowed down and made a motion to the front of his body. As his arm returned, I saw what I believed to be a revolver. I brought my revolver up and, as it cleared my body, fired."

"How many shots?"

"Three."

"What was the next thing you observed?"

"The individual staggered forward and *passed* the revolver to the other individual."

"With which hand?"

"He handed it out with both hands," Shea said, thrusting his arms forward as Walter Scott had done before the jury six days earlier.

Evseroff's remaining questions dealt largely with backup police units arriving on the scene and the presence of certain unnamed community members at the 103rd Precinct station house just prior to Shea's arrest. Then the attorney closed with a flourish.

"Patrolman Shea, in the course of this occurrence, did you ever intend to do anything other than your job?"

"No sir."

"Did you believe that Clifford Glover had a gun?"

"Yes sir."

"Did you believe that he was going to use that gun against you?"

"Yes sir."

"I have no further questions."

The direct examination of Thomas Shea had taken slightly less than fifteen minutes. "He looks like an angel," Cahill whispered as Evseroff took a seat beside him.

"Yeah," the attorney answered, casting a glance at Demakos, who was already on his feet to begin cross-examination. "But let's see how he does under fire."

The anticipated barrage never materialized. Demakos had used his best ammunition in interrogating Walter Scott, and, relying on the transcript of that confrontation, Evseroff had prepared his client well. One by one, the prosecutor fired his major salvos: Clifford Glover had been shot square in the back; the transfer of the alleged black gun appeared more implausible with every recitation; Add Armstead had flagged down the first police car he saw after the shooting. In each instance, Shea held firm to his earlier testimony. The only new ground Demakos broke concerned Shea's 1972 shooting of Felix Tarrats.

"What were the circumstances under which you used your gun then?" the prosecutor pressed.

"I was on patrol," Shea answered. "My brother officer and I observed two individuals come out of a building, look both ways, and start to run. Then another individual came running out of the same building, blood coming from his hand, yelling, 'Holdup, holdup.' I proceeded to chase one of the individuals, and he let one round go in my direction."

"You saw a gun?" Demakos interrupted.

"That's correct."

"You saw the flash?"

"Yes sir. So I put my revolver over my head and fired one round in the air, yelling 'Stop. Police.' Tarrats continued to run and, at a point on 84th Street when he started to turn behind a car, I fired one shot and struck him in the neck."

"You shot him in the neck?"

"That's correct."

"Did you find a gun on that individual?" Demakos demanded, his voice rising for one of the few times during the course of trial.

"No sir."

"Did you charge that individual with attempted murder?"

"Yes."

"And what happened?"

"The case was dismissed," Shea admitted.

"No gun was found on that individual either, was it?"

"Objection," Evseroff interrupted. "The question has already been asked and answered.

"Objection sustained," Dubin informed the attorneys.

"You were beautiful," Evseroff told Shea when the day was done. "You came across as decent, forthright, and honest."

"Was I that good?" Shea asked.

"Yes. And I'll tell you something else," the attorney chortled. "You came across as one hundred percent cop."

Evseroff's assessment was correct. Shea had been an effective witness but, unless the jury's view of Walter Scott were altered, the defense would still be in trouble.

On the morning of Tuesday, June 4, two witnesses designed to rehabilitate Scott's credibility were called to the stand. The first was a PBA attorney named Anthony Buffalano. One year earlier Buffalano had accompanied Scott to the District Attorney's office just prior to the cop's grand jury testimony. The afternoon had been ugly, and bitter words had been exchanged as Albert Gaudelli ridiculed Scott's claim of having seen Clifford Glover pass a black gun to Add Armstead. Now, over Demakos's stiff objection, Dubin allowed Buffalano to testify with regard to the confrontation.

"Mr. Buffalano," Evseroff began, "what is your occupation?"

"I am an attorney for the Patrolmen's Benevolent Association."

"Do you know a man by the name of Patrolman Walter Scott?"

"Yes, I do."

"Did there come a time on May 18, 1973, when you went somewhere in connection with Walter Scott?"

"Yes."

"Where?"

"To the office of Mr. Gaudelli."

"Did you see Mr. Gaudelli?"

"I did."

"Were you there with Patrolman Scott?"

"Yes."

In a highly unusual maneuver, Evseroff was about to attack the integrity of a fellow attorney in open court. "Would you relate to the court and jury what was said?"

"Yes sir," Buffalano answered. "Mr. Gaudelli at that time was Chief of the Homicide Bureau. He stated that he would like to hear from Police Officer Scott a certain story. If Police Officer Scott did not tell him that story, Officer Scott would be fired."

"Did Mr. Gaudelli say what story he wanted?"

"A story that would be beneficial to the District Attorney's office."

"What if anything was said to Scott with respect to prosecution?"

"Mr. Gaudelli said that Police Officer Scott would be prosecuted if he did not tell that certain story to the District Attorney's office."

"Did Scott tell him that certain story?"

"No sir, he did not."

"I have no further questions," Evseroff ended.

Walter Scott—victim of official persecution because he had held his ground. On cross-examination Demakos attacked immediately.

"Mr. Buffalano," he snapped, "you are implying that Mr.

Gaudelli asked Scott to commit perjury; isn't that a fact?"

"That is correct."

"Did you complain to anybody about Mr. Gaudelli's attitude?"

"Yes, I did."

"To whom?"

"To Mr. McKiernan, the President of the PBA."

"How about the District Attorney himself [Michael Armstrong]?"

"I did not."

"Did you complain to the Bar Association?"

"I believe our office decided against going to the Bar Association."

"Why?" Demakos roared. "Isn't it because Scott was, in fact, lying?"

Buffalano didn't answer.

"I have no further questions," the prosecutor said.

"Next witness," Dubin ordered.

On signal from Evseroff, Sergeant Thomas Donohue took the stand. Thirteen days earlier Donohue had testified as a witness for the prosecution, recounting his postshooting conversation with Thomas Shea. Now, in an effort to erase the stigma of the infamous tape, Evseroff planned to pursue a different line of questioning.

"Sergeant Donohue," the defense attorney began, "you responded to this particular lot on New York Boulevard and 112th Road on April 28, 1973, did you not?"

"Yes sir."

"Did there come a time when you were in that lot and saw Clifford Glover?"

"Yes sir," Donohue answered. "He was lying on the ground."

"And when you saw Clifford Glover on the ground, did you have a conversation with him?"

"Yes."

"What was said?"

Donohue looked around the courtroom, then back at Ev-seroff. "Glover said to me, 'I'm dying,' and I said, 'That's right, you little fuck; you're dying.' "

"Did that take place about five minutes after five?"

"Yes, sir."

"Thank you so much."

Again, it was a "good try" that didn't work. Demakos was on his feet immediately to cross-examine the witness.

"Sergeant Donohue," the prosecutor demanded, "did you have a walkie-talkie with you that day?"

"I don't think so."

"And when you were standing over the boy, what was it you said?"

" 'That's right, you little fuck, you're dying.' "

"Not 'Die, you little fuck'?"

"No sir."

"Are you sure of that?" Demakos pressed.

"Yes sir."

"The epithet came over the transmitter immediately after a green Javelin was mentioned," the prosecutor reminded the witness. "Do you recall anybody saying, 'Come over to Dillon Street, you'll see a green Javelin or something'?"

"I remember the green Javelin being mentioned," Donohue answered.

"When did you first hear that?"

"Somewhere along New York Boulevard en route to the scene."

"So, when the green Javelin was mentioned, you were still in the car; is that correct?"

"Yes sir."

Demakos had made his point. Contrary to the red herring Evseroff had sought to insert into the proceedings, it was not Donohue who had uttered the words "Die, you little fuck." It had been Walter Scott. Thomas Donohue, whom Captain

Glanvin Alveranga had once called "one of my brightest, most competent men," had sullied his own reputation for naught. In a matter of months, he would be transferred from Queens to a precinct in Brooklyn.

The remainder of the day passed quickly. Detectives Angelo Sollecitto, Michael Studdert, and Henry Sephton (who had interviewed community witnesses in the aftermath of the shooting) testified to contradictions in the testimony of Marie Young, Helen Kelly, and Doris Lyons. Lieutenant Joseph Kossmann and Executive Officer Louis Troiano of the 103rd Precinct confirmed that Armstead was considered a prisoner rather than an innocent victim when first brought to the 103rd Precinct station house. Detective William Burke recounted arresting Armstead for illegal possession of a dangerous weapon. Then Sergeant Charles De Rienzo (the Supervisor of Queens Central Booking) told the jury that, because of intervention by high-ranking police officials, Armstead was given a desk-appearance ticket rather than being fingerprinted and arraigned. Evseroff's purpose in calling the latter four witnesses was to demonstrate that, were it not for community pressure and intervention by the police brass, Armstead, not Shea, would have been indicted.

Shortly before 5:00 P.M. court was adjourned. It had been an ugly day filled with venom. As a rule, lawyers seek to keep personal animosity to a minimum. They may rant and rave for jury consumption but, when the battle is done, they remain friends. Something different though, had happened in the case of Thomas Shea. The attorneys were developing a genuine dislike for each other, and their mutual antagonism was spilling over into the trial proceedings.

For Albert Gaudelli, the escalation of hostilities was a particularly bitter pill to swallow. From the inception of the Shea case on, he had received hate mail accusing him of "coddling niggers." "Dear Sir," one letter read. "It makes my blood boil when I see how niggers are getting away with murder. That policeman was doing his duty. What was that nigger child doing out at five o'clock in the morning? Of course, you are afraid for your life if you don't convict the policeman."

That particular letter, like most of its counterparts, had been unsigned. Gaudelli was able to dismiss it as the work of a crank, but other attacks were more difficult to endure. One week into the trial, PBA President Robert McKiernan had told a reporter, "The District Attorney's office has bowed to anarchy and fear. Thomas Demakos and Albert Gaudelli have become symbols of shame."

The irony of the situation was clear. Several years earlier Gaudelli had prosecuted two blacks for the murder of a policeman shot and killed during a South Jamaica liquor-store holdup. Both men were sentenced to die in the electric chair, though their sentences were later reduced to twenty-five years to life by an appellate tribunal. Thereafter Gaudelli had been presented with a plaque, which still hung on his office wall. Painstakingly penned in black, red, and gold letters, it read:

PBA Certificate of Honor to
ALBERT A. GAUDELLI
Assistant District Attorney,
Homicide Bureau, Queens County

In appreciation of his conscientious,
courageous, prosecution of the murderers
of Patrolman Kenneth Nugent.

Robert M. McKiernan
President

On Wednesday, June 5, the final phase of the defense case began. Just prior to the trial, Evseroff had instructed Shea to compile a list of co-workers and friends who would be willing to testify as "character witnesses." "I want all types of people," Evseroff instructed. "Cops, lawyers, priests, Italians, Jews, and as many blacks and Puerto Ricans as you can find who are willing to speak out on your behalf."

Wednesday morning the parade of character witnesses began. Detective Edward Harrop was the first.

"How old are you, sir," Evseroff asked.

"Thirty-seven."

"Are you married or single?"

"Married."

"How long have you been a member of the Police Department of the City of New York?"

"Since May 1, 1961."

"Do you know the defendant in this case, Patrolman Thomas Shea?"

"I do," Harrop answered, "from working and socializing with him."

"How long have you known him?"

"Since September 1961."

"Do you know other people who know him?"

"I do."

"Have you ever had occasion to discuss Patrolman Shea's reputation for truth, honesty, and peaceableness with these other people who know him?"

"Yes sir," Harrop answered.

"And what is that reputation?"

"Good."

Harrop's direct examination took less than two minutes. On cross-examination, Demakos reminded the witness (and jury) that Shea had shot a man named Felix Tarrats in the neck in a similar incident and had allegedly pistol-whipped a fourteen-year-old boy.

"Had you heard that?" the prosecutor snapped.

"Only what I read in the paper," Harrop answered.

"Would your opinion be changed as to this defendant's reputation for peaceableness if you had known that?"

"No sir."

Harrop was followed to the stand by a Catholic priest named Ernest Reardon, Jack Lynch (a thirty-five-year-old insurance salesman and former neighbor of Shea's) and Lynch's wife, Kathy. In each instance, as he would do over the next two days, Evseroff elicited cursory biographical information about the witness and then posed six questions: Do you know Thomas Shea? How long have you known him? How did you come to know him? Do you know other people who know him? Have you ever had occasion to discuss his reputation for truth, honesty, and peaceableness with these other people? What is that reputation? Invariably, the final question was answered, "Good," "Of the highest order," "Very good."

Then Demakos would cross-examine each witness, asking two questions with regard to Shea's "reputation": "Did you know that, in April 1972, this defendant shot a suspect he was pursuing in the neck, claiming this suspect had fired a shot at him, and that no gun was found at that time either? Did you know that this defendant is alleged to have pistol-whipped a fourteen-year-old boy?"

The day's fifth character witness was Lieutenant James Gaines—a twenty-six-year veteran of the force, who had known Shea since 1966. Gaines was black. He was followed to the stand by Ron DeVito (a PBA delegate from the 103rd Precinct), William Meyer (a production control manager for the Potter Instrument Company), George Mims (a black police detective assigned to the 103rd Precinct), Vincent and Christine Nyholm (former neighbors), and Lieutenant Charles Mancuso, who had been Shea's boss in the Brooklyn North Task Force. "If he wasn't peaceable," Mancuso declared, "he couldn't have been in my outfit. We had to operate in areas where there were riot-type situations. If Tom was the type that lost his head, I would never have had him in the outfit."

After a luncheon recess, ten more witnesses, including a black patrolman named Carl Hackett, testified to Shea's "good character." Thursday morning the parade picked up again.

"He's a very truthful and honest person, a capable officer," declared Patrolman William Cutter of the 103rd Precinct. Cutter's words were echoed by Detective Victor Ortiz, who had befriended Shea thirteen years earlier at the Police Academy and later become a key figure in the Department's efforts to recruit more Puerto Ricans for the force. Another officer of Puerto Rican descent (Detective Jose Ramirez) testified that he and his family had stayed overnight at Shea's home and that the defendant was definitely not a racist. "His reputation is above reproach," declared Detective Stephen Moriarty, a twenty-year police veteran.

At the close of Moriarty's testimony, Evseroff motioned for Demakos to approach the Judge's bench and, out of earshot of the jury, complained, "If Your Honor please, there is a man with a big Afro hairdo sitting in the back of this courtroom who is laughing as I question each witness."

"I didn't notice him," Dubin said.

Evseroff stood rigid with his back to the spectators. "Directly in line from where I'm standing," he said. "On this side of the courtroom. At this point, I'm not asking Your Honor to exclude anybody from the court. I'm just asking you to observe what I say."

"All right," Dubin answered. "If necessary, I'll admonish him. Let's get on with the proceedings."

More character witnesses followed. By and large, their testimony was predictable but, on several occasions, it was apparent that the defense had come dangerously close to overreaching itself in finding people willing to testify on Shea's behalf.

"You are assigned to the 103rd Precinct, are you not?" Evseroff asked Patrolman Abraham Jenkins.

"Yes."

"Do you know Patrolman Thomas Shea?"

"I can't say that I know him," Jenkins answered. "I've seen him."

"Do you know him to speak to?"

"Maybe speaking, passing by, but I don't know him."

"Have you ever had occasion to discuss with other police officers who know him, his reputation for truth, honesty, and peaceableness?"

"No," Jenkins answered.

"Have you ever heard anything bad about him?" Evseroff asked in desperation.

"No."

By 4:00 P.M. a total of forty-seven character witnesses had been called over the two-day period: eight of them black, three Puerto Rican. The final defense witness was Patrolman Terry Salley—a black cop who had been Shea's partner on April 4, 1968, the night Martin Luther King was assassinated. Shea and Salley had been on crowd-control duty when a police rookie facing his first riot situation panicked and fired several shots in their direction. Shea had knocked Salley to the ground, possibly saving his life.

"Have you had occasion to discuss with other policemen who know Patrolman Shea, his reputation for truth, honesty, and peaceableness?" Evseroff asked.

"Yes," Salley answered.

"And what is that reputation?"

"Good."

Salley was excused, and Evseroff looked up toward the bench. "If Your Honor please, the defendant Patrolman Thomas Shea rests."

18

THE SUMMATIONS

On Friday, June 7, the prosecution called two rebuttal witnesses. Tony Minutello, Add Armstead's employer, was the first. For more than a year the wrecking yard owner had resisted a role in the proceedings. As a white man doing business in a black neighborhood, he needed both police protection and the goodwill of area residents to survive. Involvement in the case could only hurt him.

Demakos had sensed Minutello's reluctance to testify and decided against calling him as a witness during the prosecution's main case. But Evseroff had repeatedly driven home the point that Armstead had no business being on the streets at five o'clock in the morning, and some rebuttal was necessary.

"Mr. Minutello," Demakos asked after the wrecking yard owner had taken the stand, "do you know Add Armstead?"

"Yes, he works for me."

"What type of job does he have?"

"He's an auto wrecker, cutting cars."

"What are his hours of work?"

"Seven to five."

"And the days of the week that he works?"

"Five and a half," Minutello answered. "Half a day Saturday."

"Do you recall a conversation with Mr. Armstead with respect to his day's work for Saturday, April 28, 1973?"

"Right; he was supposed to get in early because we were going to ship a load of motors."

Demakos paused so the jurors would focus on the answer, then forged ahead. "Did Clifford Glover ever come to work with Add Armstead?"

"Yes."

"Can you tell us how many Saturdays Clifford Glover came to work each month?"

"Three, maybe four."

"And how often would he come to work after school?"

"Three or four times a week."

"Did you pay him?"

"I threw him a couple of dollars. He used to be my errand boy."

Alan Parente, who had assisted Gaudelli in presenting the case to the grand jury, followed Minutello to the stand. He recounted being present at the May 18, 1973, meeting attended by Gaudelli, Anthony Buffalano, and Walter Scott and denied that any threats had been made.

"What did you hear at that meeting?" Demakos asked.

Parente answered without hesitation. "Mr. Gaudelli told Officer Scott and Mr. Buffalano that we thought Officer Scott was lying, that his story was not believable, and that we wanted the truth."

"What did Scott or Mr. Buffalano say to that?"

"I don't remember Mr. Buffalano saying very much at all," Parente answered. "Patrolman Scott said, 'That's my story, and I'm not going to change it.' That was the end of the meeting."

"Did Mr. Gaudelli threaten Scott with an indictment?"

"No, he did not. No threats were made."

By midmorning the People's case was complete. All totaled, the prosecution had called forty-nine witnesses; the defense, fifty-seven. "It's the damnedest thing I ever saw," Court Clerk James Higgins told a reporter. "Usually, in a murder case, you have a pretty good idea of which way the jury will go. Right now I don't have the foggiest notion what will happen."

In truth, the outcome would hinge on the attorneys' summations. Jurors are used to watching Perry Mason on television. They have been weaned on courtroom dramas in which everything is neatly and fully explained at the end of trial. In the real world, of course, pieces seldom fall so easily into place. The job of an attorney on summation is to convince the jury that, even though some loose ends remain, the cause he has championed is just. He must weave the evidence into a scenario the jurors will accept.

Shortly after 1:00 P.M. on the afternoon of Monday, June 10, Jack Evseroff rose to face the eleven men and one woman who would decide the fate of Thomas Shea. As counsel for the defendant, he was required to sum up first. The prosecuting attorney would have the advantage of speaking last. Inside the courtroom the atmosphere was stifling. Unable to meet the demand for power brought on by an unseasonably warm burst of ninety-five-degree weather, the Consolidated Edison Company had ordered a city-wide voltage cutback. Immediately thereafter, the courtroom air conditioners had gone dead, pushing temperatures inside the windowless chamber well above ninety degrees.

"If Your Honor please," Evseroff observed, "Con Edison has decided to cut back our electricity, and it is a little warm in here. I wonder if I might remove my jacket while I sum up to the jury."

241

"Being comfortable is never an offense," Dubin answered. "If anyone wants to take off their jacket, they have the court's permission."

Gratefully the attorney removed his coat, then strode to a point directly in front of the jury and began. "Your Honor, Mr. Demakos, Mr. Gaudelli, Mr. Foreman, Madam and Gentlemen of the Jury: This is the portion of the trial known as the summation. It is my last opportunity to speak to you in connection with the case of *The People* versus *Thomas Shea.* Initially, I should like to apologize if, in the course of this case, I offended anybody. If I have argued a little too vociferously or yelled a little too loud, please forgive me. This is something that happens in the course of battle. If I yelled a little too loud, it was only in the interest of protecting my client's rights."

Having begun his summation with a touch of humility, Evseroff next sought to achieve a veneer of impartiality. "Now a summation, Madam and Gentlemen, is the time in a trial when the lawyers for both sides speak to you and try to persuade you of the merit in their particular point of view. It is argument by counsel, not evidence. Please do one thing. However you decide this case, decide it as you promised you would, solely, completely, and exclusively upon the evidence."

It takes a big ego to be a successful trial lawyer, and Jack Evseroff had one. "Where else," he once asked a fellow attorney, "can you get twelve people and maybe even a judge and assistant district attorney to listen to your every word?" Now Evseroff was onstage and loving every minute of it.

"Madam and Gentlemen, you have sat here and listened carefully for four weeks, and you have heard an aggregate of one hundred six witnesses. I want you to come and reason with me, to make a qualitative analysis. Let's look at the witnesses. Let's look at who and what they are.

"Patrolman Shea took the stand in his own defense. He

242

testified on direct and cross-examination. He told you what happened on that fateful morning of April 28, 1973. He told you that he never knew Clifford Glover was ten years old until after this was all over. He said he was involved in a chase. He said he identified himself as a police officer with his shield and his ID card, and that Glover said, 'Fuck you, you won't take me,' and took off into the lot and zigzagged back and forth. When Patrolman Shea saw a gun coming out, he fired, and he then saw Glover hand the gun to Armstead. He answered clearly, concisely, and truthfully.

"Ladies and Gentlemen," Evseroff boomed, his voice suddenly bouncing off the courtroom walls, "in listening to the testimony of any witness, you can tell, you can feel, you can sense what he is. You can tell what Thomas Shea is from the way he testifies. Is he an animal? Is he depraved? Is he a wanton killer? No! He is a policeman who was doing his job, a cop who was out on the streets of New York working to fight crime.

"I don't think there's any issue in this case between the prosecution and the defense that at five A.M. on April 28, 1973, Patrolman Thomas Shea was working, that Patrolman Thomas Shea was in a car with Patrolman Walter Scott, and they were on the job. There's no allegation that Patrolman Shea or Patrolman Scott was drunk or disorderly. There is no allegation that they were acting outside the scope of their authority when they appeared on New York Boulevard. They were policemen working, doing a tour of duty. There had been an alarm that a taxi had been stuck up in another area of Queens, and there came a time when Patrolman Scott told Patrolman Shea that he thought he saw the perpetrators. Thomas Shea got out of his police car in the furtherance of his duty, not to go into a gin mill to have a drink, not to shake down the local bookmaker, but to enforce the law.

"What should a policeman do under those circumstances?" Evseroff roared. "What duty is thrust upon a man in blue? Do you think a policeman who gets out of his car is required to make an in-depth inquiry with respect to a birth certificate, or is he required to make a split-second judgment to enforce the law?"

Suddenly Evseroff's voice softened. "The question of whether the guilt of Patrolman Shea has been established beyond a reasonable doubt has to be determined free from any passion. Let's face it, there was a ten-year-old child killed in connection with this case and, when a ten-year-old child is killed, this is tragic. But notwithstanding the fact that the deceased was ten years old, the question is whether or not the prosecution has established the guilt of Thomas Shea beyond a reasonable doubt. It is the position of the defense in this case that the defendant acted justifiably and that, tragically, a ten-year-old was killed. The District Attorney will make for you the big argument, 'Where is the gun?' Mr. Demakos will ask you, 'If Armstead had a gun, where is it?' That's true. They found no gun, but let's look at the facts. The ten-thirteen alarm was sent out about five A.M. The police responded at 5:05. There were five minutes in between that Armstead had to dispose of the gun."

And then, his voice growing louder, Evseroff came to Armstead. "Add Armstead testified here. Add Armstead is a convicted rapist, a hoodlum, a gangster, a man who keeps a gun in his place of business and takes it home on occasion. Add Armstead, this fifty-one-year-old man who says to you, 'We were walking along on New York Boulevard, my stepson and I, my son, my son and I.' How many times did we hear him refer to that boy as his son? It's not his son," Evseroff shrieked. "It's a paramour's child, the woman with whom he lives, her child. And if there is any significant factor in this case by which you can gauge the kind of person Add Armstead is, look at his conduct. He ran! He split, and he ran. He had no more concern for Clifford Glover than the man in the moon. He never looked back and never cared.

244

"Add Armstead is not stupid. Add Armstead is anything other than what he professes to be on that witness stand. He's not a sad, pathetic fifty-one-year-old worker. He is a clever, clever man, who takes ten-year-old boys out with him at five in the morning to do whatever he knows should be done. Add Armstead, this convicted rapist, would have you believe that a car pulled up, that a man exited, and that the man said, 'You black son of a bitch,' and started firing. That's what he testified to here. Do you think that Armstead really believed the men who were pursuing him were there to stick him up? You be the judges of that—two white men at five A.M. in South Jamaica. Or rather do you believe that Add Armstead knew that these men were policemen and that he had reason to run?

"Why did he run?" Evseroff thundered. "I don't know. But I know that people who run usually have a reason for running, something with respect to guilt. I don't know if he was ripping off cars; I don't know if he was doing burglaries; I don't know what he was doing. Only Armstead knows what he was doing with that little boy at five in the morning."

Dripping with perspiration, Evseroff again moderated his tone. "What are we all doing here? Does it make sense to you that Patrolman Shea would get out of that car and not identify himself as a police officer? What possible reason would a police officer have for getting out of a car and not identifying himself? Is that the act of a police officer? Is that the act of a man who is thirty-seven years old with two daughters? Is that the act of a man with thirteen years on the force, who has participated in seven hundred arrests, who himself has made some three hundred?

"Where is the evidence? We have been here for four weeks, and in four weeks we have heard Add Armstead, eight wood-work witnesses, and a parade of testimony about how the area was searched and there was no gun. The prosecution insults your intelligence by presenting the type of witnesses it did. They put a poor elderly woman by the name of Katie Robinson on the stand. You saw her—a pathetic, senile lady. They brought a woman before you by the name of Jane Boolds. Can you imagine the District Attorney bringing for your edification a woman whose brother has been arrested for killing a cop and asking you to accept as gospel her testimony in order to convict one of New York City's Finest? Come on! We don't live in the Middle Ages. That witness was here for one reason and one reason alone—to get even with every cop that walks the streets because her brother is locked up and is a cop killer. If that isn't a woodwork witness, I don't know what is. You decide whether testimony of that ilk satisfies you beyond a reasonable doubt of the guilt of Thomas Shea."

His voice choked with emotion, Evseroff pointed toward his client. "This policeman here is the kind of man who is on the street; not in an office, not pounding a typewriter, not operating a radio at the communications bureau. This is the cop on the street. This is the policeman who stands between you and me and crime. Of course, he gets involved; of course, he has to use his gun. Does that make him an animal? Does that make him vicious? Does that show that he is dangerous? No! It shows he does his job, that he is out there working.

"Forty-seven people got on this witness stand and attested to Thomas Shea's good character and reputation for truth, honesty, and peaceableness. Sure, most of those people were policemen. Who should a policeman know? Supreme Court judges? Big shots in Washington? He knows the policemen he works with and the neighbors with whom he lives. This is the measure of a man. Thomas Shea's crime is that he was doing his job. He was a policeman out there doing what he was paid to do, enforce the law and make arrests.

"Madam and Gentlemen, I speak to you for every man in blue. I speak to you for Thomas Shea. There is no murder here, only a tragedy. Go back, deliberate, and, for the sake of Thomas Shea and every policeman who walks the streets of New York, give us a verdict that speaks truth, law and order, and justice. Thank you."

It had been a virtuoso performance. Like most trial lawyers, Evseroff believed that "guilt" and "innocence" are oftentimes of secondary importance to a jury. Most cases are decided by whether or not the jurors believe the defendant *deserves to be punished.* It was now up to Thomas Demakos to convince the jury that, in Shea's case, the answer was "yes."

Following Evseroff's summation, Justice Dubin called for a brief recess. Then, shortly before 3:30 P.M., Demakos rose and faced the jurors. "Justice Dubin, Mr. Evseroff, Mr. Cahill, Lady and Gentlemen of the Jury. The first stage of the trial you heard was what we called the voir dire. And after the selection of the jury you heard the opening statements. Then there was the third stage—the taking of testimony. We have now reached the summation."

One by one, in workmanlike fashion, Demakos reviewed the testimony of various witnesses. Only when he reached the testimony of Thomas Shea did his emotions come to the surface. "Shea tells you that the two individuals ran zigzag. They went southwest, northwest, southwest, northwest, and he was behind them all the time. Can you really believe that, a police officer chasing a kid in circles? And, you know, I will tell you why he testified that they went zigzag. Because when Captain Flanagan said to him, 'It doesn't sound right that Scott could come over to 112th Road, run into the lot, and see what he said he saw,' Shea told him, 'No, they weren't really running into the lot straight; they went into the lot in a circle.' Shea then tells you that the boy reached in his pocket and came up with a gun, and he fired three times, after which the boy staggered and passed the gun to his

247

father. But Shea also said the gun was tossed. And another time he said Armstead bent over to take it."

Then, pulling the Fox map of the shooting site into full view, Demakos tore into Walter Scott with a savagery he had never before mustered. "What did Scott tell you? After the boy says, 'Fuck you, you're not taking me,' Scott gets out of the car, gets back in the car, drives down New York Boulevard, makes a right turn, and parks his car on 112th Road. He then tells you he gets out of the car, runs into the lot and sees the shooting.

"Scott never got out of his car on 112th Road," Demakos roared. "Scott drove all the way to Dillon. That's where he went into the lot. He was nowhere near when Shea shot that boy. Listen to his testimony. Walter Scott, twenty-six years of age, chasing a fifty-one-year-old man. What did Scott say? He was twenty feet behind Armstead when Armstead pegged a shot. Twenty feet behind him, and what does Scott do? He runs back to his car! He runs back to his car a distance of over two hundred feet to drive around and chase Armstead, a fifty-one-year-old man who was only twenty feet away. Incredible! And you people heard the tape. Clear across that tape comes one thing—'Die, you little fuck.'

"You are not here to judge the moral character of Add Armstead," Demakos continued. "You are here to judge whether or not he told you the truth; not whether he is a coward, not whether he is living in sin. And his testimony is corroborated by all the police officers who got to the scene. Patrolmen Panico and Alvy say they came down Dillon and spotted Armstead. Armstead was flagging them down. Patrolman Farrell and Patrolman Tom Scott came north on Dillon and saw Armstead. Armstead was flagging them down. Armstead flags down Panico and Alvy. Armstead flags down Scott and Farrell. All of them in patrol cars. Can you really believe Armstead was having a duel with another cop and was out there flagging down police cars?"

His voice cutting through the stifling air, Demakos went on. "Now, there has been a lot of talk around here about community pressure being exerted on the Police Department to arrest Shea for murder. It wasn't community pressure. The Police Department themselves, listening to the incredible story of this defendant and Scott, decided to launch an investigation. That's what started the investigation, not community pressure. And it wasn't community pressure that placed Shea under arrest. He was arrested by the Police Department, his own peers. They placed him under arrest because they couldn't believe his incredible story.

"And you heard the searchers. You heard the police officers from the Emergency Services Division. They conducted a search of the whole area with rakes and shovels. Pardon the expression, but those police officers busted their chops looking for that gun Armstead was supposed to have had. They busted their chops for three days, and what did they come up with? A starter's pistol in the sewer, a toy gun, and the gun Armstead had in the shop.

"Let's get to that starter's pistol. No fingerprints; nobody knows how long it was in the sewer. It only fires blanks. You'd have to be a maniac to duel a cop with a blank gun. Then you have Armstead's gun—the weapon he had at his place of business on New York Boulevard and 115th Road. That gun was silver, not black. And it would have been impossible for Armstead to go all the way to his place of business and get back to Mathias and Dillon before being picked up by Farrell and Tom Scott.

"And, you know," Demakos went on, his voice suddenly dripping with sarcasm, "it's the strangest thing. All the police officers talked to Armstead. Not one police officer asked Armstead, 'What did you do with the gun?' Don't you think that would have been a perfectly logical question for a police officer to ask: 'What did you do with the gun?' But nobody asked it. Do you know why? Because there wasn't a single police officer who believed Shea's incredible story.

"I can't help but feel indignation at the colossal gall, the colossal arrogance of this defendant in concocting the incredible, preposterous story of a ten-year-old boy, soaking wet ninety-eight pounds, turning around to take a shot at him and then, after he is shot, passing the gun to his fifty-one-year-old father. There are no ifs, ands, or buts about this case. That boy never turned around with a gun in his hand. He was shot square in the back. The bullet went in almost dead center. That boy never turned around. He just kept running and running and running with his back to the defendant. He ran and he ran and he ran for his dear life until he was struck down by a bullet in the back. I ask that you return a verdict of guilty."

In the wake of Demakos's summation, there was absolute silence. Finally, Justice Dubin spoke. "Lady and Gentlemen of the Jury, now that we are at the end of trial, it is more important than ever that you not read any newspapers or talk to anyone about this case. Don't go to the scene. Don't watch the news on television. When you are through with this case, you can read all the back newspapers you want but, from now until after your deliberations, I don't want anything to interfere with your verdict. We will start here tomorrow morning at ten o'clock. There is nothing more important in your whole life than that which you are going to do tomorrow. Nothing!"

19

THE CASE GOES
TO THE JURY

Shortly before 10:00 A.M. on Tuesday, June 11, Justice Bernard Dubin entered the courtroom. "Good morning," he told the assemblage. "At least it's a little more comfortable today than yesterday."

Evseroff nodded his concurrence. Then, on signal from the Judge, Court Clerk James Higgins rose and declared, "The Court is about to charge the Jury. Anybody wishing to leave must do so now. No one will be allowed to leave during the charge."

No one left. Dubin surveyed his domain and began. "Lady and Gentlemen of the Jury! We now come to that part of the trial known as the charge. The People of the State of New York have called upon you to render an important service. No other public obligation requires a greater degree of intelligence, fairness, patience, integrity, and courage. A juror assumes great responsibility when he or she sits in judgment of another person and seeks to determine the issues that arise in a trial. Although you knew that service would involve great responsibility, you responded in the spirit of cooperation. I extend to you my profound thanks.

"As you sit as jurors, we are all one color. We are all one nationality. We have no Italians, no Jews, no Negroes, no Poles, no Irish. We are Americans, and as Americans we seek justice for everyone. I am not a flag waver. Waving the flag doesn't make anybody an American. It is what you are doing now that does. You are Americans.

"Now, in a trial such as this, we have got to leave our emotions out. The Police Department is not on trial. Whether you like policemen or not doesn't enter into it. Sympathy for or against the deceased or for or against the defendant has got to be out. You must decide this case on the facts. Prejudice and sympathy were left out in the street before you entered this courtroom. Both the People and the defendant are entitled to a fair trial."

Briefly the Judge reviewed generally accepted methods for evaluating the credibility of witnesses and noted the jurors' right to study trial exhibits and have portions of trial testimony read back to them during their deliberations. Then he came to the standard of proof imposed on the prosecution. "Under our system of justice, a defendant is presumed innocent until the contrary is proven. That presumption of innocence remains throughout the trial until such time as a jury unanimously agrees that the defendant's guilt has been established by reliable and credible evidence beyond a reasonable doubt. The burden of proving the guilt of a defendant is at all times on the prosecution. If the evidence is as consistent with innocence as it is with guilt, the defendant is entitled to the innocent construction and must be acquitted.

"A reasonable doubt is an actual doubt that the jury is conscious of having after going over the entire evidence of the case. But it is not a mere whim, guess, or surmise. Nor is it a subterfuge to which resort may be had in order to avoid a disagreeable duty. It is a doubt that must be founded on the evidence. It must be a doubt founded in reason and must survive the test of reason. The People are not required to prove the defendant's guilt beyond any doubt because, in most cases, that's impossible."

Having laid the groundwork, Dubin next outlined the specific charges against Shea. Under the indictment the defendant could be found guilty on one of four charges—two of them relating to "murder," the other two to "manslaughter."

"The indictment in this case charges the defendant with two counts of murder," Dubin explained. "Let us look at the first count. A person is guilty of murder when, with intent to cause the death of another person, he causes the death of such person. There are two essential elements constituting murder under this count: intent by the defendant to cause the death of another person, and the causing of such death. To find that the defendant intended to cause the death, it is essential that you come to the conclusion that it was his conscious objective to do so. If you find only an intent to injure, then one of the essential elements constituting the crime of murder is missing and you may not find the defendant guilty of murder under this count of the indictment."

After pausing briefly to make certain that his instruction had been absorbed by the jurors, the Judge continued. "We come now to the second count of murder as differentiated from the first. A person is also guilty of murder when, under circumstances evincing a depraved indifference to human life, he recklessly engages in conduct which creates a grave risk of death to another person and thereby causes the death of another person. In order for you to find the defendant guilty under this count of the indictment, the People must establish to your satisfaction beyond a reasonable doubt that one, the defendant evinced a depraved indifference to human life; two, the defendant recklessly engaged in conduct which created a grave risk of death to another person; and three, the defendant caused the death of that person. 'Depravity' means an inherent deficiency of moral sense and rectitude. 'Indifference' means impartial, unbiased, disinterested; feel-

253

ing no interest, anxiety, or care. Murder under this count of
the indictment is the highest form of reckless homicide. It
embraces extremely dangerous fatal conduct performed
without specific homicidal intent but with a depraved indifference. It does not require a specific intent to cause death."

Several jurors nodded their understanding. Dubin noted
their response and read on. "If each of the elements constituting murder has not been proven beyond a reasonable
doubt, you may not find the defendant guilty of murder.
However, you may consider whether the defendant is guilty
of manslaughter. A person is guilty of manslaughter in the
first degree when, with intent to cause serious physical injury to another person, he causes the death of such person.
There is no requirement that there be an attempt to cause
death, but there must be an intent to cause serious physical
injury.

"You may also consider whether the defendant is guilty of
manslaughter in the second degree. A person is guilty of
manslaughter in the second degree when he recklessly causes
the death of a second person." The Judge paused to let his
instruction sink in. "That's all you need on this count—
recklessly." Shea shifted uneasily, and Dubin continued. "A
person acts recklessly with respect to a result when he is
aware of and consciously disregards a substantial and unjus-
tifiable risk that such result will occur. The risk must be of
such nature and degree that disregard thereof constitutes a
gross deviation from the standard of conduct that a reasonable person would observe in a like situation."

The four possible guilty verdicts had been fully explained.
All that remained was for Dubin to define the one set of
circumstances which would legally justify Shea's conduct—
the defense of "justification." Carefully enunciating his
words, the Judge pressed on.

"In considering whether the defendant is guilty of murder
or any lesser form of homicide, you the jury must give con-

sideration to the testimony concerning events leading up to the shooting. You must consider whether the defendant's conduct was justified. The defendant said he thought the deceased had a gun. Our Penal Law reads as follows: 'A peace officer, in the course of attempting to effect the arrest of a person whom he believes to have committed an offense, may use physical force to the extent he reasonably believes such force to be necessary to effect the arrest or defend himself; except that *he may use deadly physical force for such purpose only when he reasonably believes that the use of deadly physical force is necessary to defend himself from the imminent use of deadly physical force.*' "

Once again, the Judge paused, allowing his remarks to sink in. Then he went on. "It is the defendant's contention that whatever physical force he did use was justified. In order for you, the jury, to find justification for the defendant's act, you must conclude that he reasonably believed his conduct necessary to defend himself from what he reasonably believed to be the imminent use of deadly physical force."

The legal complexities of the charge were now complete. All that remained were a few closing remarks.

"In order for you to find the defendant guilty or not guilty under this indictment, you must vote unanimously. In other words, all twelve of you must agree as to the defendant's guilt or innocence. You can't find the defendant Thomas Shea guilty on two or more counts. It has to be guilty on one count or not guilty on all counts. Earlier I told you not to discuss the case. Now I'm telling you to reason with each other. Vote your conscience, but don't be stubborn. Your duty is to reach a verdict, fairly, justly, and equitably. No innocent man should be convicted, and no guilty man should be acquitted. The defendant has a right to a fair verdict, and the People have a right to a fair verdict; not based on sympathy, not based on prejudice, just on the facts."

At 11:30 A.M. the jurors retired to deliberate and an armed

guard was posted outside their chamber. Twenty-five minutes later, the Judge received a note signed by the foreman,
Sidney Horn, asking to examine the Fox map of the shooting
site, the gun found by Harold Cannon at the Pilot Automotive Wrecking Company, the transcript of the infamous tape,
and the trial testimony of Thomas Shea, Add Armstead,
Walter Scott, and Doris Lyons. The request for trial testimony ran counter to the general rule that witness transcripts
(as opposed to court exhibits) are not sent into the jury room.
Accordingly, Dubin asked that the jurors be brought back
into court.

"Is there any particular part you want to hear?" the Judge
asked.

The jurors offered no response.

"Do you want to hear the entire testimony or certain
portions?"

"The entire testimony," Dennis Connolly (juror number
ten) answered.

Dubin shook his head, then turned to the court reporter.
"Well, you'd better start reading. Let's start with the defendant."

One hour later, with Shea's testimony still being read, the
Judge interrupted and sent the jurors to lunch. At 3:00 P.M.
they returned, and Shea's testimony was completed, followed
by that of Doris Lyons.

"Now you want to hear Scott?" Dubin inquired, clearly
annoyed at the length of time the reading would take. "The
entire testimony?"

"Your Honor," Evseroff suggested, "it would be all right
with me if the jury took the testimony of Patrolman Scott
into the jury room and read it at their leisure rather than all
of us sitting here listening to it."

Dubin looked toward Demakos.

"It's up to the jury," the prosecutor said. "If the jury
wants to take it in, it's all right with me."

Several jurors nodded their concurrence. "Take it in," Dennis Connolly said.

A slightly worried look crossed the Judge's face. "I've never done this before in any trial. I don't know if it's legal. I want the defendant to agree to it."

"I agree," Shea said.

"And you too?" the Judge asked, turning to Gaudelli.

"Yes sir."

"I think we're all in agreement," Evseroff prompted.

"All right," Dubin responded. "Do you want to do the same thing with Armstead?"

The attorneys agreed they did, and at 4:00 P.M. the eleven men and one woman returned to their sanctum to deliberate. "You know," Evseroff said, turning to Cahill when the jurors had gone, "you never get used to it. You can try cases for a hundred years. You can pretend you don't care. You can say, 'I've done my best; there's nothing more I can do,' but you never get used to it. You grow a little older with each case, and waiting for the verdict is hell, especially when you care about a case like I care about this one."

"I'll tell you something," Cahill answered. "I'm a pretty conservative fellow, but this case has made me more of a liberal. I've had the feeling all through trial that here's a cop who just got caught up in the system and, once things went into motion, nothing could stop them. There was no way this case could have been plea-bargained away or dropped. The news media would have had a fit. But I don't think the media or the police brass or anyone else ever really cared about Clifford Glover. They're just pursuing their own interests, and Tom Shea is an insignificant figure caught up in their schemes."

At 6:30 P.M. the court clerk announced a temporary recess for dinner. Flanked by Hinchy and Curtin, the defense attorneys and Shea crossed Queens Boulevard to a restaurant called the Flagship Diner. "You know what I think?" Evseroff proclaimed over soup. "I think that black woman is all alone on the jury."

Cahill agreed.

"I hope you're right," Shea said.

The jury resumed its deliberations at 8:00 P.M. Unable to sit still any longer, Shea began pacing up and down the courthouse corridor. One at a time, his bodyguards, Evseroff, and Cahill took turns accompanying him. Upstairs Justice Dubin sat in his chambers, working on a backlog of court motions. Demakos and Gaudelli waited side by side in a spectator pew.

At 9:50 P.M. the jurors were brought back into the courtroom. Moments later Dubin mounted the bench and announced, "I have a note signed by the foreman. The jury wants a recharging on manslaughter in the first and second degree."

Evseroff turned white.

"A person is guilty of manslaughter in the first degree," Dubin began, "when, with intent to cause serious injury to another person, he causes the death of such person. Under manslaughter in the first degree, there is no requirement that there be an intent to cause death, but there must be an intent to cause serious physical injury. A person is guilty of manslaughter in the second degree when he recklessly causes the death of another person. All that is necessary here is to prove that he recklessly caused the death. You don't need intent."

Briefly, the Judge redefined "intent," "recklessly," and the defense of justification. Then the jury was sent back to continue its deliberations.

"Congratulations," Evseroff said shakily, approaching Demakos and Gaudelli. "I think you've got a winner." Then, walking back to Shea, the defense attorney hung his head. "I'm going to die," Evseroff said.

Hugh Curtin went to a pay telephone in the courthouse corridor and dialed his home number. For the past month

Shea's wife had spent five days a week at the Curtin home.
"Give Bonnie the strongest drink you can," Curtin told his
wife. "It looks like they're coming back with a verdict of
guilty on manslaughter."

At 10:50 P.M. Dubin ordered the jurors brought back into
the courtroom. One day earlier, they had been advised that
they would be sequestered overnight if unable to reach a
verdict by a reasonable hour.

"Madam and Gentlemen," the Judge said, "you have had
a very rough day, so we are going to send you to a hotel to
rest. From now until tomorrow morning when you come to
court, don't discuss this case. When you go to your hotel
room, don't turn on your television or radio or read any
newspapers. Have a good night's sleep, have a nice breakfast,
and get here tomorrow about nine-thirty A.M."

The jurors left the courtroom and were shepherded to a
bus which would take them to the International Hotel at
John F. Kennedy Airport. Soon afterward the lawyers, reporters, and spectators began their journey home. Dubin
retired to his chambers to tend to a few more court matters,
then left the building via the front entrance. As he descended
the steps, a young white woman approached and looked him
straight in the eye. "God help us if they find that cop guilty,"
the woman said.

On Wednesday morning, June 12, the defense team gathered
as usual at Ann's Café across the street from the Queens
County Criminal Courthouse.

"Guilty on manslaughter," Shea said, staring at his coffee.
"That's what the verdict will be. I know it."

Evseroff didn't answer. He had spent much of the night
downing martinis with a friend, and his assessment of the
situation was equally bleak. Curtin and Hinchy were just as
morose. Only Cahill was optimistic.

At 9:00 A.M. the five men rose and left the diner. The sky was bright blue. A gentle breeze would moderate temperatures throughout the day ahead.

"Look at them," Evseroff muttered, pointing to a dozen mostly white pickets on the courthouse steps. "Even the goddamn whites are picketing."

"Screw them," Hinchy said.

It was one year to the day after Evseroff had been notified by the Queens County District Attorney's office that his client had been indicted for murder.

Moments before 9:30 A.M. the jury resumed its deliberations.

"How long do you think it will take?" Shea asked.

Evseroff shrugged his shoulders. "I don't know. Not too much longer."

An hour later, still awaiting a verdict, the lawyer and his client left the courtroom and began pacing the halls. At 11:15 a court officer approached. "The Judge wants to see you inside," he instructed.

The two men returned to the courtroom, where Dubin was seated. "I have received a communication, signed by Sidney Horn, the foreman," the Judge said. "We have reached a verdict."

On signal, the twelve jurors were ushered into court.

"Jurors," Court Clerk James Higgins ordered, "please answer when your name is called."

One by one, the members of the jury affirmed their presence.

"Mr. Foreman," Higgins asked, "has the jury agreed upon a verdict?"

"We have," Horn answered.

"Will the defendant please rise and look upon the jurors," the clerk commanded.

His face bright red, Shea rose, struggling to maintain his composure.

"Mr. Foreman," Higgins intoned, "what is the jury's verdict?"

The world was frozen in one awesome, terrifying moment. "NOT GUILTY," Horn said.

Shea collapsed in his chair and began to sob uncontrollably. A half dozen reporters rushed for the courtroom door.

"Quiet," Dubin ordered, banging his gavel hopelessly amidst the increasing tumult. "Quiet, please!"

The roar continued.

Again, the Judge sought to make himself heard. "The defendant is discharged."

Lifting his head from his hands, Shea looked toward the jurors. "Thank you," he said.

"Come on," Evseroff shouted, grabbing hold of his client's shoulder. "Let's go celebrate."

Joyously the victors trooped from court, surrounded by a flock of cameramen and reporters. "I feel as though I've been reborn," Shea said, his voice still choked with emotion. "Thank God for the jury system. I did my job, and that's all I ever did. All I want is to do my job again. I don't care where they send me. I just want to be a cop."

On the courthouse steps an angry bystander charged forward and shouted, "We'll get you, you white motherfucker, you and your fucking lawyer. Just wait!"

Pushing by, the defense entourage swept down Queens Boulevard to Luigi's Restaurant, where they had lunched for much of the past four weeks. As they entered, the proprietor handed Shea a congratulatory snifter of brandy. "I feel as though I've been reborn," the cop said again. "This past year has been a nightmare. I couldn't have survived if I didn't have the greatest wife in the world. In the end, when a lot of other women wouldn't have, she stood by me."

A half dozen jurors, Ederica Campbell among them, entered the restaurant. Shea rushed to the black woman's side and planted a kiss on her cheek. "She's going to go through

261

hell for this," he said, returning to his compatriots. "I give
her a lot of credit."

Immediately several reporters cornered the jurors and
asked about their deliberations. The verdict had been
reached after hard, sometimes bitter debate. The initial vote
was six to three for acquittal with three abstentions. Then,
after Shea's testimony was reread, the vote changed to nine–
three in the defendant's favor. By dinner Tuesday night, only
Mrs. Campbell and Dennis Connolly (the telephone company cable splicer who sat next to her) favored conviction.
Then, at Mrs. Campbell's request, the jurors asked for a
rereading of the Judge's charge on manslaughter, after which
Connolly joined the majority. "Armstead said he didn't look
back to see what happened to the boy," Connolly explained
to the reporters. "But when he flagged down the police, he
said, 'My son is shot!' His testimony wasn't right." The
morning after Connolly's defection, Mrs. Campbell's resolve
had weakened and she agreed to go along with the others.

"There were too many guns," juror Martin O'Brien later
added. "You had the starter's pistol the cops found in the
sewer, the toy gun, and the revolver Armstead kept at work.
Where there's smoke, there's fire."

"Nothing would have happened if Armstead hadn't run,"
juror Daniel Ehring said, explaining his vote. "And the fact
that he kept running after his son was shot had a lot to do
with my decision. He had something to hide if he kept running like that, and it gave him time to get rid of the gun."

Strangely, in light of their verdict, five jurors disbelieved
Walter Scott's testimony that he had witnessed the shooting.
But, except for Mrs. Campbell, these same jurors also felt the
"woodwork witnesses" were lying. Perhaps juror George
Stell summed up his colleagues' feelings best: "The Judge
told us that, in order to convict Thomas Shea, we had to find
him guilty beyond a reasonable doubt. We all had that doubt.
Outside of Shea and Armstead, I guess only God really

knows whether the boy had a gun. But I think Shea was a very fine cop. He had seven hundred arrests, and that's some record. He was always there. He didn't fear nothing. We need more cops like that so there will be less crime."

"It's the old plantation philosophy," a black reporter observed bitterly. "White folks are conditioned to believe that the police are their last line of protection against the black hordes. Convict a cop, and you'll live to regret it. The hands of the police must not be tied. The police arrested Shea. The grand jury indicted. The District Attorney's office prosecuted the case. It was the jury that let him go—eleven men and one woman telling us exactly where they stood. That says something about America."

Add Armstead and Eloise Glover sat on the steps of their ramshackle house at 109-50 New York Boulevard as police cars cruised periodically by. Armstead had learned of the verdict while listening to the radio at work and come immediately home. A contingent of reporters arrived minutes later.

"The trial wasn't right," Eloise Glover said. "No justice has been done. There are a lot of people who don't want to work, but Clifford was learning at an early age how to earn a living. My son's blood is on Shea's hands. He can't wash it off."

Then she and Armstead turned their backs to the reporters and retreated inside after one tormented burst of bitterness. "For that one kid," Armstead proclaimed, "there's going to be a thousand whites die. God hasn't told me how, and I won't raise my hand to do anything, but God's going to see that I get justice. God don't like ugly."

The celebration at Luigi's was under way. "You know what I'd like," Evseroff shouted above the din. "Someday I'd like to defend a black cop who kills a white kid. Then I wouldn't be called a racist."

Several onlookers roared their approval.

"A toast," someone cried. "We need a toast."

All eyes turned toward Thomas Shea. Majestically Evseroff rose to his feet and hoisted a glass on high. "Gentlemen," the attorney said. "To victory! It's better than getting laid."

20

EPILOGUE

On August 28, 1974, after presiding over a ten-day trial of departmental charges, Deputy Police Commissioner Philip Michael recommended that Thomas Shea and Walter Scott be dismissed from the New York City Police Department— Shea for "failing to use utmost care in handling and discharging his service revolver," Scott for "wrongfully and knowingly impeding an investigation into the death of Clifford Glover by false and misleading statements." Pursuant to the Michael recommendation, on August 30, 1974, Shea and Scott were dismissed by Police Commissioner Michael J. Codd. No further criminal proceedings were instituted against them.

In relevant part the Michael recommendation read:

> Perhaps the most demanding of all professions is that of police officer. We do not suggest that police officers cannot return gunfire directed at them. We do not suggest that they must be restrained in the necessary action they take to protect themselves. Nor do we suggest that their mission is other than to pursue criminals aggressively. However, the case of

Shea and Scott entails none of these precepts.

Shea and Scott were not shot at, they were not chasing persons who were armed, they were not in any personal danger, and they had no possible cause to use their guns. Glover was wrongfully shot, and Shea and Scott thought deceit and fabrication could extricate them. They were the hunters, not the hunted. They were not imperiled by the situation that developed, and needed assistance only to deal with the results of their hasty and ill-conceived actions.

Shea is not a wanton killer [but] he did display an attitude of reckless abandon and consummate carelessness. Scott, from badly misdirected and unjustified loyalty, elected to cover-up his partner's wrongful use of deadly force. Shea and Scott do not have the maturity and judgment that is required of all police officers. Their continued employment is unacceptable.

STATEMENT OF THOMAS SHEA

"So you're writing a book. Okay, Jack Evseroff says you seem like an all-right guy, so I'll talk with you. You don't have to pay me. You can write what you want. All I ask is that, along with everything else, you tell my side of the story.

"I'm not a racist. Whatever else you write, I want people to know that. What I did as a cop never depended on a person's color. If someone did something wrong, I locked him up whether he was black, white, red, yellow, or green. I've lived with black people all my life. Brentwood has one of the largest black populations on Long Island. Look at the character witnesses I had at trial. Eight of them were black; three were Puerto Rican. These men had to go back to their communities when the trial ended. They had to justify their testimony to their family and friends. Do you think for one minute that any one of them would have gone out on a limb and testified on my behalf if I was a racist? No way!

266

"I'm not perfect. I'm vulnerable and, like everyone else, I make mistakes. I don't belong on a pedestal, but I can think of quite a few other people who don't belong on one either.

"Look at Add Armstead. The press built him up to be the perfect father, a loving husband. No one reported that the day after Christmas 1974 Mrs. Glover went to the 103rd Precinct station house and asked the police to serve a Family Court warrant on Armstead for assault. At my departmental trial, two former boarders in Mrs. Glover's home testified that Armstead played with guns in front of the children. One witness testified that Armstead pointed a gun at his stepson Henry and told the boy to get down on his knees and pray. Then a truck driver testified about some work he had done hauling motors for the Pilot Automotive Wrecking Company. He told the Trial Commissioner that Armstead let Clifford Glover run around the wrecking yard without any supervision at all; how one day Clifford washed his hands in a pail of gasoline and held them over a barrel with a fire in it so they could dry. Some loving father.

"I wonder how many of the people who put my name on the front page of the *New York Times* and wrote editorials about my going to jail have ever walked through South Jamaica or Harlem. I wonder how many of them have ever gone to a cop's funeral and seen a widow bend over to kiss her husband's face when it's surrounded by flowers. My case was a classic example of reverse discrimination. If I was black, I would never have been prosecuted. Because I was white, the shooting became a media extravaganza.

"I saw this television show not too long ago about two kids who were muggers. It was a panel discussion, and they treated these kids like they were heroes. I almost destroyed the television. The kids were black. One of them said, 'I never mug anybody who's not my equal. I never mug unless there's a challenge.' That's a lot of crap. Look at the statistics. Ninety percent of the people who are mugged are elderly men or women who get knocked down, beaten, and stomped if they don't turn over their money. Then the other kid says, 'I mug people because of my cultural background.' I almost died. People like Booker T. Washington grew up in slums, but they didn't go out and mug anyone. Thurgood Marshall was the grandson of a slave. Now he's on the United States Supreme Court. When the Italians came here, they had rotten neighborhoods. They didn't all go out and join the Mafia. If someone came into court and said, 'I'm a member of the Mafia because of my cultural background, my next-door neighbor was a don, my friends are in the Mafia, I grew up around it,' the judge would still send him to jail. Why should black people be treated different? Sure, a mugger who goes to jail might come out a hard-core criminal. But I got news for you. Someone who gets away with mugging fifty people on the street becomes a hard-core criminal, too. So what happens? They put these kids on a TV talk show. They're probably paying them too, and they let them lie. Nobody tells them where to get off because the kids happen to be black and the host doesn't want anyone to think he's a racist.

"Well, I've got news for you. I'm not a racist. Three cops were killed in the 103rd Precinct in the 1970s—Kenneth Nugent in 1971, William Capers in 1972, and Timothy Hurley in 1974. The only year missing in that sequence is 1973. That could have been me. I shot Clifford Glover because he had a gun. I didn't know he was only ten, but a ten-year-old can kill you just as dead as an adult. Look at that student up at Columbia University who was shot to death by a twelve-year-old last year.

"I know my story stinks. You probably don't believe it either, but it's true. Look, I had twelve years on the force. If I was going to lie and make up a story, I would have made up a good one. I could have said that I was aiming for Armstead, missed, and hit the boy. I had a knife in my pocket that morning. I could have turned the kid over and put it in his hand. For that matter, I could have turned him over, put a bullet in his chest, and then said the first shot hit square and spun him around, which was why the second bullet was in the back.

"I can see it upsets you, my talking like that. Well, I didn't do it. I told the truth, and you can see where it got me. As for Walter Scott, let me put it this way. Even if Walter lied about what he saw, and I'm not saying he did, that wouldn't mean I was guilty of murder. Suppose Walter drove straight from New York Boulevard to Dillon without stopping. Just suppose he didn't see the shooting. That wouldn't mean I was in the wrong. It would just mean that Walter didn't see what happened.

"Incidentally, in case you're wondering about Felix Tarrats—that supposedly innocent man I shot in the neck back in 1972—he was shot and killed in July of 1974 while committing an armed robbery. That's how innocent he was."

———

"Five days? Is that how long we've been talking? I probably don't seem as tough to you now as I used to. It's funny, the other day I saw three kids kicking up a car that was parked on the street. You know, denting the sides, breaking off the antenna, just for the hell of it. I started towards them. Then I realized there was nothing I could do. I'm not a cop anymore. That's been the hardest thing for me to accept these past five years. All my life all I ever wanted to be was a cop. I didn't even want to be a sergeant or a detective, just a street cop pounding a beat. If the president of a corporation is acquitted of a crime, he's back at his desk the next day. Not me. I was acquitted by a jury, then bounced off the force two months later. At first I was angry. Then I was scared; after that, bitter. Now all I am is lonely. I feel empty about the whole thing.

"Let me tell you what happened to me after I was acquitted. First I got kicked off the force. Then my wife and I were formally separated and divorced. We'd argued a lot before that—I guess all husbands and wives do—but the pressure of this case broke us apart. No regular paycheck coming in, living in constant fear, my name in the newspapers all the time. Then my oldest daughter got married at age sixteen. She wasn't pregnant. She had a child, but that wasn't until a year later. She had a nice wedding with a cake and a gown and all that, but it wasn't what we wanted. She was too young. All I can hope is that it works out for the best. You don't have to be a psychiatrist to know that my problems were one of the reasons she got married.

"Then I tried to find a job, but no one would hire me. Walter Scott made out okay. His father bought him two tow trucks and set him up in a business reclaiming autos for car rental agencies. I couldn't get a job. I remember one incident a couple of weeks after I was kicked off the force. Someone told me about a job as a porter in a building up in the Bronx. It wasn't what I wanted to do, but hey, I had to make a living. I went up to the Bronx and filled out an application, did it honestly. I put down exactly why I had been thrown off the force and told them I was prepared to answer any further questions they might have. They wouldn't hire me. The President of the union told me, 'We'd love to have you. You're a great guy, but forty percent of our members are black.' You show me one decent unskilled job in the city of New York where they don't hire blacks. They have to. It's the law.

"You know what job I finally got? Jack Evseroff hired me to paint his house. God bless that man, I love him. He's been like a father to me. I don't think the house even needed painting. I was embarrassed to take his money. Finally, I got a job working nights in a printing plant out in Queens. It's the worst job I ever had. I've been doing it for three years now. All my life I worked outdoors. Even with the airline,

I was outdoors loading planes from underneath the ramp. Now I spend twelve hours a night, five nights a week, inside. I work sixty hours a week for one hundred eighty dollars.

"The workers in the printing plant are mostly black and Puerto Rican with a few Italians thrown in. They know who I am, and it doesn't bother them. They're strugglers like me. We get along fine. Except I hate the work. It's twelve hours of nothing that goes nowhere. Twelve hours a night for me to sit and think about what happened. I have some pretty bad sessions with myself. The only thing that saves me is sometimes I'll see some guy in a wheelchair whose legs were blown away in Vietnam, and I say to myself maybe life's not so bad for me after all.

"You know, back in April of 1973, I was sitting on top of the world. I had a nice house with ten years on the mortgage already paid and a swimming pool in the backyard. I owned two cars and was getting ready to trade one of them in on a '73. I had a wife and two kids who loved me. The guys I worked with were my friends.

"I lost it all. Financially I've been destroyed. My cop's salary and pension are gone. As far as family is concerned, I'm pretty much alone. My mother and father are dead. My grandmother is in a nursing home. My wife is gone. My granddaughter is two years old and I've never seen her. I don't even have my own apartment. Sometimes I stay at my cousin's, sometimes with a friend. Every possession I own is in the trunk of my car. I wasn't criminally convicted; I wasn't sent to jail. But everything I worked for my entire life is gone. In case anyone is sitting around wondering whatever happened to Thomas Shea, now they know."

AUTHOR'S NOTE

The Trial of Patrolman Thomas Shea is the second book in which I have sought to reconstruct events subsequent to their occurrence. Here, as with my first effort, the heart of my research has been extended interviews with my subjects. Other data has derived from public records, historical texts, and documents found in the files of the Queens County District Attorney's office, New York City Police Department, New York City Patrolmen's Benevolent Association, and the attorneys for Add Armstead, Eloise Glover, and Thomas Shea.

Where conversations are included in quotation marks, they are the result of verbatim transcripts obtained by me or a reconstruction based on the memory of one or more participants to a given conversation. In some reconstructions, such as the police deliberations leading to the arrest of Thomas Shea, I benefited from the input of many participants. In other instances, such as the conversations between Martin Bracken and Frederick Ludwig on the day of and the day following Shea's arrest, I was limited to one direct source, since Mr. Ludwig would not grant me an interview. In this regard, I should also note that it has been necessary to edit a number of transcripts down to manageable size. For example, the Shea trial transcript runs well over two thousand pages, much of it repetitive and devoted to procedural matters. I am confident that in excerpting this material I have done nothing to compromise the fairness of my manuscript.

On those occasions where the memories of participants differ, I have attempted a judgment as to which version is the most credible. I should also note that the statements of Add Armstead and Thomas Shea, which form the bulk of Chapters 1 and 20, are composites of numerous remarks made by them during the course of my interviews rather than uninterrupted extemporaneous comments. However, the thoughts and words are their own.

In the Author's Note to my first book, I mentioned several family members and friends who were particularly supportive during the preparation of my manuscript. Continuing this practice (and without excluding others), I would like to express particular appreciation to my parents (the best in the world), my brother and sister, Ed Nordlinger, Ruth and Peter Baylinson, Catherine Hazard, Vera and Albert Reegen, Patricia Kiernan, Robin Zuckerman, Melody Lawrence, Donald Morris, E. Joseph Schmachs, and Bruce Sloman. Special thanks are again due Christine DiFrancesco.